Inside Judaism

How Jews Live the Torah

Volume I

Inside Judaism

How Jews Live the Torah

Volume I

Rabbi Eliezer Melamed

Contents

Introduction 1
Foreword 6
Preface 9

Chapter 1: The Jewish Vision 12
Chapter 2: From Genesis Through the Revelation at Sinai . . . 21

Interpersonal *Mitzvot* **41**
Chapter 3: Interpersonal *Mitzvot*. 42
Chapter 4: The Value of Human Life. 73
Chapter 5: Justice 84
Chapter 6: Charity 95
Chapter 7: The Justice System 110

Family **117**
Chapter 8: Marriage. 118
Chapter 9: Nidda. 130
Chapter 10: Protecting Marriage 138
Chapter 11: The Wedding. 154
Chapter 12: Parents and Children 166
Chapter 13: Family Celebrations 177
Chapter 14: Mourning 186

Faith, the People, & the Land 203

Chapter 15: Fundamentals of Faith.....................204
Chapter 16: Torah Study.............................228
Chapter 17: The Land and the People 247
Chapter 18: Conversion 277
Chapter 19: The Holy Temple........................283

Glossary of Hebrew Terms

THROUGHOUT THIS BOOK, you will encounter several Hebrew words that may be unfamiliar. While most Hebrew terms are translated in context, the following words either recur frequently or carry meanings that merit clarification here. This glossary provides brief definitions to help you navigate the Jewish concepts explored in these pages.

Mitzva - Commandment, also sometimes used to mean a good deed or act of kindness.

Mitzvot - The plural of mitzva

Halakha - Jewish law

Halakhically - According to Jewish law

Halakhic - Pertaining to Jewish law

Kavana - Intention, focus, or concentration, often used in the context of prayer

Mikveh - Ritual bath

Introduction

By Rabbi Tuly Weisz

"I made you for a people's covenant, for a light to nations."
Isaiah 42:6

THIS VERSE CAPTURES the mission statement of the people of Israel. For most of Jewish history, the role of "light unto the nations" has been understood primarily as a private call to have a positive influence on the world by living an ethical life and setting a personal example of righteous behavior. Rarely was anyone on the outside ever interested in what the people of Israel as a nation had to say. But Isaiah is calling for so much more. The Bible, the "light" that God gave to the people of Israel at Mt. Sinai, is meant to illuminate the entire world. God's light is capable of opening the eyes of the blind and leading the imprisoned out of darkness.

The establishment of the State of Israel and the return of God's people to God's land is a sign that the day has finally come to put Isaiah's words into action. The people of Israel, a strong nation in its ancestral homeland, are ready to fulfill their destiny and share God's light with the world.

At Israel365, we believe that strengthening Israel requires building genuine bridges between people of faith. As Orthodox

Jews, we have discovered that sharing the wisdom of the Torah with the broader world creates meaningful connections with Christians and others who share our biblical values. Our mission is rooted in friendship and mutual respect—we seek to build relationships with those who support Israel while honoring our differences and remaining committed to truth regardless of cultural pressures or popular ideologies.

It is in this spirit that we proudly present Rabbi Eliezer Melamed's work, *Inside Judaism: How Jews Live the Torah*. This precious book offers a unique window into the heart of Jewish tradition, revealing how Jews have understood, interpreted, and lived according to the Bible for thousands of years. For Christians seeking to understand the roots of their own faith, there is perhaps no more valuable resource than this comprehensive exploration of Jewish thought and practice.

Rabbi Eliezer Melamed

Rabbi Eliezer Melamed stands among Israel's most important religious leaders and thinkers today. As the Rabbi of the city Har Bracha and Dean of Yeshivat Har Bracha, he has dedicated his life to making the profound wisdom of Jewish law and tradition accessible to all people. A leading religious Zionist thinker, Rabbi Melamed seamlessly bridges the ancient wisdom of the Torah with the practical challenges of modern life in the Jewish state.

Rabbi Eliezer Melamed's scholarship is both deep and broad. His multi-volume work *Peninei Halakha* (Pearls of Jewish Law) is a staple in Israeli homes. The popular series is the cornerstone of contemporary Jewish legal literature, offering clear and comprehensive guidance on Jewish law while weaving together insights of faith and practice. Rabbi Melamed's ability to distill complex religious concepts into accessible language has made him one of the most influential spiritual voices in Israel today.

What makes Rabbi Melamed particularly significant for this work is his understanding and appreciation of Christian Zionism and the vital role that Christian supporters play in strengthening the State of Israel both practically and prophetically. He recognizes the miraculous nature of the relationship that has developed between the Jewish people and millions of Christians worldwide who have awakened to their biblical calling to bless Israel.

As Rabbi Melamed himself has written:

"Since the foundation of the State of Israel, the numbers of philo-Semitic evangelicals have increased. They see with their own eyes how the Jewish people is returning to its land after its awful, two-thousand-year-long exile, and is creating a prosperous country. They see new settlements and vineyards flowering in the very areas described by the Bible, and they are excited by our miraculous return to Zion. They are overwhelmed by the fulfillment of the ancient prophecies of the prophets of Israel...

Sometimes I see these honored guests walking on our roads and paths, and I am filled with great love; I am deeply moved and have to hold back tears. How beautiful are these people, who volunteer enthusiastically, crossing oceans and continents to express their wonderful connection with us. How they shine with joy at being privileged to see the miraculous return to Zion, to walk on holy ground, and to contribute to making the desert bloom."

Rabbi Melamed sees in Christian support for Israel the fulfillment of Isaiah's prophecy that "in the end of days, the Mountain of the Lord's House shall stand firm above the mountains and tower above the hills, and all the nations shall stream to-wards it... For Torah shall come forth from Zion, and the word of the Lord from Jerusalem."

A Bridge Between Faiths

Inside Judaism: How Jews Live the Torah represents far more than an academic exercise in comparative religion. It is a gen-uine attempt to build bridges of understanding between Jews and Christians based on our shared reverence for the Hebrew Bible and our common commitment to biblical values. Rabbi Melamed's work reveals how Jewish tradition has preserved and transmitted not just the text of the Bible, but its living spirit—the way it shapes daily life, informs moral decisions, and creates meaning in both individual and communal existence.

For Christians, understanding how Jews read and live the Bible provides valuable insight into the world that gave birth to Christianity. The festivals, laws, and spiritual practices described in these pages are not mere historical curiosities, but living tra-ditions that continue to shape Jewish life today. They represent an unbroken chain of tradition stretching back to Mount Sinai, offering a unique perspective on the biblical text that has been lovingly preserved and refined over millennia.

The book explores the fundamental principles of Jewish interpersonal ethics, family life, faith, and ritual observance. It reveals how Judaism prioritizes the social commandments—those relating to justice, kindness, and human dignity—while showing how ritual observance serves to sanctify daily life and strengthen the bonds between the individual, the com-munity, and the Divine.

The Purpose of This Book

Rabbi Melamed's work aligns perfectly with our calling to be a light unto the nations. *Inside Judaism: How Jews*

Live the Torah serves as a bridge of understanding, allowing Christians to see how Jews have lived with and interpreted the Bible for thousands of years. It honors both traditions while revealing their shared biblical foundations.

We offer this work with respect for the Christian faith and no desire to change anyone's beliefs. Our purpose is simply to educate and inspire. When Christians understand how Jews read and live the Bible, it can enrich their own faith journey while building the mutual respect and friendship that strengthens both our communities.

It is a great honor for Israel365 to work with Rabbi Melamed in making this important work available to a broader audience. Rabbi Melamed's willingness to share the treasures of Jewish tradition with Christians around the world reflects both his scholarly generosity and his deep appreciation for the Christian commitment to Israel and the Jewish people. His vision aligns perfectly with our mission to fulfill Isaiah's calling of Torah going forth from Zion—sharing God's light with all nations while honoring the distinctiveness of each faith tradition.

As you embark on this journey through Jewish tradition, we invite you to approach it with an open heart and mind. Allow yourself to be enriched by the wisdom of the ages, to gain new insights into the biblical text, and to develop a deeper appreciation for the Jewish people and their remarkable contribution to the world.

May *Inside Judaism: How Jews Live the Torah* serve as a bridge of understanding, a source of inspiration, and a testament to the beautiful friendship that can flourish between Jews and Christians when we recognize the role of the Jewish people to serve as a light unto the nations.

Rabbi Tuly Weisz
Founder, Israel365

Foreword

By Rabbi Elie Mischel

WHEN I FIRST encountered the writings of Rabbi Eliezer Melamed, I was struck by their clarity and vision. Here was a rabbi who didn't just explain Jewish law — he showed how Torah shapes the way a people lives on its land, in its own country, after two thousand years of exile. Over time, I came to understand that Rabbi Melamed is not only one of the most respected experts on Jewish law in Israel, but also one of the few rabbinic leaders who has articulated, with rare consistency, what Religious Zionism really means in practice.

Rabbi Melamed serves as the rabbi and head of Yeshivat Har Bracha, the Mount of Blessing, in the hills of Samaria. From that mountaintop, overlooking the same landscape where Abraham once walked, he teaches that Torah and the Land of Israel are inseparable — that the fulfillment of God's word happens not in theory but through the daily life of the Jewish people rebuilding their homeland. He writes and speaks about settling Judea and Samaria not as a political position but as an expression of faith, a commandment of the BIble to be lived and advanced without hesitation. His teachings are steady and measured, but also deeply inspirational.

Through his monumental series *Peninei Halakhah, "Pearls of Jewish Law,"* Rabbi Melamed has become a household name across Israel's Religious Zionist community. These volumes are studied in religious schools throughout Israel and across the world. They are written in simple, precise Hebrew, but the ideas behind them are vast — presenting Jewish observance as something whole and joyful, a way of sanctifying every aspect of life. More than a million copies have been sold in multiple languages, and it's not an exaggeration to say that *Peninei Halakhah* has shaped how modern Jews study and practice Jewish law.

What stands out most about Rabbi Melamed is his courage. In a time when many rabbis avoid controversy, he has consistently spoken and acted according to conviction, not convenience. He has taken positions that others hesitate to take — not to provoke, but because he believes the Torah demands honesty and strength. That same courage has defined his approach to the relationship between Jews and Christians.

Years ago, he welcomed the Christian organization HaYovel to the edge of his community, inviting volunteers from around the world to help Jewish farmers plant vineyards and cultivate the land. For Rabbi Melamed, this was not a publicity gesture. He saw in their efforts the fulfillment of Isaiah's vision — that strangers would one day help tend the fields of Israel.

He has written publicly and courageously in defense of these Christian friends, acknowledging both the painful history of Christian antisemitism and the remarkable change taking place in our time. He has said plainly that Christians who love Israel and honor the Jewish people are undergoing a spiritual awakening, and that Jews must respond to it with gratitude and respect. In a religious world that often defaults to suspicion, his clarity and generosity stand out.

I saw this firsthand in the months after the October 7 massacre, when Israel was still in shock and mourning. We at Israel365 brought a group of Christian leaders to Har Bracha to meet Rabbi Melamed, and I had the privilege of translating between his Hebrew and their English. Even in that painful moment, his warmth and gratitude toward these visitors were unmistakable. He spoke to them about faith, courage, and the meaning of standing with Israel when so much of the world had turned against us. He made no effort to hide the differences between Judaism and Christianity, but he expressed those differences with such honesty and respect that every person in the room felt elevated by the encounter. When we left, several of the pastors told me that they had never met a rabbi who embodied such strength and kindness at once.

For me, Rabbi Melamed represents something essential about our generation: confidence in Torah, devotion to the Land of Israel, and a sincere love for those who bless the Jewish people. His life's work shows that faith does not have to be defensive or narrow; it can be strong, clear, and open at the same time. That balance — of conviction and humility, of commitment and generosity — is what gives his voice such authority.

It is a privilege for Israel365 Publishing to present this English edition of Rabbi Melamed's work. For our Christian readers, it opens a window into Jewish life as it is actually lived — how Torah guides daily action, family, community, and the ongoing story of the people of Israel. My hope is that this book deepens understanding, strengthens friendship, and brings more people to see how the words of the Bible continue to unfold, here and now, in the Land of Israel.

I want to express my sincere gratitude to Rabbi Yogev Cohen, Director of the *Peninei Halachah* Project, whose efforts helped bring Rabbi Melamed and Israel365 together, and to Rabbi Maor Cayam, Head of the Yeshivat Har Bracha Research Institute, for his invaluable support throughout this process.

Rabbi Elie Mischel
Director of Education, Israel365

Preface

By Rabbi Eliezer Melamed

I THANK MY COLLEAGUES at Israel365 for preparing and adapting my book *Jewish Tradition* for readers of different faiths—especially for Christians who love Israel and seek to understand Judaism. The book you are now holding, *Inside Judaism: How Jews Live the Torah*, is a version of that earlier work, revised and presented for a non-Jewish readership.

Jewish Tradition was originally written about six years ago for the Jewish people, and many have already studied it. I was pleased to hear that, in the view of my colleagues at Israel365, its presentation of Judaism is faithful and clear—so much so that even those who did not grow up within the Jewish tradition can learn about Judaism directly and authentically through it.

The purpose of this book is not to persuade its readers to adopt a Jewish way of life, nor to engage in argument or polemic. Rather, it seeks to present an accurate and coherent account of Jewish faith, values, and law as they have developed throughout Jewish history. Special emphasis is placed on the ethical and interpersonal commandments—justice and charity, kindness and moral responsibility—which stand at the heart of Jewish tradition.

In recent generations, alongside the emergence of the first

rays of redemption for the Jewish people in the Land of Israel, devoted members of the Christian faith have begun to express love and support for Israel's return to its land, and have even provided significant assistance. A notable example is Lord Balfour, the Foreign Secretary of the British Empire, who, out of his Christian faith, led the decision to establish a national home for the Jewish people in the Land of Israel.

In light of the dreadful memories of a blood-soaked history, some Jews find it difficult to believe that a genuine change has truly taken place—that there are tens, and perhaps hundreds, of millions of Christians who sincerely love the Jewish people and seek their good. Yet the wonder is indeed happening. The hand of God, which guides history, has touched the hearts of good people throughout the world. The words of the holy prophets who foretold the redemption of Israel stir within them, and they accompany the return of the people of Israel to their land with awe and love.

The position of Christians who look upon the people of Israel and Judaism with sympathy is very precious to us, and our hearts are filled with love toward them. In the face of waves of darkness and hatred, they uphold a stance of faith and moral conviction—a stance that expresses one of the signs of the redemption that is drawing near.

As King David said (Psalms 126):

"A Song of Ascents. When the LORD restored the captives of Zion, we were like dreamers. Then our mouths were filled with laughter, and our tongues with song. Then they said among the nations, 'The LORD has done great things for them.' The LORD has done great things for us; we rejoiced. Restore our fortunes, O LORD, like streams in the Negev. Those who sow in tears shall reap in joy. He who goes out weeping, bearing the seed for

sowing, shall surely return with songs of joy, carrying his sheaves."

"These sheaves" are the great blessing that God promised to our father Abraham, as it is written (Genesis 12:2–3): "I will make you into a great nation... and through you all the families of the earth shall be blessed."

It is my hope that this book will deepen understanding, strengthen mutual respect, and contribute to the blessing promised to all the families of the earth.

Rabbi Eliezer Melamed
Har Bracha, Israel

CHAPTER 1

The Jewish Vision

1. The Vision of the Jewish Nation

The appearance of the Jewish people began with God's commandment to our forefather Abraham to go up to the Land of Israel. There he would establish a large and blessed nation – a nation that would reveal God's word to the world and bring blessing to all.

> *The Lord said to Abram: "Go forth from your native land and from your father's house to the land that I will show you. I will make of you a great nation, and I will bless you: I will make your name great, and you shall be a blessing. I will bless those who bless you and curse him that curses you; and all the families of the earth shall be blessed through you" (Genesis 12:1-3).*

Similarly, our forefather Isaac was promised: "All the nations of the earth shall be blessed through your offspring" (*ibid.* 26:4). Also our forefather Jacob was told: "All the families of the earth shall be blessed through you and your descendants" (*ibid.* 28:14).

In other words, as we say in the *Aleinu* prayer, the mission of the Jewish nation is to perfect the world under the sovereignty of the Almighty. We are meant to reveal to the world faith in God and the path to live a life of blessing, illuminated by the divine values of truth and goodness. This will gradually shower goodness and blessing on all nations, families, and individuals.

2. The Jewish Character: Endless Pursuit of Kindness and Justice

The gateway to Judaism is striving to add goodness and blessing to the world, and to insist upon justice. Several Bible stories illustrate this point.

When Abraham opened his tent to guests, he did not do so because he was commanded to, or because he was seeking profit. Rather, he was motivated by his love of people and his desire to help them. Later, we find Abraham and his son, Isaac, digging wells, an essential activity which provides water to people and animals. Jacob worked diligently and faithfully as a shepherd, not only to benefit himself, but also to increase the world's food and clothing supply. When Jacob's son, Joseph, was sold into slavery, he could easily have fallen into despair over his fate. However, he did not let it sap his spirit. Rather, wherever he went, he tried to improve the situation of those around him, eventually saving Ancient Egypt from a terrible famine.

Jewish scientists and social activists today, whose primary goal is to contribute to society's welfare and prosperity, are following in our ancestors' footsteps.

When Moses left Pharaoh's palace and saw an Egyptian overseer striking an Israelite slave, he hit the Egyptian and saved the slave, even though he knew he was endangering himself. As a result, he lost his status as an Egyptian prince and was forced to run for his life to Midian. There, when he witnessed shepherds harassing young women (Jethro's daughters), he could not stand by silently. He fought for their right to provide their sheep water from the well, even though he risked a conflict with the locals. Due to this intervention he merited marrying Zipporah, Jethro's daughter. Moses continued improving himself until he was worthy to lead the Jewish nation to receive the Torah at Sinai.

After Ruth the Moabite was widowed, she decided to leave her home in Moab and move to Bethlehem with her mother-in-law, Naomi, rather than leave her alone in her pain. Naomi, who had come from a very prominent family, was about to return to her homeland – downtrodden, as a widow who had lost her wealthy husband and both of her sons. Ruth felt a moral obligation to accompany her and stand by her. As a result of this, Ruth's heart opened to faith in God. She converted to Judaism and became the progenitor of the Davidic line.

The Sages tell us that three traits characterize the Jewish people:

- "merciful" – they are emphatic to the pain of others.
- "modest" – they possess a God-fearing nature.
- "compassionate" – they strive to act kindly.

3. Faith as a Jewish Characteristic

All people have a basic faith. For most people, this is expressed as belief in God, the source of all life and the values which make life meaningful. Devoting one's life to these ideals - truth and goodness, love and kindness, justice and law, dignity and loyalty, courage and good-heartedness – greatly elevates daily living. These values are expressed in various combinations and degrees in most individuals and nations.

Beyond the basic faith of most humanity, among Jews, faith is exceptional. It is such a fundamental characteristic, that all of our national-historical processes revolve around it. This is why the Jews are referred to as "believers, the children of believers." No other nation has had so many of its people devoting their talents and their lives to their faith. This manifests itself in the unwillingness of Jews to be satisfied with a basic goodness and truth, but rather strive for growth and depth. They aspire to more, hoping to make everything more profound, more lasting, more meaningful. Therefore, the Jewish nation deserved to receive the divine Torah which is rooted in the Infinite. It is always possible to discover infinite ideas and meanings in Torah.

Jewish faith includes the certainty that the universe and everything in it can be improved and uplifted. This is because everything contains a spark of the divine within it. When we use the Torah and mitzvot to reveal this divine spark, we can elevate reality. To accomplish this, we must reject idol worship and any other conventions which limit or distract us from our aspiration to improve the world.

The astounding optimism of the Jews is rooted in this faith. Despite the incomparable pain and suffering the Jewish nation has experienced throughout the ages, it has retained its belief in the possibility of perfecting the world. The power of this belief fostered many Jews who became revolutionaries, entrepreneurs, and innovators in science and the humanities. The first two of the Ten Commandments, which we heard directly from God at Sinai, demand faith in God and the renunciation of idols. Together, these two commandments provide the foundation for the Jewish nation's activism in the world.

4. The Unity of All

The most common and serious mistake made when understanding life and faith is adopting the pagan worldview, which deeply disconnects heaven and earth. Heaven is the 'ideal' – absolute truth and lofty morality, while earth is the 'real' - daily necessities and physical pleasures, with all their problems and limitations. This forces people to choose between heaven and earth, splitting the spiritual and mundane.

By contrast, the Jewish view is unified: heaven and earth are connected, enhancing each other in a symbiotic relationship. This is because God is One. He is the Creator of heaven and earth and everything within them, and He gives life to all things. Therefore, the divine message must manifest itself everywhere, from the heights of heaven to the depths of the earth. It is intended to elevate all areas of life: the intellectual and the emotional, the spiritual and the mundane; agriculture, industry, and business; the sciences and the arts, including literature, poetry, music, and painting. This unity also informs relationships – husband and wife, parents and children, siblings, and other relatives – as well as communal and national life.

5. The Role of the Jewish Nation

Actualizing divine values in all facets of life requires an entire nation. The mission shared by all its participants is to reveal divine faith on every level. That is the ultimate purpose of the Jewish nation who left Egypt, received the Torah at Sinai, and entered the Promised Land.

According to a pantheistic ideology which divides the world and its elements, only spiritual people can be suffused with faith. Whereas among the Jewish people, faith can be revealed by anyone – including spiritual people and practical people. Spiritual people may explain the divine message more profoundly, while practical people are more skilled at materializing it. Other religions tend to limit or narrow their scope, and this may be attributed to their pagan outlook. In contrast, Judaism maintains that everything is important and all talents and types must unite to discover godliness in the world. The manifestation of the Divine Presence (*Shekhina*) is thus dependent upon the nation connecting to God in unity, as the Jews did when the Torah was given.

The role of the Jewish people is to be a "a kingdom of priests and a holy nation" (Exodus 19:6) and "a light unto the nations" (Isaiah 42:6). This means living a life grounded in truth and faith, goodness and blessing, which exemplifies how to reveal God's word in the world. This will result in the continuity of God's blessing on all nations. Many faiths learned the foundations of goodness, truth, and morality from Jewish history and heritage. Consequently, the defining values for those nations includes the recognition of human life, created in the image of God. This continues to be our destiny as a Jewish nation – to enact divine values, which will improve the world and bring about its redemption.

6. The Nation and Its Land

All the divine revelations experienced by our forefathers Abraham, Isaac, and Jacob included the promise that their descendants would multiply, inherit the Land of Israel, and put divine values into practice there, thus bringing blessing to all the nations. When Abraham was in Bethel, he was told, "I will make your offspring as the dust of the earth, so that if one can count the dust of the earth, then your offspring too can be counted. Get up, walk about the Land through its length and its breadth, for I will give it to you" (Genesis 13:16-17). As a result, "All the families of the earth shall be blessed through you" (*ibid.* 12:3). A similar promise was made to Isaac: "Reside in this land, and I will be with you and bless you. I will assign all these lands to you and to your offspring . . . I will make your descendants as numerous as the stars of heaven, and give your descendants all these lands, so that all the nations of the earth shall be blessed through your offspring" (*ibid.* 26:3-4). Jacob received his promise in the famous dream of the ladder: "The ground on which you are lying – I will assign to you and your offspring. Your descendants shall be as the dust of the earth; you shall spread out to the west and to the east, to the north and to the south. All the families of the earth shall be blessed through you and your descendants" (*ibid.* 28:13-14).

The Land of Israel plays a central role in the Jewish vision and in the expression of monotheism. A binary worldview imagines a chasm between heaven and earth, in which heaven is so holy that it is alienated from everyday earthly matters. However, God created the Holy Land of Israel which is conducive to the revelation of faith, Torah, and *mitzvot*, and was given to the Jewish nation. When Jews dwell in their Land and observe the Torah and its *mitzvot*, heaven is not estranged from earth, and earth is not sealed off from heaven. Rather, they undergo a unique synergy which fosters the expression of divine values in all areas of life. This results in holiness and blessing bestowed upon the whole world.

The Jewish nation's reward and punishment are also connected to the Land of Israel, as stated many times in the Torah and Prophets. When the Jews follow in God's ways, divine blessing is revealed in the Land, which flows with milk and honey. When the Jews sin, they are exiled from the Land, which becomes desolate. This continues until either the Jewish people repent, or they are cleansed of their sins through suffering, at which point the exile will end. God will gather the Jews from all over the world and return them to their Land, which will once again be fertile and fruitful.

7. Torah Study

To enable the Jewish people to actualize the grand vision of perfecting the world, God gave His nation the Torah. The

Torah instructs them how to live life properly – specifying what is permitted and what is forbidden, what is obligatory, what is preferable, and what is optional – in order to reveal the unique value of every entity in the world. This is why each Jew should study the Torah to understand what it has to say on issues of faith, morality, and *halakha*.

Ordinarily, we can understand the Torah's message by studying it in depth. At times, often when we face crises, questions arise which require us to study Torah in even greater depth to arrive at answers. Whether the crises are personal, familial, societal, national, or international, they force us to delve deeper into the Torah and discover its light. As a result, life continues to be blessed, until we merit a complete redemption, when we will no longer need to grapple with evil in the world. Even then we will still be presented with an amazing challenge – to continue discovering deeper layers of meaning and infinite gratification found in Torah.

8. A Blessing to All Nations and Societies

It is not part of the Jewish vision to dictate to other nations how they should govern themselves or organize their societies. Rather, blessings that emanate from the Jewish people reach other nations by way of example and inspiration. Each nation and society can choose what to adopt from Judaism to increase truth, goodness, and blessing in their particular cultures.

The worldview of the Jewish nation maintains that all values are important, and each has its place. Thus, the Jewish people must carefully consider what is uniquely positive in each nation's character and culture, respect it, and learn from it, thereby empowering and elevating it. The Jewish nation needs to perfect itself by absorbing the faith, truth, and good found in Torah and *mitzvot*, and combine that with what is positive in other cultures, integrating them into one harmonious whole.

If they succeed at this, the more the other faiths will be blessed, bringing the whole world closer to redemption.

That is when the words of the prophet will be fulfilled:

> *In the days to come, the Mount of the Lord's house shall stand firm above the mountains and tower above the hills; and all the nations shall gaze on it with joy. And the many peoples shall go and say: "Come, let us go up to the Mount of the Lord, to the house of the God of Jacob; that He may instruct us in His ways, and that we may walk in His paths." For Torah shall come forth from Zion, the word of the Lord from Jerusalem. Thus He will judge among the nations and arbitrate for the many peoples, and they shall beat their swords into plowshares and their spears into pruning hooks. Nation shall not take up sword against nation; they shall never again know war (Isaiah 2:2-4).*

Furthermore, "The wolf shall dwell with the lamb, and the leopard lie down with the kid... In all of My sacred Mount, nothing evil or vile shall be done. For the land shall be filled with devotion to the Lord as water covers the sea" (*ibid.* 11:6, 9).

CHAPTER 2

From Genesis Through the Revelation at Sinai

1. The Creation

In six days God created the heaven and earth and all its contents, resting on the seventh day. The purpose of creation was to provide 'good' to all creatures, as the verse states, "And God saw all that He had made, and found it very good" (Genesis 1:31). In order for people to merit that goodness, God created people in the divine image. He left humans room to partner with Him in improving the world, as we read, "And God created man in His image, in the image of God He created him; male and female He created them" (*ibid.* 1:27), and "The Lord God took the man and placed him in the garden of Eden to work it [to improve it] and tend it [so that it would not be ruined]" (*ibid.* 2:15).

How long were these six days? That question can be answered in a number of different ways. Since the sun and moon were not created until the fourth day (*ibid.* 1:16), it is clear that Genesis is not speaking about days as we know them. Rather, the six days represent the hierarchy of creation on a conceptual level. Is this compatible with the theory of evolution popular in modern thought? Yes, it could be, since "days" can refer to epoch time periods. The significance of the creation of man containing a soul that God breathed into him (*ibid.* 2:7) enables people to choose to move the world forward. In any event, even if we accept the theory of evolution, the creation of the world reflects a planned, purposeful process at the hands of the Creator. The destiny of humanity, created in the image of God, is to choose what is right and thereby become God's partner in perfecting the world.

2. Adam's Sin

"Of every tree of the garden you are free to eat; but as for the tree of knowledge of good and evil, you must not eat of it; for as soon as you eat of it, you shall die" (Genesis 2:17). Human survival depends on what is absorbed – ideas as well as food. God commanded man to eat and enjoy all the trees in the Garden of Eden. Because Adam was able to "digest" the fruits, he could discern what was good and reject what was bad, without being drawn to it. However, God warned Adam not to eat from the tree of knowledge, because its fruits contained an intense mixture of positive and negative dimensions too powerful for him to distinguish. Eating those fruits would allow the evil elements they contained to pierce his body and soul, causing his death. As an aside, this is the concept underlying a positive type of conservatism, which is cautious of being led astray by potentially dangerous revolutionary ideas; even if such ideas have positive aspects, their negative ones might destroy all that is good.

Unfortunately, Adam sinned and ate from the tree of knowledge of good and evil. He was punished with expulsion from the Garden of Eden into the land cursed due to his sin. His survival depended on harsh physical labor which continued until his death. Only then would his body return to the earth from which it came. Generation after generation, his descendants would eat by the sweat of their brow (*ibid.* 2:17-19) and undergo a grueling journey rife with crises until they could achieve progress. The goal of this punishment is for humanity to fulfill its original mission which was intended to be easy, pleasant, and self-taught. Instead, it is a lengthy process filled with trials and tribulations, whereby humanity learns how to progress.

Eventually, once perfection is attained and evil is transformed into good, humanity will reach a level even loftier than that of Adam in the garden. The status of penitents – who can change from evil to good, – is greater than that of the righteous, who have never been exposed to temptation and have been good all their lives.

3. The Flood and Noah

After the expulsion from the Garden of Eden, humanity began to master the art of survival in this world. However, the evil ingested by Adam started to "grow", leading to a wave of murders, sexual immorality, and idol worship. Worst of all was the corruption and thievery of the powerful which destroyed everything good. They exploited nature rather than developing it, bringing humanity to the brink of collapse. With the land replete with corruption, their judgment was sealed (Genesis 6:13). Everyone was to be wiped off the face of the earth by a flood.

While all other people deteriorated into sinfulness, Noah remained perfectly righteous. He was not drawn after the ways of his corrupt society, but continued to develop through plowing and planting. Therefore, God commanded him to build an ark to save himself and his family, along with the animals and birds – a male and female of every non-kosher type, and seven pairs of all kosher creatures.

4. The Seven Noahide Laws

After the flood and the lessons learned from it, God made a covenant with Noah, his children, and the animals. He promised that He would never again subvert the natural order and flood the earth. He also commanded the human survivors to be fruitful and multiply and develop the world, while observing seven commandments that reflect natural law. They are:

The prohibitions of:
1) Idol worship.
2) Murder.
3) Sexual immorality.
4) Stealing and theft.
5) Cursing the Creator.
6) Cruelty toward animals, specifically cutting off part of an animal to eat while it is still alive.

And the obligation:
7) To establish a judicial system to govern society and social interactions.

These are referred to as the Seven Noahide Laws.

5. Noah and Abraham

Noah was perfectly righteous and he distinguished himself from the rest of his generation, whose sins destroyed the world, by staying honest and working hard. Yet, Noah did not expend any effort to help the people of his generation repent. He was satisfied with knowing that he was behaving properly and productively. Perhaps Noah realized there was no chance the people would repent, so he preferred to preserve his integrity and serve as an example of a life properly lived. As a result, Noah's legacy reflects good deeds, and honest living and being careful not to cause harm. But it lacks the grand divine vision of continuously striving to perfect the world.

By contrast, Abraham, born 10 generations after Noah, used his very being to make the world a better place. He saw the good in humanity and tried to improve their lives. If people were sinful, Abraham sought to help them repent, guiding them on the path of truth and virtue. His essence was a strong protest against idol worship and human exploitation. That is the legacy of the Jewish nation: not satisfied with just a partial improvement, but always striving to bring the world to complete perfection. This begins with the soul that God gave the Israelites, Abraham's heirs, a soul that strives to cling to God using divine ideals and values to perfect the world.

6. Our Father Abraham and Our Mother Sarah

The Jewish people have three patriarchs and four matriarchs: Abraham, Isaac, and Jacob; Sarah, Rebecca, Rachel, and Leah. We will briefly summarize their lives and legacies.

Abraham and Sarah were the first ones to introduce belief in monotheism to the world. They had a firm faith in one God and they personified kindness. They welcomed travelers into their tent, supported their family in times of trouble, and attracted many to believe in the one God. Unfortunately, Sarah was unable to give birth and she and Abraham endured many childless years. This was a tremendous test, since these models of faith did not seem to merit what ordinary people do. Abraham was not interested in taking an additional wife despite it being common practice at that time. God revealed Himself and made him a promise: "'Look toward heaven and count the stars . . . So will your offspring be.' And because he put his trust in the Lord, He credited it to him as righteousness" (Genesis 15:5-6).

Many years passed and realizing that she had still not

conceived, Sarah brought her Egyptian maidservant, Hagar, to Abraham. Sarah hoped that Hagar would bear a child whom they could raise together, an early form of 'surrogacy'. When Ishmael was born, however, Sarah's hopes that Hagar would continue to act respectfully and raise the child in accordance with Sarah's values were not fulfilled.

Abraham and Sarah continued teaching faith and kindness to everyone. God had also commanded Abraham to undergo circumcision. One hot afternoon, God sent three angels disguised as travelers and Abraham and Sarah invited them in to eat and drink, as usual. Jewish tradition explains that the angels arrived three days after Abraham had been circumcised and when he would have been in great pain. Since it was also a particularly hot day, we would have expected him to be resting in his tent. Yet, Abraham was unwilling to miss the chance to welcome guests out of the heat into the shelter provided by his tent. Therefore, he was sitting and waiting at the entrance and when he saw the three travelers he ran to greet them and invite them in. During the meal, one of the guests revealed he was an angel and relayed the news that they would give birth to a boy next year.

After their son Isaac was born, his half-brother Ishmael was drawn towards perverse behaviors and culture. Sarah saw that he was likely to be a negative influence on Isaac and destroy their spiritual endeavors. She therefore demanded that Ishmael be expelled, along with his mother Hagar, who had been responsible for his education. This request greatly pained Abraham. However, God appeared to him and said, "Do not be distressed over the boy or your maidservant; whatever Sarah tells you, do as she says, for it is through Isaac that offspring shall be continued for you. As for the son of the maidservant, I will make a nation of him too, for he is your seed" (Genesis 21:12-13). Sarah's initiative ensured that Abraham and Sarah's legacy would continue.

7. The Binding of Isaac

"Some time afterward, God put Abraham to the test...He said, 'Take your son, your favored one, Isaac, whom you love, and go to the land of Moriah, and offer him there as a burnt offering on one of the hills that I will point out to you'" (Genesis 22:1-2). The test was frightening, but Abraham retained his belief in God. Since the divine imperative he had received through prophecy was clear and categorical, he humbly obeyed it. Although Abraham did not understand the reason or purpose behind the command, he knew it emanated from God – Creator of the world and source of life, goodness, truth, justice, and morality – so he accepted it. He woke up early, took his only son to Mount Moriah, and bound him on the altar in preparation for the sacrifice. Suddenly, an angel called to Abraham from heaven with a message from God:

> "Abraham! Abraham!...Do not raise your hand against the boy or do anything to him. For I know now that you fear God, since you have not withheld your son, your favored one, from Me...By Myself I swear, the Lord declares: Because you have done this and have not withheld your son, your favored one, I will bestow My blessing upon you and make your descendants as numerous as the stars of heaven and the sand on the seashore; and your descendants shall seize the gates of their foes. All the nations of the earth shall be blessed through your descendants, because you have listened to My voice" (Genesis 22:11-12 and 16-18).

It was clear in retrospect that God never intended for Abraham to sacrifice his son Isaac. Such was the practice of the surrounding idol worshipers, who would sacrifice their children to appease their gods. Rather, God wanted to reveal the power of Abraham and Isaac who were willing to sacrifice everything in order to reveal God's word and bring blessing to the world. Centuries later, the Divine Presence dwelled on Mount Moriah, the place of the binding, and the Jews built the Holy Temple there. For generations, the binding of Isaac has served as a stellar model of faith, a symbol of self-sacrifice to sanctify God's name and the ultimate portrayal of faith and morality in the world.

8. Our Father Isaac and Our Mother Rebecca

The challenge Isaac faced was to continue the legacy of his great father, who had revealed the light of faith to the world. It is often easier to start a revolution than to sustain it over time. Isaac carried on the legacy, faithfully and with fortitude. It is a characteristic fact of Isaac's life that he was the only one of the forefathers born in the Land of Israel and never left it. Even when famine struck and Isaac sought to go to Egypt as his father had done, God instructed him to remain in the Land. In his agricultural endeavors he was diligent and successful. Isaac even managed to return and open the wells his father had dug, after the Philistines had sealed them.

The story of the quest to find a wife for Isaac, epitomizes the legacy of kindness in Abraham and Sarah's family. Abraham's servant Eliezer needed criteria to evaluate a worthy candidate to become Isaac's wife. So he traveled to Haran, stood near a spring, and decided to ask the young women there to give him a little water to drink. The woman who would not only give him water, but also offer water to his camels, she would be the right one for Isaac. God arranged for Rebecca – Abraham's relative – to be there and when Eliezer asked, she quickly gave it to him. Then, out of her own diligence and goodness, she hurried back to the well and drew more water to provide for all of the thirsty camels.

Initially Rebecca was also infertile, and after years of prayer, she gave birth to twins, Jacob and Esau. The boys paths diverged: Jacob was a humble person who stayed at home, while Esau was a hunter and man of the field, willing to kill to get what he sought. When Jacob saw that Esau was not suited to continue the family's legacy and how he demeaned his role to lead as the firstborn – Jacob acquired the birthright from his brother in exchange for a bowl of lentils.

When Isaac was old and partially blind, he wished to bless his firstborn son. Rebecca was aware of Esau's misconduct and understood he was not suited to continue their mission. She ordered Jacob to dress up as his brother and receive the blessing meant for Esau and that is how Isaac blessed Jacob. After Isaac became aware of his mistake, he did not rescind his blessing. Rather, he accepted that the blessing was destined for Jacob. It seems that Isaac also knew Esau was sinful but since he was the firstborn, he assumed that there was no choice but to bless him. When Isaac understood that he had accidentally blessed Jacob and that Esau had already sold the birthright to his brother, Isaac was pleased that God had arranged things in such a way so that Jacob received the blessing.

9. Our Father Jacob

When Rebecca realized that Esau was planning to kill his brother in revenge for the blessing incident, she sent Jacob to her family in Haran. She hoped he would find a wife there and eventually return home. Rebecca even asked Isaac to bless Jacob before his departure. Isaac granted him the blessing of Abraham – to be fruitful and multiply and inherit the Land.

When Jacob arrived in Haran, he met and fell in love with Rachel, the daughter of his mother's brother, Laban. In order to marry her, Jacob agreed to Laban's demands that he work for him for seven years. After completing those years, on the night of their wedding, Laban switched Rachel with his older daughter Leah. In the morning, Jacob discovered he had married Leah instead, and confronted Laban about the deception. Laban suggested he could marry Rachel too, in exchange for another seven years of work. Jacob complied since Laban had the upper hand and was capable of destroying those who stood in his way. After fulfilling his contractual years for his wives, Jacob worked another six years as Laban's partner in order to accumulate assets before returning to the Land. Despite being repeatedly cheated by Laban, Jacob worked steadily and faithfully for 20 years, shepherding the sheep during the hot summer days and the cold winter nights. This merited God protecting Jacob and blessing his labors.

10. Our Mothers Rachel and Leah, and the Twelve Tribes

Leah loved Jacob very much and was blessed to have seven children with him, six sons and a daughter: Reuben, Simon, Levi, Judah, Issachar, Zebulun, and Dinah. Rachel, whom Jacob loved more than Leah, was barren for many years. When Rachel lost hope of having children, she gave Jacob her maidservant Bilhah, hoping she would merit children that way. Jacob and Bilhah had two sons, Dan and Naphtali. Leah followed in her sister's footsteps and also gave her maidservant Zilpah to Jacob. They had two sons, Gad and Asher. Ultimately, Rachel herself gave birth to two sons, Joseph and Benjamin, but she died while giving birth to Benjamin. Thus, Jacob fathered 12 sons, each of whom became the leader of a tribe of Israel. When Jacob returned to the Land, he wrestled with an angel and was given the name "Israel" (based on the Hebrew for "wrestled"). The Jewish nation has been called Israel ever since.

Many insights can be derived from the traits of Rachel and Leah. There are numerous commentaries which discuss the characters of their children, each following a distinct path. As the children grew into adults, strong tensions increased between Leah's sons and Rachel's son Joseph, who was particularly capable and favored by their father Jacob. The brothers believed that like Ishmael and Esau, Joseph was not suited to continue their father's legacy. They sold him into Egyptian slavery, and told their father he had been devoured by a wild animal. Jacob's grief was endless over the loss of his beloved and talented son, the orphaned child of his beloved wife Rachel.

Following a long and complicated journey, Joseph the slave ultimately met Pharaoh the king of Egypt. Joseph interpreted Pharaoh's dreams and saved the kingdom from starvation. As a result, he was appointed second-in-command in Egypt. When the famine struck the Land of Israel (Canaan), Joseph's brothers traveled to Egypt to buy food. When they arrived, Joseph set up a situation whereby he could test his brothers and determine whether they regretted their actions. Without knowing who he was, they expressed their regrets for having sold their brother. When Joseph saw this, he burst into tears, revealed his identity, and forgave them for selling him. He asked his brothers to tell their father Jacob that he was alive and second to the king in Egypt. Consequently, Jacob's entire family moved to Egypt.

Over the course of his life, Jacob endured many hardships: his struggle with his brother Esau, his complicated marriages created by Laban's trickery, the death of his wife Rachel in childbirth, and the difficulties of raising and educating his children. Worst of all was the rivalry between his sons that drove to them selling Joseph into slavery. Nevertheless, due to the merit of Jacob's adherence to his faith and service to God, ultimately all the sins were rectified, and his sons were reunited. All of them, without exception, stood together around his deathbed and accepted his last request – to cling to their ancestors' legacy.

According to Jewish tradition, Jacob was worried on his deathbed that one of his children might not sustain the path of faith. His twelve sons reassured him by reciting together the words of the Shema: "Hear, O Israel! The Lord is our God, the Lord is one." They were saying: "Israel, our father! Do not worry. The Lord your God is our God as well. He is one and there is no other." This put Jacob's mind at ease and he responded: "Blessed be the name of His glorious kingdom forever and ever." With his last words, Jacob requested that his children return his body to the Land of Israel and bury him with his ancestors in the Cave of the Patriarchs in Hebron. This would be the last time the Israelites visited the Land before they began their long, harsh years of slavery in Egypt.

11. The Meaning of the Egyptian Enslavement and the Exodus

In the prophetic vision referred to as "The Covenant between the Parts," Abraham was informed that his descendants would be enslaved by a foreign nation but would ultimately depart triumphantly, with great wealth. As long as Joseph was alive, the Egyptians treated the Israelites well. After his death, they forgot what he had done for them, and proceeded to enslave them, a situation which lasted about 120 years. The Israelites retained their faith that God would redeem them from Egypt and bring them to the good Land which He had promised their ancestors. This belief enabled them to preserve their identity as they continued to be fruitful and multiply, becoming a large nation.

Since the mission of the Jewish people is to lead the redemption of the world from its tyranny and troubles, the Jews first needed to suffer every type of evil humanity is capable of. This is why the Israelites were enslaved to the Egyptian Empire which was the most powerful, pagan society then in existence.

The Egyptians philosophy valued only the material, believing that as long as the body exists, the person lives. Thus, to ensure themselves a dignified eternal existence, they had their bodies mummified and placed in ornate tombs in massive pyramids. The Egyptians' pagan worldview believed in the powers exhibited in nature. Yet while nature can possess power, beauty, and wisdom, it lacks justice and morality. The strong devour the weak and powerful people control weaker ones, enslaving them. Rather than striving for greater morality, paganism glorifies the natural order, including its abuse of power. This led the Egyptians to depravity. Their moral failings ranged from ingratitude toward Joseph by enslaving his descendants, to drowning innocent Jewish baby boys.

Thus, the Exodus of the Israelites from Egypt was more than their freedom from physical enslavement. It was also an exodus from a pagan culture that had "enslaved" morality. Monotheism, in contrast, fosters the free expression of humane values. God struck the Egyptian deities with signs and wonders during the Exodus to teach us that the spiritual can rule over the natural to shape the world in accordance with divine ideals. Despite their physical redemption, if the Israelites were still enslaved spiritually and culturally, they would have remained in Egypt, ruling over their former owners, as other nations have done in similar circumstances. However, the Israelites were also freed from the Egyptian pagan ideology, revealing the value of faith and freedom to the world. Therefore, they did not harm the Egyptians' freedom.

Moreover, God actually commanded the Jews that if an Egyptian wished to convert to Judaism, he should be accepted: "You shall not abhor an Egyptian, for you were a stranger in his land" (Deuteronomy 23:8). Jews are commanded to remember the positives that existed even when they were slaves in Egypt. They must not behave like the ungrateful Egyptians who enslaved Joseph's descendants, acting as if they had forgotten how Joseph saved their people from famine and the empire from collapse.

As a result of their terrible enslavement, Jews learned the horrific moral depths to which people can sink, even using violence to enslave human beings for financial gain. This experience forced them realize how essential it is to cling to faith in God, the Torah and *mitzvot*, which liberates us from pagan worldviews that lead to moral degeneracy. For this reason, when the Torah prohibits causing pain to the stranger or the weak, it refers to our experience in Egypt: "When a stranger resides with you in your land, you shall not wrong him. The stranger who resides with you shall be to you as one of your citizens; you shall love him as yourself, for you were strangers in the land of Egypt; I the Lord am your God" (Leviticus 19:33-34), and "You shall not oppress a stranger, for you know the feelings of the stranger, having yourselves been strangers in the land of Egypt" (Exodus 23:9).

12. How the Exodus Led to Faith

Due to their prolonged slavery, the Jewish people were able to absorb pure faith in God and to accept the Torah and *mitzvot*, whose goals are perfecting the world via God's ways. Other nations have undergone a gradual process of development – from family to tribe to nation. Along the way, they created cultures and religions which provided a framework for their natural beliefs, fostering their ideology. In contrast, the Israelites developed into a nation while they were enslaved without any culture or nationality of their own. This left them receptive to adopting faith and the divine Torah, as they were not tethered to any lifestyle or culture developed over generations.

The Exodus was accompanied by signs and wonders never previously seen in the world. This phenomenon was meant to reveal to the Israelites and to the world at large, the power of God, Creator of heaven and earth. All of nature is a divine creation under God's control. According to Jewish tradition, God created the world by means of ten statements (*Ethics of the Fathers* 5:1).

When He decided to reveal Himself to humanity through the Israelites, and the Egyptians refused to listen to Him and free their slaves, God to send ten plagues (parallel to the ten statements). Later, God used those ten statements at Mount Sinai transformed into the Ten Commandments, which provide fundamental meaning to sustain the world. (See section 17 below.)

13. Leaving Egypt with Great Wealth

In order to avoid being "enslaved" by the desire for money and pleasure, certain spiritual and philosophical types go to the other extreme by belittling the material world and striving only for spiritual truth. However, Judaism believes that everything is important. The physical and material aspects of life have a role to play, as long as they are used as tools in the service of spiritual values, and not seen as the ultimate goal.

To help the Israelites understand this, God decreed that they be enslaved to the wealthy nation of Egypt. Whereas the Egyptians intended to exploit them, the Israelites triumphed in physical and material ways. During the early slavery years, they were fruitful and multiplied until they became a massive community. Later, when the Israelites were redeemed from Egypt, they left with great wealth. This served as partial payment for their hard work over many years, and as partial compensation for their great suffering. Ultimately, justice prevailed. The material values cultivated by Egypt served as a platform for the manifestation of the Divine Presence: the silver and gold vessels the Israelites received from the Egyptians provided materials to build the Tabernacle, and later the Temple.

14. Splitting the Red Sea

After the Egyptians surrendered and agreed to release the Israelites, God hardened their hearts. Only if the decision was truly an expression of repentance would the Egyptians agree to emancipate their slaves. Otherwise, the Egyptians would be filled with arrogance and seek to enslave the Jews again. And so it was. The Egyptian army chased the Israelites, and caught up with them near the Red Sea. When the Israelites saw the Egyptians, they screamed out to God. God responded that they should act to save themselves, by entering the sea, rather than cry for help. Under Moses' leadership the people entered and a great miracle occurred. The sea split and the Israelites passed through it on dry land, with the Egyptian army in hot pursuit. When the last of the Israelites emerged from the sea, the waters returned to normal, and the entire Egyptian army was drowned.

Ordinarily, a miracle is not something desirable. God created nature and its rules so that people would use their abilities to harness its laws in the best way possible. Despite this, in order to reveal to the world His might, His providence, and the protection of His nation, God struck the Egyptians with the ten plagues, split the Red Sea, and led His children through it.

15. "Na'aseh VeNishma"

Following the Exodus, God brought His nation to Mount Sinai, and commanded His loyal emissary Moses to prepare them to receive the Torah:

Thus shall you say to the house of Jacob and declare to the children of Israel: You have seen what I did to the Egyptians, how I bore you on eagles' wings and brought you to Me. Now then, if you will obey Me faithfully and keep My covenant, you shall be My treasured possession among all the peoples. Indeed, all the earth is Mine, but you shall be to Me a kingdom of priests and a holy nation (Exodus 19:3-6).

All the people answered as one, saying, "All that the Lord has spoken, we will do (na'aseh)!" Later, they expanded this commitment and proclaimed, "All that the Lord has spoken, we will do (na'aseh) and we will listen (nishma)!" (ibid. 19:8 and 24:7).

In other words, the Israelites' great faith in God led them first to agree to perform all the *mitzvot* even if they did not understand their significance. Later, they agreed to study the Torah in order to understand the meaning of the *mitzvot*. Ever since, the expression "*na'aseh ve-nishma*" serves as a declaration of faith and a statement of identification with the divine mandate.

16. The Revelation at Mount Sinai

After the Israelites agreed to accept the Torah, what followed was the most inspiring, wonderous event in the history of the world. An entire nation stood and listened to the voice of God addressing them:

> *There was thunder and lightning, and a dense cloud upon the mountain, and a very loud blast of the shofar; and all the people who were in the camp trembled. Moses led the people out of the camp toward God, and they took their places at the foot of the mountain. Now Mount Sinai was all in smoke, for the Lord had come down upon it in fire; the smoke rose like the smoke of a kiln, and the whole mountain trembled violently. The sound of the shofar grew louder and louder. As Moses spoke, God answered him in thunder. The Lord came down upon Mount Sinai, on the top of the mountain... God then spoke all these words (Exodus 19:16-20:1).*

The words that God spoke were the Ten Commandments. This occasion was so powerful and transcendent that the Jews were afraid they would not survive it:

> *All the people witnessed the thunder and lightning, the sound of the shofar, and the mountain smoking; and when the people saw it, they fell back and stood at a distance. "You*

*speak to us," they said to Moses, "and we will understand;
but let not God speak to us, lest we die" (ibid. 20:14-15).*

Moses reassured the people, explaining that this other-
worldly occasion was meant to elevate them and imbue them
with a deep-rooted faith, in order to overcome the evil inclination and avoid sin (*ibid.* 20:16). The revelation at Sinai also
certified that Moses' prophetic ability was far beyond that of
all other past and future prophets, since he was chosen to receive God's Torah and transmit it to the Jewish people.

After the revelation, Moses spent 40 days on the mountain.
During that time, God presented him with the tablets of the
covenant (on which the Ten Commandments were engraved)
and taught him the foundation and essentials of the entire
Torah. Throughout the forty years that the Jews wandered in
the desert, Moses continued to receive sections of the Torah
from God, until the Torah's closure with the death of Moses.

17. The Ten Commandments

Because the Ten Commandments (Exodus 20:2-13) are so
important, we will present them here with brief explanations.

1) "I the Lord am your God Who brought you out of the
land of Egypt, the house of bondage." Faith is learned
through the story of God's revelation to the Israelites.
2) "You shall have no other gods besides Me. You shall not
make for yourself a sculptured image, or any likeness of
what is in the heavens above, or on the earth below, or
in the waters under the earth. You shall not bow down
to them or serve them. For I the Lord your God am an
impassioned God, visiting the guilt of the parents upon
the children, upon the third and upon the fourth generations of those who reject Me, but showing kindness to

the thousandth generation of those who love Me and keep My commandments." (See chapter 15 below, especially sections 6-7 and 13, on the commandment to have faith and the prohibition of idol worship.)

3) "You shall not take the name of the Lord your God in vain, for the Lord will not hold guiltless one who takes His name in vain." We are instructed to respect and honor God by not taking His name in vain, especially in the context of oath-taking. It is a natural outgrowth of the two previous commandments, which deal with faith in God and the rejection of idols.

4) "Remember the Sabbath day and keep it holy. Six days you shall labor and do all your work, but the seventh day is a Sabbath of the Lord your God; you shall not do any work – you, your son or daughter, your male or female slave, or your cattle, or the stranger who is within your settlements. For in six days the Lord made heaven and earth and sea, and all that is in them, and He rested on the seventh day; therefore the Lord blessed the Sabbath day and made it holy." Faith in God must be expressed in all dimensions, including the dimension of time. The Sabbath (Shabbat) is the day when we are commanded to abstain from productive labor, to focus on the fundamentals of faith, and to study Torah in a relaxed state of enjoyment. (See chapters 26-28 below for more about Shabbat.)

5) "Honor your father and your mother, that you may lengthen your days on the Land that the Lord your God is assigning to you." Respecting parents is an extension of respecting God and an outgrowth of gratitude. Gratitude is a core value, a moral necessity. When a person is grateful to one's parents, it opens one up to be grateful to everyone, and especially to the Almighty. (For more about this commandment, see chapter 12 below.)

6) "You shall not murder." This commandment teaches us about the sanctity of human life. Since each person is created in the image of God, it is forbidden to shorten a life. This leads to many other commandments aimed at protecting and preserving human life. (See chapter 4 below for more on this commandment.)

7) "You shall not commit adultery." This commandment is aimed at preventing damage to the sanctity of the marriage covenant. (See chapters 8-11 for more on this commandment and the other laws of marriage.)

8) "You shall not steal." The value of a human being is also expressed through respecting the product of one's labor and creativity. Therefore, it is forbidden to steal anything that belongs to someone else. (Clearly, then, it is also forbidden to "steal" a person and make one a slave.) Theft does damage on three levels. It harms the individual victim from whom something was stolen; it undermines the foundations of society, weakening people's motivation to labor and create, and it moves society in the direction of poverty and shortages. (See chapters 3 and 5 below for laws related to this commandment.)

9) "You shall not bear false witness against your neighbor." It is prohibited to testify falsely in court. This commandment, like many others in the Torah, is meant to reinforce the status of the judiciary and ensure justice is done. (See chapter 7 for more about this commandment.)

10) "You shall not covet your neighbor's house; you shall not covet your neighbor's wife, or his male or female slave, or his ox or donkey, or anything that is your neighbor's." Greed and desire are at the root of many interpersonal sins. Therefore, the Torah commands us to quash them at the very outset, before the thoughts are translated into actions. (See also 3:33 below.)

Interpersonal *Mitzvot*

Chapter 3: Interpersonal *Mitzvot*................42
Chapter 4: The Value of Human Life.............73
Chapter 5: Justice...........................84
Chapter 6: Charity...........................95
Chapter 7: The Justice System.................110

CHAPTER 3

Interpersonal *Mitzvot*

1. "Love Your Fellow as Yourself" – A Major Torah Principle

Two general *mitzvot* serve as the basis for all interpersonal relations. The first is the *mitzva* of loving every Jew. The second is the prohibition of hating any Jew. These *mitzvot* are rooted in the concept that the entire Jewish people is one big family, hence we must all feel like siblings. As it says, "You shall not hate your brother in your heart . . . Love your fellow as yourself" (Leviticus 19:17-18). These *mitzvot* are the foundation of the entire Torah, as Rabbi Akiva said: "Love your fellow as yourself – this is a major Torah principle." According to the Talmud (*Shabbat* 31a), Hillel the Elder made a similar statement when a prospective convert asked him to teach him the whole Torah on one foot: "What you hate, do not do to your fellow. This is the essence of the Torah. The rest is in the details."

Our lives are lived primarily within the interpersonal arena – relationships with our family, friends, and neighbors. Thus, most of the *mitzvot* we encounter are contained in these two general categories. If these principles guide us, we will spend most of our time doing *mitzvot*. Let us take this a step further.

Even the *mitzvot* that relate to our relationship with God depend on interpersonal *mitzvot*. If we do not care about other people and do not try to avoid hurting them, we are self-absorbed, living in our own selfish bubble. We are unable to see the world as it really is, so we are unable to open ourselves up to faith in God. Breaking out of the narrowness of egotism and experiencing the vastness of faith can be accomplished through love, love through which we identify with the other and want good for them in the same way we want good for ourselves. This in turn allows us to connect to the vision of perfecting the world through Torah and *mitzvot*.

2. Defining the *Mitzva* to Love

In practice, it is impossible for us to know every one of our broader Jewish family and to actively express our love for them all. Rather, love and a sense of responsibility towards others are manifested from the inner circle outwards: first to one's spouse, then immediate family, friends and more distant family, acquaintances and neighbors, and so on. How then does "Love your fellow as yourself" apply to the entire Jewish people? We are meant to feel kinship with all Jews, and to want the best for each one of them just as we want the best for ourselves. That way, if we do come across a fellow Jew in trouble and we are able to help, we will do so, just as we would want to be helped if the situation were reversed.

3. Defining the Prohibition to Hate

"You shall not hate your brother in your heart" means it is forbidden to hope that something bad will happen to a fellow Jew. This is true even if we neither speak nor act against them. Additionally, if we hate another so much that we refuse to say hello or speak to them, we transgress this prohibition.

4. Jews and Non-Jews

As we said above, love is manifested from the inner circle outwards. Beyond the Jewish people is the circle that includes all of humanity, irrespective of opinions, religions, and nationalities. Accordingly, Jews should care about non-Jews. However, when it comes to fellow Jews, all Jews must feel like family, so the love and commitment towards them are expected to be greater than towards others.

One may not hate a fellow Jew even if that Jew is a sinner. A sinner must be criticized and sometimes even punished, yet not hated, just as in a family one must not feel hatred towards a sibling even if he or she has behaved badly. By contrast, when it comes to non-Jews who are evil, it is justified and sometimes even advisable to hate them and view them as enemies.

5. The Inherent Worth of a Human Being Created in the Image of God

According to Ben Azzai, there is an even greater principle than that of loving your fellow, namely the principle of human worth (*kevod ha-adam*), which derives from humans having been created in the image of God. The Torah clearly states, "This is the record of Adam's line. When God created man, He made him in the likeness of God; male and female He created them" (Genesis 5:1). Similarly, "And God created man in His image, in the image of God He created him; male and female He created them" (*ibid.* 1:27).

Man is created in the image and likeness of God – what does that mean? It means that humans, like God, have free will. Each person can better (or worsen) his or her own condition as well as the condition of the world at large. Since we have the ability to improve the world, we have the responsibility to do so. Thus, the principle of human worth would seem to be qualitatively greater than "Love your fellow as yourself," because it touches the very definition of our humanity. This principle is also quantitatively greater, as it applies equally to all of humanity.

6. The Interpersonal is the Gateway to God

Despite the importance of the principle of human worth and responsibility, it is generally accepted that the principle of "Love your fellow as yourself" is more important, in the sense it is more demanding. While we should respect others for their ability and responsibility to choose goodness, respect is not enough. We must love our fellow human beings and act in their best interests.

Beyond this, love allows us to break through the barrier of our own selfishness, revealing the image of God within ourselves. God created us with a divine soul. However, to protect our free will and enable us to be independent, God concealed our soul's divine light. When we interact lovingly with other people, helping them in times of trouble or rejoicing with them during times of joy, the image of God in them becomes apparent to us. In turn, our soul begins to shine too, allowing us to grow spiritually and improve our connection with God. The interpersonal *mitzvot* guide us in this direction.

The independence and uniqueness of every human being has negative consequences as well, namely the tendencies to separation, competition, and war. The great challenge facing us all is to reveal our inner unity, which is rooted in the oneness of God Who created everything and gives life to everything. Through faith, love, and cooperation, everyone receives blessing from the divine source. And it all starts with the *mitzva* to "Love your fellow as yourself."

7. Providing Aid

Helping someone in need is a *mitzva*. This includes helping a neighbor move heavy furniture, helping a mother having difficulty pushing a stroller up the stairs, offering a ride to a friend or helping someone whose car has broken down.

Even if the person in need is an enemy, the Torah stresses that the *mitzva* to provide aid still applies. Therefore, if one sees an enemy's donkey staggering under its load, one must help unburden the donkey and repack the load (Exodus 23:5). With this, the Torah establishes a norm – even when two people are at odds, they need to set limits as to how far they take their feud. When someone needs help, provide it. If people follow this norm, the hatred will eventually dissolve, and love will again assume its rightful place.

8. Returning Lost Objects

If we find an item someone has lost or forgotten, we must return it. We should feel a strong enough sense of kinship and responsibility towards our fellow that we cannot ignore this lost object. As it says, "If you see your fellow's ox or sheep gone astray, do not ignore it; you must take it back to your fellow... And so too shall you do with anything your fellow loses and you find; you must not remain indifferent" (Deuteronomy 22:1-3). Similarly, if we see thieves about to break into a car or a home, we cannot ignore it but must call the police. If we see water flooding a neighbor's apartment, we cannot disregard it. We must call the neighbor and work to find a solution to the problem before there is serious damage.

If we find a lost object and do not know to whom it belongs, we should look for the owner using accepted methods, as long as the item is valuable enough to make it worth the effort. The more valuable the lost item (whether financially or emotionally), the more of an effort must be made to return it. When there is no chance of finding the owner, and one can assume the owner has given up on getting the item back, it becomes the property of the finder.

9. Not Belittling People

Since people are created in the image of God, we must treat them with respect. No one may be belittled, even if they are not aware of it. As it says, "You shall not insult the deaf" (Leviticus 19:14). This means it is prohibited to demean anyone even if they cannot hear you and do not know they are being disparaged.

An employer must be careful to treat his or her employees respectfully. Don't give them humiliating work or order them around in a demeaning way. Anyone who sees or hears a person disparaging someone else should be horrified and feel as if they themselves were hurt. The Sages state that one who raises his hand to strike another, even if they do not carry through, is considered wicked. Slapping another person's face is like slapping the face of God. Even after a person has died, the respect due their body demands we bury them in a timely fashion. There is even a *mitzva* to bury enemy soldiers respectfully (Ezekiel 39:13).

10. Honoring the Wise, the Elderly, and Community Leaders

There is a *mitzva* to honor the wise and the elderly, and to stand up when they enter or exit the room. As it says, "You shall rise before the aged and show deference to the wise" (Leviticus 19:32). Those who honor the elderly and the wise are privileged to learn from their wisdom and experience. A community that honors its elders and sages is blessed and enriched by them.

The Torah commands us to treat judges and community leaders with respect, as long as they are not wicked. Even a person who loses a court case or is harmed by a communal ordinance must take care not to mock or curse the judge or leader (Exodus 22:27), even in private. Since leaders represent the community, honoring them is honoring the community, and the community's wellbeing depends on them.

11. Human Dignity

Because human life is so valuable, it is right to honor mothers, especially those who have been blessed with many children, and pregnant women who are nourishing new lives. Additionally, it is proper to honor people who excel in their fields, whether scholars, scientists, entrepreneurs, artists, or anyone else. For talented people give expression to the greatness hidden in humanity. Honoring them is honoring the entire human race. In fact, every person is deserving of respect, as every person, created in the image of God, brings something unique to the great tapestry of life.

12. Not Hurting or Embarrassing Anyone

It is forbidden to cause a person pain through words or actions. As it says, "Do not wrong one another, but fear your God; for I the Lord am your God" (Leviticus 25:17). This prohibition includes calling anyone an offensive nickname, making fun of something about them (e.g., being fat or stupid), or making fun of something they did or said. Additionally, it is forbidden to hurt a person by reminding them of their mistakes, which they now regret.

The greater the hurt, the greater the sin. Therefore, someone who publicly embarrasses another is committing a serious transgression. In a sense, it is considered murder, as a psychological wound may destroy a person's life. Sometimes, traumas a person experienced as a child or teen leave them fearful of forming relationships. As a result, they never marry and remain alone, missing out on love and happiness. Sometimes, a person insulted by colleagues stops believing in themselves and their ability to succeed, so they fail at work and lose their livelihood. When someone elderly is hurt, they may well think life is worthless, which can lead to premature death. In light of such cases, the Talmud states, "It is better to throw oneself into a fiery furnace than publicly shame anyone" (*Bava Metzia* 59a).

13. Sensitivity to the Orphan, Widow, and Others Who Suffer

It is a *mitzva* to be sensitive to people who have suffered through crises, disasters, or very painful events. These include orphans, widows, the disabled, the ill, and those who have lost children. We should treat them with great sensitivity and friendship. We should make every effort to give them good advice, help them find work, and do anything else necessary to bring them some happiness. Obviously, it is very important not to take advantage of their vulnerability. As it says, "You shall not wrong a stranger or oppress him, for you were strangers in the land of Egypt. You shall not ill-treat any widow or orphan . . . I will heed their outcry as soon as they cry out to Me, and My anger shall blaze forth and I will put you to the sword, and your own wives shall become widows and your children orphans" (Exodus 22:20-23).

14. Treatment of the Convert

The *mitzva* to "Love your fellow as yourself" applies to every fellow Jew, including a convert. In addition, the Torah includes a special *mitzva* to love the convert, as it says (Deuteronomy 10:19), "Love the *ger*." (The word *ger* is generally translated "stranger," but Jewish tradition understands it to refer to a "convert.") Similarly, as we saw above, the Torah prohibits hurting any Jew, as we read, "Do not wrong one another" (Leviticus 25:17). It also specifically prohibits hurting a convert, as we read, "You shall not wrong a *ger*" (Exodus 22:20).

Showing extra love for converts makes sense, since they

relinquished their previous identity and joined the Jewish people of their own free will. Furthermore, it makes sense to be extra careful not to hurt them, as they lack the feeling of security in their natural surroundings. If people are not especially vigilant to treat converts respectfully, there is real concern someone may hurt them without realizing it. Due to their vulnerability, they may well feel great pain even if no one meant harm, but they may not have the courage to confront the offender and resolve things. All this explains the Torah's extra commandment to avoid causing a convert distress.

The extra love we must feel for converts should be expressed in additional willingness to help them. Boaz is a good example of this. Well-respected and wealthy, he saw Ruth, the impoverished convert, picking up the sheaves left behind by the harvesters. Not only did he take pity on her, but he noticed her exceptional character and married her. Ruth and Boaz became the ancestors of the Jewish royal family. King David was their great-grandson.

These *mitzvot* can also apply to returnees to religion, who need to integrate into a new community with unfamiliar behavioral norms. To some extent, these *mitzvot* can even apply to new immigrants, who have left their comfortable homes to come to Israel. They are now vulnerable foreigners with the challenge of establishing themselves in a new country with a foreign language. Therefore, they must be shown much love. Israelis in their natural surroundings must be extra vigilant not to offend them.

15. Including the Poor and Lonely in Our Celebrations

A person planning a celebration, such as a wedding, should remember to first invite acquaintances who are widows, poor, or despondent. It is only by including friends and relatives who are struggling that one can experience true joy and find favor with God. In contrast, if one forgets to invite them, they will feel unwanted, as if their presence poisons the atmosphere, and this will make them feel even worse.

Similarly, at holiday time, we must think of relatives, neighbors, and acquaintances. Perhaps they are having a hard time celebrating, whether due to financial difficulties, loneliness or something else. We should make a point of including them in our holiday celebrations, as it says, "You shall rejoice in your festival, with your son and daughter, your male and female slave, the Levite, the stranger, the fatherless, and the widow in your communities" (Deuteronomy 16:14).

16. Reprimanding When Offended

If a person hurts or insults someone else, it is a *mitzva* to reprimand the offender. This makes him or her aware that what they said or did was hurtful and gives them a chance to repair the relationship. As it says, "You shall not hate your kinsfolk in your heart. Reprove your kinsman but incur no guilt because of him. . . Love your fellow as yourself; I am the Lord" (Leviticus 19:17-18). If instead we hide our upset and hate the person in our heart, we transgress two *mitzvot*: the prohibition to hate and the *mitzva* to reprimand and to love.

Since the goal is to correct, not to attack or to assert superiority, criticism must be delivered respectfully. Care must be taken to minimize any insult or distress. Sometimes, upon being informed our behavior was hurtful, we say we did not intend to hurt or insult. We apologize and promise not to repeat the behavior. When this happens, it turns out there was never a reason to be angry in the first place. A gentle, loving rebuke was all that was necessary. Other times, it becomes clear the offense was the result of a misunderstanding, and if there is anyone who should take offense it is the other person.

In this case, the person who started to reprimand must apologize for the misunderstanding and for thinking badly of the other person without cause. Therefore, when giving rebuke, one must always offer it tentatively, and be ready to hear what the other person has to say in their defense.

Even if the injured party is positive the reprimand will not help because the offender often acts insensitively and hurtfully, there is still a *mitzva* to rebuke them respectfully, because there is always a chance they will take the words to heart. Even if the criticism is rejected, it is safe to assume that if everyone this person insults speaks to them about it, they will improve, at least slightly, over the course of time.

17. Avoiding Revenge and Grudges

When we have been hurt by another person and not reproached them, we are likely to start hating them. We often harbor a desire for revenge, or at least hold a grudge. Therefore, the Torah commands us, "You shall not hate your brother in your heart. Reprove your fellow but incur no guilt because of him. You shall not take vengeance or bear a grudge against the members of your nation. Love your fellow as yourself; I am the Lord" (Leviticus 19:17-18).

How does the Torah define "vengeance" and "grudge bearing"? Let us say Reuven asks Shimon to lend him a hammer and Shimon refuses. Later, Shimon asks Reuven to lend him a screwdriver. If Reuven responds, "I'm not going to lend you the screwdriver because you didn't lend me the hammer," he is guilty of taking revenge. If instead he responds, "Look, I'm not mean like you. You didn't lend me the hammer, but I have pity on the pathetic person you are, and therefore I will lend you the screwdriver," he is guilty of bearing a grudge. The Sages offer an analogy to explain how such behavior is self-defeating. A person trips and hurts his hand. Is it conceivable his hand would then pick up a hammer and break his foot as revenge? Of course not, because the hand and foot are part of one whole. So too, every Jew is an essential part of one whole. If one of us hurts another, it makes no sense for the other to retaliate, as that simply adds to our total pain and misery.

What should we do instead though? The best thing is to rebuke the other person gently and lovingly, to pre-empt any bad feeling developing. Preferably one should do this before the other person needs to ask for a favor, as by that point any type of reproach is likely to be hurtful. If, despite the importance of the *mitzva* of rebuke, we prefer to avoid it, either due to embarrassment or because of fear it would just make the situation worse, we must let go of our hurt feelings. Since we have not rebuked the other person, we have no right to be angry with them. While we may choose to distance ourselves from the person so as not to get hurt again, we cannot ignore them or treat them as an enemy. If we meet them by chance, we should greet them cordially, and help them wholeheartedly if they request a favor.

Observing these *mitzvot* puts an end to most feuds. Even if one side behaves badly, a feud cannot be sustained as long as the other side abstains from revenge and grudges. When we succeed in overcoming the evil inclination and avoid hating others, bearing grudges, and exacting revenge, we acquire the trait of humility. This allows us to look benevolently upon the world, to enjoy life, and to direct our energies towards developing our talents and carrying out our mission. As an extra benefit, we will have more friends and fewer enemies.

18. Judging Favorably

It is a *mitzva* to judge people favorably, as we read, "Judge your fellow with righteousness" (Leviticus 19:15). This means that when another person's actions are ambiguous and can be interpreted either positively or negatively, there is a *mitzva* to interpret them positively. Every person is a mix of good and bad, so almost every action can be interpreted positively or negatively. The question is which is primary. Through this *mitzva*, the Torah teaches us that virtue is primary, as people truly aspire to do good. Let us take this a step further. By judging one's fellow favorably, we change reality for the better, because we are reinforcing the positive elements within ourselves and within the other person.

The obligation to judge favorably is conditional upon the positive interpretation being reasonable. If it is very difficult to put a positive spin on another person's action or speech, one does not need to judge favorably unless the other person is righteous. If they are, then even if they have done something difficult to interpret in a positive light, there is a *mitzva* to judge them favorably as long as there is some way to do so. This is logical, since for a righteous person the terrible thing one thinks one is seeing would be out of character. The more righteous a person is, the more reason demands we make efforts to judge them positively.

By contrast, when judging a wicked person, it is reasonable to assume the worst, even when the action can be interpreted favorably. Even though a wicked person may deep down aspire to be good, since they have chosen an evil path, it is reasonable to assume they are being consistent. Therefore, one should not judge them favorably.

19. Rebuking for Bad Behavior

If we see someone about to sin, we have a *mitzva* to admonish them. These potential sins might include committing adultery, cheating at work, or getting involved in a pointless dispute.

The rebuke must be motivated by a sense of responsibility

and love, not by arrogance or hatred. As it says, "You shall not hate your brother in your heart. Reprove your kinsman but incur no guilt because of him . . . Love your fellow as yourself; I am the Lord" (Leviticus 19:17-18). Therefore, we must first make it very clear that we value and love the other person. Only after this has been done may we reprimand. We must do so very carefully, privately and with great sensitivity, as one never knows what might be a delicate or painful issue. We should also bear in mind that we may have misinterpreted something.

Rebuking is always somewhat unpleasant and complicated. Nevertheless, as long as there is some chance it will be effective, it is a *mitzva*. Sometimes a rebuke can save someone from unknowingly destroying their family or from other catastrophes. Sometimes a person does not know proper work etiquette; if someone does not let them know what they are doing wrong, they will be fired and ignorant of what needs to change to avoid the situation repeating itself. Sometimes a person is unaware they have body odor, or that they speak in a hurtful way. They do not understand why they have no friends and why their spouse is growing distant. Therefore, the *mitzva* of rebuke is to help the person, in this world and the next.

The Sages tell us that if we might be able to help someone by criticism but do not do so, in a sense we are an accomplice to sin. The more influence we have with someone, the greater our obligation to rebuke them. In the words of the Talmud (*Shabbat* 54b), "If someone is in a position to object to the bad behavior of his household members but refrains from doing so, he is punished for the behavior of the household members. If it is the people of his city, he is punished for the behavior of the people of his city. If it is the people of the entire world, he is punished for the behavior of the people of the entire world."

20. Protest

Even if there is no chance the person being rebuked will listen, sometimes it is still necessary to take a stand. Even if the reproach will not be accepted, one's words may have a long-term impact – if not on the sinner, then at least on others (who heard directly or indirectly about the confrontation). Therefore, if we see someone being cheated or humiliated, we must object even if we know the offender will pay no attention. However, after objecting, we do not need to say anything more. The Sages inform us (*Yevamot* 65b) that "Just as it is a *mitzva* to say something that will be accepted, so too it is a *mitzva* not to say something that will not be accepted."

21. The Prohibition of Excessive Flattery

It is forbidden to pander to a wicked person, meaning to justify or praise their actions. Doing so encourages them to continue and makes the flatterer an accomplice. Therefore, even when it is impossible to rebuke a wicked person because they are violent and dangerous, one must be careful not to praise them, at the very least. The Sages tell us that the punishment of people who pander to the wicked is that they or their children will be victimized by someone like the wicked person whose actions they reinforced. Even someone who does not praise the evil deeds of the wicked, but simply honors or praises them in general, has transgressed the prohibition of false flattery. Therefore, someone who must mention something good done by a wicked person must also mention the evil deeds, so that people will not emulate them. A person must even be prepared to suffer a financial loss or a loss of status to avoid pandering to someone undeserving of respect. Only in a case in which one's life is in danger is it permissible, for lack of choice, to flatter someone wicked.

22. Negative Speech, Slander, and Gossip

It is forbidden to speak badly of others (*lashon ha-ra*). This is the case even when the statement is true. Even worse is telling lies and slandering someone (*hotza'at shem ra*). Less evil, but still prohibited, is simple gossip (*rekhilut*) – talking about someone else's private life. Even when gossip is not negative, it is forbidden because it compromises privacy. Nobody wants people gossiping about their private lives. Nevertheless, well-known information may be shared, as long as the sharing is motivated neither by animosity nor a desire to mock.

23. The Severity of Negative Speech

People who think badly of others are often guilty of speaking *lashon ha-ra* about them. Both of these are usually manifestations of baseless hatred, a terrible epidemic. Since *lashon ha-ra* has the power to poison social interactions, in a sense it is equal to all of the most serious transgressions. Therefore, one should train oneself to think well of other people and make a habit of not speaking badly of them. Someone who succeeds in this will merit living a good, long life, as we read, "Who is the person who is eager for life, who desires years of good fortune? Guard your tongue from evil, your lips from deceitful speech. Shun evil and do good, seek peace and pursue it" (Psalms 34:12-15).

If we listen to *lashon ha-ra* and accept it, we become partners in the sin. Therefore, if we hear *lashon ha-ra*, we must judge its subject favorably and resolve not to believe what we have heard. This is also a very reasonable approach, as the listener is not in possession of all the facts. Often it becomes evident that the story was missing a crucial detail which dramatically alters everything. Additionally, even if the story was a hundred percent true and the subject did act badly, it is possible that he or she has since repented and expressed regret. Since repentance has the power to change a person for the better, the subject is now a different person. Thus, the person who believes *lashon ha-ra* is making a poor decision.

One should avoid people who regularly speak badly of others, especially those who tell seemingly innocuous stories but subtly inject poisonous innuendos. If we have no choice but to talk to such people, we must keep our guard up and resist believing their nasty stories.

24. When Speaking Badly of Someone is Permitted

There is a *mitzva* to save people from harm. Therefore, if a person witnesses someone's property being damaged (whether intentionally or unintentionally), and it is clear the perpetrators will not take the initiative to admit guilt and pay, one may report this to the injured party, thus enabling them to sue for damages. As a general principle, the prohibition of *lashon ha-ra* is meant to prevent causing people needless pain, not to protect criminals and hooligans.

Let us say Reuven wants to do business with Levi, and asks Shimon if Levi is honest. If Shimon knows Levi is dishonest, he must tell Reuven to protect him. At the same time, Shimon should make sure not to overstate his criticisms. If his information about Levi is not definite, he must make that clear. Shimon should also not speak out of animosity. Rather, he should be motivated by his desire to save Reuven from making a mistake and suffering the consequences. When Reuven receives the negative report, he must thank Shimon for his help. At the same time, he should not take Shimon's word as absolute truth. For even one who is extremely righteous may still misjudge another person. Similarly, it is possible Levi was dishonest in the past, but has since corrected his ways. Therefore, even though Reuven will make sure not to do business with Levi to avoid getting cheated, he should still retain a positive attitude towards him and treat him with respect.

The same thing applies to people running for office. It is permitted to report facts about them for the public benefit. This is on condition that a full picture is presented that includes both virtues and vices, without animosity or exaggeration. All this applies when the candidate is someone who is fundamentally decent like most people, but who has serious flaws which might lead others to prefer a different, better candidate. However, if a candidate is truly wicked – whether the wickedness stems from corrupt character or hatred for all that is sacred – they may be spoken of with hostility, to keep people from mistakenly following them. Yet even in such a case, it is still forbidden to lie or overstate the candidate's shortcomings.

25. Journalists and Lashon Ha-Ra

The role of journalists and the media is important but complex. As long as they are careful about what they say and provide information the public needs to know, such as information about political candidates or information aimed at protecting consumers, they are doing a *mitzva*. Similarly, when they criticize the decisions and actions of public figures in a fair and precise way, presenting a balanced portrait of the positives and negatives, they are doing a *mitzva*. However, if the journalists are motivated by animosity or a desire to mock, they are sinning even when what they say benefits the public. And if they overstate the case or deviate from the truth, they are guilty of a serious sin, as this does not benefit the public. Rather, it hurts the public by providing only a partial picture, which will lead people to weigh things incorrectly and arrive at inappropriate decisions. Furthermore, if journalists publish negative information about a private individual, and there is no public benefit, they are transgressing the severe prohibition of *lashon ha-ra* (speaking negatively about someone else). The graver the embarrassment, the graver the sin.

26. Media as Watchdogs

When idealistic journalists condemn wicked people with the aim of putting a stop to their wrongdoing, they are fulfilling the *mitzva* to rebuke, which is vital for the improvement of the world. If people of integrity do not condemn the wicked, it is impossible to defeat them. For it seems every confrontation between someone righteous and someone evil will end in victory for the bad person. This is because they are willing to use lies and other illegitimate means to win, while the righteous person's hands are tied by the rules of fairness. Nevertheless, the righteous person has one advantage – being on the side of morality. He or she can label the sinful person as bad. And since morality does prevail in the long run, the moral declaration that someone is wicked will pave the way for the ultimate triumph of the righteous. However, if the righteous cede their right to label and condemn the wicked, they have no chance of defeating them at all.

Thus, members of the media have a major responsibility. They must analyze situations in a fair, balanced way, and analyze people correctly. If they make a mistake though, labeling someone righteous as bad and condemning them, they are sinning twofold. Not only are they hurting someone righteous, they are also damaging the public by making it less likely people will learn from this individual, their opinions, and their good deeds. The same thing applies if journalists condemn a group which is in fact mostly good. Beyond the *lashon ha-ra* involved, they are also harming the public by preventing people from learning from the group's positive example.

27. Dispute vs. Disagreement for the Sake of Heaven

Hating people is prohibited; fighting or feuding is even more strongly prohibited. For a feud is a deep-seated, long-running dispute which leads to multiple confrontations and draws more and more people into the vortex of hatred. When the animus is directed against a righteous Torah scholar, it is even worse, because it causes the public to turn away from Torah and *mitzvot*. Worst of all is when a student feuds with his or her teacher. This is why it was so extremely serious when Koraĥ (and his followers) fought against Moses, teacher of all Israel, and humblest of men.

Sometimes people think they are helping their friends or family by joining their vendetta against someone. However, they are really hurting them because they are worsening the feud and fanning the flames of hatred. Real friends try to save their friends from quarrels that will just be painful and sap their energy.

At the same time, there is value in a disagreement focused on actual ideas, which is not motivated by hatred, and is carried out respectfully. While it can still cause tension and hurt feelings, it does help clarify issues. This type of disagreement is called a "disagreement for the sake of heaven," and it endures because its purpose is to clarify the truth. Ultimately it will become clear there was some truth on both sides. This is why the Talmudic debates of Shammai and Hillel have staying power. However, when a disagreement is motivated by personal grudges and hatred, neither side has value. Hence it will ultimately not prevail. Before it fizzles out though, it will sap the energies of all those involved.

28. Making Amends

If someone realizes they have hurt another person, it is a *mitzva* to repent and to make things right before confessing one's sin to God. There are three primary stages of repentance:

1) Feeling bad, regretting, and resolving to change. We must understand that what we did was a sin, feel bad about it, and resolve not to do it again.

2) Making it right. We must do our best to repair the negative consequences of our actions. If we spoke *lashon ha-ra* about someone, we should do our best to undo the damage by disavowing the derogatory comments and repeatedly praising the person.

3) Asking forgiveness of the other person. When we ask for forgiveness, we must spell out what we did wrong, apologize, and commit ourselves not to repeat it. In cases in which spelling out the sin will likely cause the other person great pain, it is preferable not to do so. However, in such cases, we must try even harder to undo the damage.

Forgiveness may be requested in person, by phone, or in writing. If we think the other person might be more receptive if the request is made through an intermediary, we should use an intermediary. If the person was so badly hurt they are not willing to forgive, the offender should request forgiveness three more times, each time in front of three people. If the offended person still refuses to forgive, the offender does not have to make any further effort.

The injured party should be forgiving and not cruel, as all people are liable to make mistakes and to sin. Just as we want those we have hurt to forgive us, so too should we forgive those who have hurt us. However, if someone causes another monetary damage, there is no *mitzva* for the injured party to forgive before the damage is paid for. Similarly, if someone damages another's good name, there is no obligation for the injured party to forgive the offender until they correct the damage they caused.

29. Telling the Truth

Of all human abilities, speech most expresses what is unique about humanity. Without speech, society could not develop. Each person's mind would be seething with ideas, with no way to share these ideas and put them into practice. To protect this uniquely human ability, we must relate to speech with reverence and distance ourselves from any type of lie, as it says, "Keep far from a false matter" (Exodus 23:7). The more damage a lie causes, the more severe the transgression. Lying often involves additional transgressions as well, such as when someone who owes money denies it, or when a salesperson lies to customers about the quality of the merchandise.

Even a lie which does not hurt someone else is forbidden, because truth is so precious. Truth allows a person to make sense of the world. By contrast, lying creates a false picture of the world. It becomes impossible for the liar to understand the world and to connect with the Creator, the source of truth, faith, and morality. This is why the Sages tell us that liars and panderers will not have the privilege of seeing the Divine Presence.

Cheating on a test is also included in the prohibition of lying. Even though the cheater might benefit in the short term, those who cheat lose in the long term. Instead of working hard to truly succeed, they get used to looking for the easy way out. This will ultimately contribute to their downfall.

Included in the obligation to speak the truth is keeping one's word. If we commit to help a friend out or to give a relative a gift, we should honor our commitment. If we are worried we might not be able to honor a commitment, we should say we will try to help, but not make any promises, thus avoiding being unreliable.

30. Deception

It is forbidden to deceive (*geneivat da'at*). For example, we may not falsely flatter someone in order to receive something from them. We may not present ourselves to someone as a friend while actually disliking them. Similarly, we transgress this prohibition if we agree with someone's complaints about their boss or colleague while we do not actually feel the complaints are justified. Instead of helping our friend to see the situation as it is, we are misrepresenting it to curry favor. A salesperson who compliments a piece of clothing a customer is trying on, while knowing full well it is not suitable, is guilty of *geneivat da'at*. Someone who invites a friend for a meal hoping he or she will decline or knowing they can't come anyway is also guilty of *geneivat da'at*.

31. Lying to Preserve the Peace

When truth and peace come into conflict – for example, when telling the truth will hurt someone's feelings or cause hositlity – the Sages tell us there is a *mitzva* to deviate from the truth to preserve the peace. They point out that God Himself did this. When the elderly Sarah was informed she would have a child, she laughed inside and wondered (Genesis 18:12), "How will I have a child when I am worn out and my husband is old?" Then, when God retold this to Abraham, He mentioned only what Sarah said about herself. He left out what she said about Abraham being old, as any man is liable to feel hurt if he hears his wife thinks he is old.

If we look a little more deeply, we see there is really no conflict between the values of truth and peace. Rather, the tension is between profound truth and surface truth. Deep down, people want to live in harmony with one another, for one Creator created us all. It is only the disorder of the world which leads to disagreements and discord. The Torah instructs us to prefer the profound truth to the surface truth. Of course, this is on condition that deviating from the truth will not hurt someone else. However, if we know someone is harming a friend, we must tell the friend the truth to enable them to protect themselves.

32. Other Times When Lying Is Permissible

It is permitted to deviate from the truth out of humility, or to protect one's privacy or avoid embarrassment, although there is no *mitzva* to do so (as there is to preserve the peace). For example, we may cover up details of our intimate life for modesty's sake, we may hide the fact we are going to hospital for medical treatment if this embarrasses us, and we may conceal our impressive knowledge or good deeds to keep ourselves humble.

33. Do Not Covet

The last of the Ten Commandments is "You shall not covet your neighbor's house; you shall not covet your neighbor's wife, or his male or female slave, or his ox or his donkey, or anything that is your neighbor's" (Exodus 20:14). Following this injunction prevents a myriad of sins. For greed and desire are at the root of many interpersonal sins. First, someone wants what his neighbor has and starts trying to figure out underhanded ways to get his hands on it. Then things escalate and he puts his plan into action to acquire what his neighbor has. Sometimes he even descends to force, theft or rape.

"Do not covet" is not just a commandment but good advice for anyone who wants to live a contented life. If we are jealous of friends and desire what they have, we become used to thinking that our happiness depends upon acquiring what we do not have, when in truth our happiness depends upon our ability to be happy with what we do have.

Our Sages state, "Envy, desire, and thirst for honor destroy a person's world" (*Ethics of the Fathers* 4:21). These bad traits cause us to be dissatisfied with what we have. No matter what we do to satisfy our yearnings, it will never be enough. We will always want more and more, because our life is hollow and empty of values and meaning. The cure for coveting is faith in God and gratitude for everything good in life. To reinforce our happiness and gratitude, the Sages instituted blessings to be recited before enjoying food and other pleasures. (See 23:1 below.)

34. Gratitude

We have a *mitzva* to focus on everything our family and friends do for us, whether providing help, compliments, or encouragement. It is a *mitzva* to acknowledge them too. Thanking shows we are grateful and understand their goodwill is not to be taken for granted. Gratitude increases blessing, as it reinforces good deeds and positive speech, and encourages people to carry on in this vein. In contrast, an ingrate is arrogant and blocks the flow of blessing. Also, ingrates will never be happy because they will always feel people do not treat them well enough and that they deserve more.

There is also a *mitzva* to be grateful to strangers and graciously thank them for any help or kind gestures as well. This includes thanking people whose kindness is performed in the course of doing their jobs: cashiers, salespeople, clerks, and the like. It is right to value every person who works and helps others.

35. Sharing in Joy and in Sorrow

We have a *mitzva* to share in our friends' and relatives' joy. We should go to their weddings and their children's weddings, to bar and bat mitzvas, circumcisions, and birth celebrations. If they need help organizing or financing these celebrations, we have a *mitzva* to help them. A gift, traditionally given to honor the occasion, is a significant element of one's participation. The more needy the hosts, the larger the gift should be. No less important is that when attending a celebration, we should try to make our hosts and the other guests happy. We should think about something meaningful and complimentary to share that will make them feel good. The less they pay attention to whether people are honoring them sufficiently, the happier they will be and the happier we will make them (and people will think more of us as well).

There is also a *mitzva* to share in the sorrow of one's friends and relatives. If someone dies, we have a *mitzva* to mourn and to participate in the funeral to honor the deceased and the family. If we know the people sitting *shiva*, we should visit them and offer comfort, so they know they are not alone – their friends and acquaintances share in their pain. (See 14:12 below.)

36. Speaking Kindly

A person should be kind in speech, complimenting people to make them feel good and to encourage and support them. However, a compliment must be both accurate and honest, because only then will it reinforce their strengths. Insincere compliments are a type of lying and false flattery, and do more harm than good. There are times when a compliment is called for, like when a woman shows off a new dress to her friend. Then, even if the friend does not like the dress, she should find something nice to say about it to avoid hurting her friend. But even then, she should not be too effusive, so as not to encourage her friend to keep making bad choices in clothing.

If someone finds out a friend has been unfairly hurt, there is a *mitzva* to offer them moral support. One should also admonish those responsible, while being careful not to fan the flames of the conflict.

37. Greeting

We have a *mitzva* to relate to everyone respectfully and lovingly, and one way to show this respect is by greeting them. This is especially important in interactions with the elderly and dignified. We are told that Rabbi Yohanan ben Zakkai, the leader of his generation, made a point of extending greetings to everyone, even random non-Jews in the marketplace. Jews customarily greet each other with the word "shalom," which means peace and is also one of God's names. This is because the interaction of two people owes much to the divine unity that energizes their souls. As it says, "Love your fellow as yourself; I am the Lord" (Leviticus 19:18). Because of this unity, the interaction of two people can be symbiotic and productive, and the divine spark can shine forth from within them both.

38. Being Sensitive

There is a *mitzva* to be sensitive to others and not cause them pain. For example, we should not push people out of the way, cut in line, or open a window on a cold day if it will make someone else uncomfortable. As Hillel said, "What you hate, do not do to your fellow." This does not mean someone who personally is not bothered by noise may make noise near other people. Rather, just as there are some things which really disturb us, we should recognize there are some things other people find annoying. Therefore, we should be cautious about noise near others.

Different norms and varying circumstances will affect the required levels of sensitivity. For example, if someone needs to concentrate on work or studies, those around must be especially careful to avoid making even minimal noise. If we are in our yard, we should not yell so loudly that the neighbors have no choice but to hear. Late at night, in residential areas where people are sleeping, we must make sure to keep our voices down and not slam car doors. A person should not litter, and certainly should not leave glass shards or other dangerous items in busy areas, where passersby could get hurt.

39. *Derekh Eretz*

Part of "Love your fellow as yourself" is the mandate to treat people in a way that honors the divine image within them. This includes all aspects of *derekh eretz* (good manners, civic virtue, and social responsibility). Therefore, we must behave pleasantly and in a dignified manner. For example, we must conform to accepted hygienic norms. After we use the facilities, we must wash our hands properly.

A person should not walk around smelling bad, whether the smell comes from body, breath, or clothing. We should not do anything which people find offensive or disgusting, such as picking our noses, spitting out food, or picking at scabs. Anyone who does such things when around people, has not only disregarded the *mitzva* of "Love your fellow as yourself," but has also degraded themselves and transgressed the prohibition of "You shall not defile yourselves" (Leviticus 11:43). The observance of Derekh Eretz is determined by the norms of wherever we are. Even when we are at home alone, it is preferable to respect our own humanity, keeping ourselves clean and dressed respectably, and not doing anything repulsive.

40. Speaking Coarsely

It is forbidden for us to degrade ourselves by speaking coarsely. Profanity is referred to as *nibul peh*, which literally means "making the mouth disgusting." This is because it takes speech, a source of blessing and life, and destroys it. The resulting speech is like a *nevela* (the carcass of an animal not slaughtered ritually and too disgusting to eat). Since it is well-known that coarse speech is particularly prevalent among soldiers, the Torah specifically admonishes them about this. (See 17:20 below.) When coarse speech includes cursing someone, the speaker is also guilty of belittling a fellow human being.

41. Hospitality

There is a big *mitzva* to welcome guests into one's home, to honor them, to offer them good food, and to make them feel good. When the guests leave, there is a *mitzva* for the hosts to walk them out, to show they enjoyed having them and are sorry to see them go. If the way back is dangerous and there is concern the guests might get lost, there is a *mitzva* to accompany them until they reach safety.

The Torah describes at length how Abraham and Sarah welcomed tired guests and gave them food and drink. In the merit of this hospitality, they were told they would have a child (Isaac) even though they were old (Genesis 18). Similarly, the Torah tells us how Rebecca welcomed a stranger and volunteered to water his camels. As a reward, she merited marriage to Isaac and became one of the four matriarchs (Genesis 24).

In the past, the *mitzva* of hospitality was primarily fulfilled by hosting the poor and travelers, both of whom needed something to eat and somewhere to sleep. Nowadays, thank God, there are fewer people who are actually hungry. Nevertheless, there are still many people who suffer from loneliness, alienation, and depression, who need support and encouragement. It is a great *mitzva* to pay attention to them, to invite and host them. Showing them people enjoy being around them gives them strength and reminds them their lives are valuable and meaningful. Similarly, it is a big *mitzva* to host new immigrants, especially those who are single and on their own. Though they might not be lacking something to eat and somewhere to sleep, they are lacking family and community.

42. Being a Good Neighbor

We have a *mitzva* to be good neighbors. Someone who lives in an apartment building should not litter in the hallways, the communal areas, or the street. We should not leave items lying around which will get in the way of other residents or make the building look rundown.

If a neighborhood has times of the day generally accepted as rest times, we should be sure not to make any noise then. At any time of day, we should not be noisier than is generally accepted. We should not play music so loudly the neighbors will hear it, and not own a dog that barks all the time, disturbing the neighbors. We should also avoid doing anything that will cause smoke or a foul odor.

Included in being a good neighbor is making sure to pay maintenance fees and municipal taxes on time.

43. Being Part of a Good Community

Friends and neighbors have a strong influence. Therefore, the Sages instruct: "Distance yourself from a bad neighbor, and do not become friends with someone wicked" (*Ethics of the Fathers* 1:7). Often society has a subconscious influence on us. It sets norms and indirectly affects how we think and behave. Therefore, if we live in a community with good values – Torah and *mitzvot*, education and work, honesty and kindness, initiative and diligence – the odds of our living by these values increase.

This does not mean we may separate ourselves from broader society. All citizens must work together in the service of shared values, such as settling the Land [in Israel], education, health, army service, immigrant absorption, economic development, and helping the underprivileged. However, when an individual needs to choose where to live, it is proper to choose a community set up in accordance with the values of Jewish tradition. The more interest is expressed in joining such communities, the more they will proliferate. This in turn will elevate larger society. At the same time, idealists are doing a big *mitzva* when they volunteer to live in underprivileged neighborhoods and undertake to teach everyone, young and old, about civic virtue and Torah values.

CHAPTER 4

The Value of Human Life

1. Do Not Murder

The severity of the prohibition of murder is clear. A murderer transgresses all the *mitzvot* – those relating to God and those relating to people. Murder destroys everything good the victims could have experienced had they lived longer. Additionally, the murderer sins against God. God gifted the victim with life, and the murderer took it away. The entire human race originated with Adam, which shows us that a single individual can contain an entire world within themselves. In the words of the Sages, "This is why God created only one person – to teach us that anyone who destroys one life is considered to have destroyed an entire world, and anyone who saves one life is considered to have saved an entire world" (*Mishna Sanhedrin* 4:5).

The scope of the prohibition is broad. It makes no difference whether the victim is young or old, sick or healthy. Every minute of life has infinite value, so one who takes any life transgresses the prohibition of murder.

2. Inadvertent Killers

If one person kills another as a result of carelessness, the killer bears some responsibility for the death, because it wouldn't have happened if not for negligence. During biblical times, when the Jews lived in the Land of Israel, the Torah instructed the nation to designate six Levitical cities to serve as cities of refuge. Unintentional killers would be sent there, and this exile would atone for them. They would not be released until the death of the High Priest. In the meantime, the Torah-infused atmosphere of these cities would lead the killers to repent and to realize how important it is to be extra-careful when it comes to human life. The *mitzva* to set up cities of refuge should serve as a model for us today. It should inspire us to set up a process of atonement for unintentional killers, including some sort of exile as well as an educational framework to help them internalize the severity of their sin.

3. The Beheaded Calf: The Responsibility of Community Leaders

The ceremony of *egla arufa* (the beheaded calf) is one of the *mitzvot* meant to inculcate the value of safeguarding human life, and the responsibility of community leaders to uphold this value. What was this ceremony? If a corpse were found in a field, and no one knew who was responsible for the victim's death, the leaders of the closest city took a year-old calf and beheaded it near a stream. Then they publicly declared, in their own name and in the name of the entire community, that they were in no way responsible for this tragedy, either directly or indirectly. This was followed by a request that God forgive them as individuals and as a community. This dramatic ceremony was meant to inspire the leaders and all community members to do everything possible to prevent murder. There was also hope that as a result of the ceremony, someone might come forth with testimony that would help catch the murderer.

This *mitzva* applied when the Sanhedrin (High Court) was housed near the Temple. Although that is no longer the case, the *mitzva* can still inspire us. We can and should resolve that any murder will result in a public reckoning. Following a murder, the police chief, community leaders, representatives of the education system, and local clergy should assemble together. This meeting would allow them to review their policies and discuss whether everything possible was done to prevent the homicide. They would also focus on what steps should be taken to prevent future murders, such as dealing with underlying societal dysfunctions.

4. The Prohibition of Suicide

Just as it is forbidden to murder another person, it is forbidden to murder oneself. From a certain perspective, suicide is even more severe, since people who kill themselves also show a lack of gratitude towards God and a lack of belief in divine providence. Moreover, repentance is possible for all other sins, but not for suicide, as the sinner is now dead. The person may imagine suicide will put an end to their suffering, but they ignore the punishment awaiting them in the world of Truth, which will be worse than any suffering in this world.

To condemn the sin and to prevent other people from following in the dead person's footsteps, classic *halakha* dictates that someone who commits suicide receives only a minimalistic funeral, without a eulogy. They are buried in a separate section of the cemetery, in keeping with the general rule that the wicked should not be buried alongside the righteous. Nevertheless, when a suicide occurs against a background of mental illness (which is true of the vast majority of cases today), the deceased is judged favorably and the suicide is treated as a tragedy rather than a sin. We bury the person and mourn normally, though the funeral is usually kept lowkey.

5. Do Not Stand Idly by the Blood of Your Neighbor

It is a great *mitzva* to save a person in danger. As we mentioned above, our Sages state that "Anyone who saves one life is considered to have saved an entire world." Therefore, someone who sees others drowning or about to be attacked by criminals must try to rescue them, as it says, "Do not stand idly by the blood of your neighbor" (Leviticus 19:16). One is even required to endanger oneself if necessary. To what extent? To the extent reasonable people are prepared to endanger themselves to save their own property. Going beyond this level of danger to save a person is not an obligation. It is a *mitzva* though, assuming the lifesaving action will most probably succeed.

6. Public Safety

A community has a greater obligation to protect lives than an individual. Therefore, it must set up a medical system to care for the sick, a police force to prevent crime, and a fire department to fight fires. Unlike private individuals, medical professionals and first responders must do their job even when it involves endangering themselves. Since these people are public servants, they must act in accordance with official guidelines, including risking their lives when their rescue work will most likely succeed. The calculation involved in following procedure is that overall, human lives are saved despite the risks assumed by the public servants.

The obligations of soldiers and first responders are even greater during a defensive war. They must follow military orders even if chances are they will die. They must sacrifice their lives to save the nation. In other words, in a state of war, the calculation is on a national scale. Only this type of calculation will preserve the nation and ensure the lives of the maximum number of citizens.

7. Redeeming Captives

In the ancient world, slaves were a significant percentage of the population. Jews too were sometimes sold as slaves, due to wars, kidnappings, or tax debts. Other nations ridded themselves of the burden of redemption when their people were enslaved. For example, if a Roman soldier was taken captive, he was abandoned: his wife was considered a widow, his possessions were taken by the government, and no one bothered to redeem him.

However, among Jews, the *mitzva* of redeeming captives was considered the priority of interpersonal *mitzvot.* Donating money to help free a captive was considered the epitome of charitable giving. This was because a captive or slave suffered everything a poor person did – hunger, thirst, cold, and degradation. Additionally, his or her life was in danger, as the law in many times and places allowed masters to beat their slaves to death. Therefore, the Sages mandated that we spare no efforts to free captives. For example, the marriage contract (*ketuba*) obligates a husband to spend everything necessary to redeem his wife should she be taken prisoner.

If this *mitzva* was meant to save people from slavery, why is it referred to as redeeming captives (*pidyon shevuyim*)? Because the time when one could realistically save a person from this bitter fate was before a captive was brought to the slave market to be sold. Once sold it was often too late, as a master was not always willing to give up his slave.

Despite the tremendous value placed on redeeming captives, the Sages forbade paying more than the going rate in the slave market. This was "in order to repair the world," i.e., to prevent governments or criminals kidnapping Jews indiscriminately just to extort exorbitant amounts of money from the community. Since the obligation to redeem captives was combined with the caveat not to pay inflated prices, Jews throughout history succeeded in redeeming a large percentage of those taken captive.

8. Risk to Life Supersedes All *Mitzvot*

The purpose of Torah and *mitzvot* is to preserve life. As it says, "Keep My decrees and laws, which a person shall do and live by; I am the Lord" (Leviticus 18:5). God gave us the *mitzvot* to live, not to die. Therefore, risk to life (*piku'aḥ nefesh*), meaning the obligation of saving life, supersedes all other *mitzvot*. This occurs most frequently when people's lives may be in danger, and saving them would involve desecrating Shabbat. In such cases, one must desecrate Shabbat in order to save the life.

9. Be Killed Rather Than Transgress

Piku'aḥ nefesh (saving a life) supersedes all *mitzvot* except for three extremely serious transgressions. Violating them inflicts critical damage to the divine image and the fabric of life, so the tradition demands *"yehareg ve'al ya'avor"* (one should allow oneself to be killed rather than transgress them). People faced with the choice – "Either kill this person or we will kill you" –should choose to be killed rather than to kill. This is the case not only for murder, but for idol worship and certain sexual wrongdoings as well. Of course, one should do one's best to avoid such awful situations, but if they are unavoidable, one must allow oneself to be killed rather than transgress. Keeping these three *mitzvot* is a way to preserve the divine image. Through its dedication to these three *mitzvot*, the Jewish nation has succeeded in bonding to eternal values and surviving all its exiles. It continues to create, and to add blessing and life to the world.

10. Abortion

The status of an unborn fetus is unclear. On the one hand, it is on the way to becoming a person; on the other, it is not yet there. Therefore, if a pregnancy puts the mother's life at risk, the fetus may be aborted to save her life. If the fetus suffers from a serious defect that would make its life one of continuous suffering, there is disagreement about whether abortion is permitted. Some authorities do not permit aborting even in this case. Others say the fetus may be aborted to prevent suffering. I am among them. Since the topic of abortion is very complex, it is advisable to consult with a rabbi when a question arises. It is permitted for a couple to choose to consult with someone they know will be lenient. If a fetus does not suffer from a serious defect that will lead to continuous suffering, all agree that an abortion is forbidden.

11. Roof Guardrails

There is a *mitzva* to build a guardrail on your roof to make sure nobody falls off. As it says, "When you build a new house, you shall make a parapet for your roof, so that you do not bring bloodguilt on your house if anyone should fall from it" (Deuteronomy 22:8). The roofs which require railings are flat ones where people sometimes walk, so there is a real danger of falling. Similarly, a railing is required for someone's pit or well which is ten *tefaḥim* deep (76 centimeters), for a split-level yard where more than 10 *tefaḥim* separate the levels, and for a flight of stairs more than 10 *tefaḥim* high. In public areas, we must be even more careful to ensure safety.

12. Avoiding Danger

Just as there is a *mitzva* to put up guardrails, there is a *mitzva* to remove anything likely to endanger human life, as it says, "But take utmost care and guard your life scrupulously"

(Deuteronomy 4:9). Therefore, it is forbidden to leave a broken ladder in one's home, in case someone climbs up and falls off. Similarly, one may not leave a broken electrical appliance lying around which might electrocute someone, or leave something poisonous within reach of children. It is also forbidden to participate in a dangerous hike, or to own a dangerous dog likely to scare or hurt the neighbors. (It is allowed only if the dog is tied up in a way that people will not be afraid.)

13. Traffic Safety

The Torah obligates every driver and every pedestrian to follow traffic laws. Even if drivers break traffic laws without hurting anyone, they still sin by endangering themselves and others. Even if drivers are so skilled that they do not actually endanger people by speeding, they have still sinned. Because by breaking the traffic laws, they are contributing to the normalization of reckless driving, which certainly causes injuries and deaths. Parents of young adults with driver's licenses must warn them to drive carefully so as to avoid injuring or killing others. If anyone sees a friend driving recklessly, it is a *mitzva* to point out the danger.

14. Taking Care of One's Health

It is a *mitzva* to look after one's health and not do anything that damages it. God created our bodies healthy, and it is our responsibility to keep them that way. People who endanger themselves whether by eating, drinking, or smoking will have to answer to God for their behavior. As it says, "But for your own blood, your own life, I will require a reckoning" (Genesis 9:5). Persons already addicted to smoking must make every effort to quit. Furthermore, until they do so, they must make sure not to smoke around others, because secondhand smoke – or passive smoking – is also damaging to people's health and wellbeing.

When it comes to our health, we must follow the medical consensus. Currently, it recommends limiting the consumption of processed foods, sugary foods, margarine, salt, and trans fats. Included are soft drinks, commercial snack foods, deli meats, bourekas, and cakes. In contrast, it is recommended to eat plenty of fruits and vegetables and to drink several glasses of water a day. Most important is to avoid overeating, and to get enough exercise and sleep. At the same time, extreme diets and other extreme health practices should be avoided. A healthy lifestyle includes being happy and living naturally, which are incompatible with extremism.

15. Visiting the Sick

Visiting people who are sick person is a major *mitzva* and serves two purposes. The first is to share the patients' pain, to encourage them, and to pray for them. Sometimes a sick person in pain becomes despondent and loses the will to live. This in turn saps his or her ability to deal with the disease. Having visitors can reassure the ill that their lives have value, thus helping them beat the disease. Even among people who are terminally ill, having visitors can inspire them to see the value of every additional day of life, thus helping them attain peace. The second purpose is to see if the infirm need help. Perhaps they need someone to stay with them, accompany them to a medical test, or help pay for professional care.

People who work in the health system have a wonderful opportunity to do this *mitzva* every day. The more they relate respectfully and lovingly to their patients, and the better and more effectively they care for them, the greater their fulfillment of the *mitzva*. However, it is not enough for the system to care. Even when hospital staff are doing their job well, there is still a *mitzva* for family, friends, and acquaintances to do what they can to help and support.

Anyone can become sick or disabled. But as long as we are healthy, we should try to help those who are sick or injured. In the merit of doing so, perhaps God will be merciful to us, and we ourselves will not become sick or injured. But if we do get sick or hurt (God forbid), when people want to help us, we will be able to accept their help graciously, remembering the help we were privileged to offer the sick while we were still healthy.

16. The Terminally Ill

Persons who are terminally ill and expect to die shortly, should confess their sins. (The standard confession can be found in the traditional prayer book.) This way, having repented, they can face the heavenly court. It is also proper to take leave of children and relatives and encourage them to cling to the ways of truth and goodness, the Jewish heritage.

There is a concern though, that if doctors and relatives tell someone that his or her days are numbered, it could break the person's spirit and shorten their life even more. An additional reason not to tell someone is that it cannot be known with certainty. Therefore, people should not tell patients they have no chance of getting better. Rather, it is a *mitzva* for the people around them to relate to them based on what they know of their character. They should inform the person gently and with sensitivity that they are dangerously ill, so they can recite the confession and take leave of their family. At the same time, they should express hope that the situation might improve, and that the person's life might be extended in the merit of their confession and separation.

Someone who shortens the life of a terminally ill patient is guilty of murder, since every minute of life has absolute value. Even if someone sick begs people to put him out of his or her misery, it is forbidden to do so. Furthermore, anyone who actively removes a patient's food and water is considered a murderer. However, if it is known the patient does not want efforts made to extend his or her life, or if it is known they are suffering greatly and want to die, one should passively refrain from giving them life-extending treatments. These laws are very detailed, and this is not the place to discuss them at length.

CHAPTER 5

Justice

1. Choice, Responsibility, and the Right of Ownership

God created human beings in His image. This is primarily expressed in our ability to choose, to think, to plan, and to initiate. Our ability to choose means we are responsible for our choices and actions. If we choose goodness, we benefit ourselves and the world; if we choose evil, we harm ourselves and the world. Since we are responsible for our actions, we have the right to benefit from them and enjoy the fruits of our labors, our talents, and everything with which God blesses us. Accordingly, what we create with our talent and labor belongs to us. Similarly, when we buy things (with money we have come by honestly), those things belong to us.

2. Dividing the Land Equally

Equality is another value which results from God having created all people in the divine image.

Ultimately, all land belongs to God. In the case of the Land of Israel, God promised it to the Jews and commanded that it be distributed equally among all the Jews who left Egypt.

(Dividing the land equally among the Jews rather than among all human beings is similar to the way things work on the individual level. When a person dies, the estate is divided equally among the children rather than among all other relatives.)

In the past, over 90% of people made their living from agriculture. Since land was the primary means of production, dividing it equally created an equal starting point for all. This equality applied to all the Jews who had suffered in Egypt. Each was entitled to an equal part in the land God gave His nation. Just as the right to land is shared by all of a nation's members, so are mutual responsibilities, such as serving in the army and paying taxes.

3. The Jubilee

After the land was divided equally in biblical times, some people made good choices; they worked their fields diligently, had plentiful yields, and prospered. Others made poor choices; they were lazy, neglected their fields, produced little, and went without. If they did not overcome these negative traits and start working hard, eventually they were forced to sell their home and land. Their families ended up living in poverty, as land was the primary source of production. God had mercy upon these people, and especially upon their families, and established the Jubilee. This *mitzva* meant that once every 50 years, all land reverted to its original owners. If the people who sold the land had already died, it was returned to their heirs. This ensured that poverty would not be perpetuated. Rather, every 50 years a family could start anew and escape the cycle of poverty.[1]

---

1   People who made poor choices, were forced to sell their land. One unable to work hard as hired help, drowned in debt. When one got down to the last crust of bread, one was forced to sell oneself into slavery. Yet, sometimes people became impoverished through no fault of their own, due to accidents or illnesses. In such cases though, when Jewish society was in reasonably good shape, the collective fulfillment of the *mitzva* of charity was enough to help

4. Equality and the Right of Ownership

Let us review. Both equality and the right of ownership are based on the fact that human beings were created in the image of God. Since this means that people have free choice and are responsible for their actions, and since they have the ability to take care of the world and to improve it, it follows that what they create or buy belongs to them. Since every person is created in the image of God, it follows that every person has equal rights and equal responsibilities. This equality includes national concerns such as dividing the land and obligations such as serving in the army. It also includes equality before the law, as it says, "You shall have one standard for stranger and citizen alike; for I the Lord am your God" (Leviticus 24:22).

5. Applications for the Future

In the future, when the entire Jewish nation returns to its

---

the poor so they did not need to sell themselves or their land. But charity was not enough to help those who could not overcome their laziness or desires. After they were bailed out, they failed again. These were the Jews who ended up selling their land and then themselves as slaves.

A question arises about such slavery. One of the lessons taught by the Exodus from Egypt is that all people are created in the image of God, and thus deserve to be free. How then can the Torah accept the institution of slavery? This question presents us with the opportunity to explain an important principle. The Torah does not force people to go against nature. For nature, with all its flaws, is a divine creation, the platform provided for people to improve themselves. Therefore, for example, the Torah does not interfere with market forces. Rather, it provides moral direction and ethical boundaries so these very forces can be corrected and elevated. In the past, if the institution of slavery had not existed, what would have happened in periods of great scarcity? People who were unable to support themselves (whether due to laziness, or a lack of savvy, or because their land had been taken from them) would have starved to death. Slavery allowed them to survive and to have children who would be free. Sometimes the enslaved poor were more successful at staying alive than the free poor. So, the Torah did not prohibit slavery, but rather established ethical boundaries for it. For example, the only people permitted to sell themselves as slaves were those who had sold all they owned and were still hungry. In a period like ours, though, when society can supply food to the poor and ensure that they do not die of hunger, there is no excuse for the institution of slavery, and the world must take steps to wipe it out. (See *Peninei Halakha: Shevi'it Ve-yovel* 10:7-11.)

Land, the Sanhedrin will be reestablished. This high court, composed of 71 sages knowledgeable in Torah and other subjects, will be responsible for dividing the land equally among the Jews. This will include the descendants of converts, who have suffered in exile together with those born Jewish.

However, land is no longer the primary source of production, so an equal division of land will not provide everyone with an equal basis. Fortunately, we can extrapolate two guidelines from the *mitzva* of Jubilee. First, just as agricultural land was distributed equally, so too should the rest of our God-given natural resources be allocated equally. These resources include land (plots for building), air (the space over the land), sunlight (solar energy), water, crude oil, natural gas, beaches, and the radio spectrum. Second, just as the Torah commands us to divide the source of production equally, so too we should try to give everyone equal opportunity. This can be accomplished by providing all children with an education that will let them support themselves through their abilities and efforts.

These two guidelines can be integrated by taking the revenues from the sale of natural resources and dedicating them to providing the best vocational training for each person. This will allow us to actualize the Jubilee idea of equal opportunity. Originally this meant dividing the land equally (with the correction achieved by returning the land to its original owners at the Jubilee). Now it would involve providing quality education to all. All children, including those of poor families, would be able to support themselves through their talent and hard work.

There may be an additional suggestion based on the Jubilee idea. In the past, fields were returned to their owners and slaves were set free during the Jubilee. So too, sages working within the modern economic system might consider reinvesting a certain percentage of the country's accumulated wealth in education and vocational training during the Jubilee. This would be another way to equally divide resources.

6. Theft, Robbery, and Damage

It is a serious sin to steal or rob, whether from an individual or from communal funds. *Geneiva* (stealing) is done clandestinely, while *gezeila* (robbery) is done openly, generally within the framework of a violent crime. Taking even a single cent is prohibited by the Torah. "Borrowing" something without permission, even for a short time, is also included in this prohibition.

Since stealing is fairly common, it causes vast accumulated damage. When stealing becomes widespread, it injures society and damages people's willingness to work and create to contribute goodness and blessing to the world. What point is there in people working if they know a thief is going to profit from their toil? This is why in the generation of the flood, even though people were guilty of murder, sexual immorality, and idol worship, the sins which sealed their fate were theft and robbery, as it says (Genesis 6:11), "The earth became corrupt before God; the earth was filled with *ĥamas* (theft)."

Someone who damages another person's property must pay for it. This is true even if the damage is done unintentionally, such as when one breaks something when turning over during sleep.

7. When "Stealing" is Permissible

When people are absolutely sure the owner of an object would not mind their using it without permission, they may do so. However, there are those who are inflexible and do not permit this unless the person wants to use the item for a *mitzva* purpose. This is because when an object is used for a *mitzva*, its owner gets some credit. We can assume this is something to which the owner would happily agree.

If people are at risk of dying of hunger (God forbid), they may steal to stay alive. This is on condition they plan to reimburse the person they stole from as soon as possible. Similarly, a person may make use of someone else's property without permission to avoid suffering a sudden large loss, even if this will damage the property. This too is on condition they compensate for the damage immediately.

8. Withholding and Delaying Wages

The Torah requires employers to pay an employee or contractor. Someone who withholds wages is not only stealing from his or her workers, but also harming the quality of the work. Workers who eagerly anticipate their pay will work more diligently. Without the assurance they will get paid, they will find it more difficult to work efficiently and energetically.

Paying late is prohibited as well. An employer who agreed to pay an employee at the end of the day, must pay then. Payment may not be delayed – even overnight – without the employee's consent. As it says, "You shall not defraud your fellow. You shall not commit robbery. The wages of a laborer shall not remain with you until morning" (Leviticus 19:13), and "You must pay his wages on the same day" (Deuteronomy 24:15).

9. Honesty in Business and Paying Taxes

Sellers may not take advantage of their customers' naivete by overcharging them or misrepresenting the quality of their merchandise. Rather, they must act with honesty and integrity. As it says, "When you sell property to your neighbor or buy anything from your neighbor, you shall not wrong one another" (Leviticus 25:14). This *mitzva* includes the requirement that all weights and measures be properly calibrated, as it says, "You shall not falsify measures of length, weight, or capacity. You shall have an honest balance, honest weights, an honest *ephah*, and an honest *hin*. I the Lord am your God Who freed you from the land of Egypt" (Leviticus 19:35-36). Taking this a step further, our Sages forbid us even to keep an inaccurate scale in our home, in case we are tempted to use it to cheat people.

There is a *mitzva* for business people to tell the truth. They may not even exaggerate the quality of their merchandise. Furthermore, if they committed themselves to sell at a certain price, or to supply a product or a service by a certain time, they should honor their commitment. Sometimes competition is fierce and the temptation to cheat is hard to resist. However, a person who is honest will be blessed with success because trustworthiness is the true foundation of success, both in this world and the World to Come.

It is forbidden to cheat on one's taxes, as this is stealing from the community. Tax fraud is forbidden for buyer and seller alike. Therefore, if salespeople ask someone if they prefer to pay 1,000 shekels (i.e., including taxes) and get a receipt, or pay 900 NIS without a receipt, they should pay 1,000 NIS and get a receipt.

10. Putting a Stumbling Block in Front of the Blind

Tripping or misdirecting a blind person is a serious transgression, as it says, "You shall not put a stumbling block before the blind. You shall fear your God; I am the Lord" (Leviticus 19:14), and "Cursed be he who misdirects a blind person on his way" (Deuteronomy 27:18). Everyone understands that tripping a blind person is evil. The Torah teaches us it is equally evil to mislead a person in any manner. For example, if an insurance agent or financial advisor persuades someone to invest in a way that is good for the advisor but bad for the client, he or she is transgressing this prohibition (as well as the prohibitions against lying and speaking hurtfully). Also included in this prohibition is causing a person to sin, for example giving non-kosher food to a Jew.

11. Being a Faithful Employee

It is forbidden for an employee at work to spend time doing anything else – talking on the phone, texting, surfing the internet, and the like – without his or her employer's approval. If they agreed the employee is to have a half-hour lunch break, the worker should not take longer, as anyone who wastes time at work is stealing from the employer. It is proper for employees to make sure they eat and sleep properly. If they are tired or hungry at work, they will not be at their best, and thus are "stealing" from their employer. This is illustrated by our forefather Jacob. The Torah makes a point of telling us of his great righteousness in devotedly watching Laban's sheep, even during the cold winter nights and hot summer days. As a reward, when Jacob was in danger, God saved his life and the lives of his family members. For in God's eyes, doing one's work well is a tremendous thing. Additionally, being reliable and industrious at work is a tried-and-true recipe for economic success.

12. Frugality and Financial Independence

Torah values encourage people to spend less on current expenses than what they earn. A person who uses self-control to successfully delay gratification and to save money is freed from the servitude of materialism. It uplifts us and brings us closer to eternal values. It allows us to tithe, to establish ourselves financially and even become wealthy, to use our money to expand our families and to help our children get an education and start their own families.

Additionally, individuals who waste their money become

enslaved to their job. Their fear of being fired may force them to flatter, lie, and act against their conscience. Those who habitually save have more freedom to do as they please. If the employer demands they act in an unethical way, they can let themselves be fired and then calmly look for a more ethical workplace.

13. The *Mitzva* to Pay Taxes

Paying taxes is an ethical and halakhic obligation of the highest order. After all, taxes enable the provision of critical public services, including security, police, education, health, social security, welfare, water, sewage, electricity, transport infrastructure, and environmental protection. Those who cheat on their taxes are stealing from the community, which is much worse than stealing from an individual.

Many people have issues with the government and the services it provides, but these issues should not detract from their tremendous importance. Our Sages state: "Pray for the welfare of the government. For if not for fear of it, people would eat one another alive" (*Ethics of the Fathers* 3:2). This directive was referring to the wicked Roman government, which destroyed the Temple and exiled us from our Land. It is even truer when we are talking about the State of Israel, whose government is guided by the principles of justice and integrity that are part of our Jewish heritage. Every resident of Israel is the beneficiary of the good things generated by tax revenue. Those who cheat on their taxes are theives, exploiters, and ingrates repaying good with evil.

True, there are ethical disagreements about how heavily to tax whom, and how to distribute the revenue among all the different institutions and sectors. However, the decisions reached by the representatives of the people are decisions that obligate us all. Every community grants its representatives the authority to make these decisions, and the decisions made by the Knesset (Israel's parliament) and the government obligate everyone in the State. The same is true of course in all law-abiding democracies.

14. Preventing Tax Evasion and Money Laundering

Within the framework of modern life, global commerce, and e-commerce, huge black markets have developed for drugs, weapons, gambling, prostitution, counterfeit goods, and human trafficking. To deal with tax evasion and society-corrupting organized crime, many laws have been passed that require carefully reporting money transfers to and from authorized bank accounts. This is to prevent criminals from spending money on illegal activities and bribing government officials. Therefore, each citizen has an absolute obligation to follow all the rules to prevent tax evasion and money laundering. These include reporting international money transfers and not making cash payments in amounts exceeding the legal limits.

15. The Justice in Charity

Although the Torah defends the right of ownership and does not mandate individuals to divide the fruits of their labors equally, it does command us to help the poor with charity. This charity involves an element of justice as well. Farmers who work hard and see the fruits of their labor, must remember that the land and the rain come from God, as does their skill and their health. Additionally, the fact their crops escaped damage is thanks to God. The justice system, transportation system, and educational system also play a role in their success. They too are thanks to divine mercy and societal support. Therefore, it is only just for a person to take some of the blessings God granted and give them to others who have been less blessed. This is why there are many commandments relating to charity, which will be explained in the next chapter.

At the same time, since the wealth people earn belongs to them, they have the right to choose to which poor people and charitable institutions they want to donate. When necessary, if the charity people voluntarily give is not enough to meet the critical needs of the impoverished, communal leaders must obligate the entire community to donate. In the State of Israel, tax revenue contributes greatly towards meeting the critical needs of the poor.

CHAPTER 6

Charity

1. Helping the Poor

The Torah mandates four frameworks to help the poor.

The first (and formerly primary one) was agricultural.[2] The poor were entitled to harvest five agricultural gifts for themselves. (See the next section.)

The second was charity, which took care of their remaining needs.

Third was the tithe for the poor (*ma'aser ani*). Field owners, after giving a tithe (tenth) of their produce each year to the Levites (as we will explain in 17:7 and 24:4), were required to tithe again. During the third and sixth years of the seven-year cycle, this second tithe was given to the poor. This allowed them to live in relative comfort for two years out of every seven. (See section six below.)

Fourth was the inclusion of the poor in holiday celebrations hosted by the pilgrims to Jerusalem. These included offerings brought then, as well as food that could be eaten only in Jerusalem (such as the second tithe in the first, second, fourth, and fifth years of the cycle), which the poor were invited to eat.

---

2   These agricultural *mitzvot* were exclusive to the Land of Israel.

2. The Five Agricultural Gifts

The Torah commands farmers to share their wealth with the poor by leaving them five gifts:

1) *Pe'ah*. Approximately two percent of the crop was to be left for the poor. The produce was left at the end of the field or at the end of each row within the field.
2) *Shikhe^ha*. Sometimes the harvesters forgot to cut the grain or pick the fruits within a certain area. Other times, overlooked small amounts of produce. If this forgotten produce was less than the volume of 14 liters, it had to be left for the poor.
3) *Leket*. During the harvest, a few sheaves of grain might be dropped. These had to be left for the poor.
4) *Peret*. During the grape harvest, a few grapes might be dropped. These had to be left for the poor.
5) *Olelot*. If any grape clusters were incompletely formed, they had to be left for the poor.

3. The Importance of These Gifts in the Past

A cautious estimate would be that gifts for the poor constituted between three and four percent of the harvest (and a little more of the grape harvest). In the past, when agricultural produce made up over 90 percent of the economy, these gifts could have supported, if minimally, the five percent or so of the population who were so poor as to be short of food. Nowadays, thanks to the tremendous decrease in food prices and the increase in the standard of living, agricultural produce is only about one percent of Israel's total GDP. It is no longer worth it for the poor to gather the five gifts, and consequently the field owners may harvest all their produce. Nevertheless, we can derive principles from these *mitzvot* which can shed light on appropriate ways to help the poor nowadays as well.

4. Applications for Our Times

First of all, the Torah commanded the poor (including the elderly) to come to the fields and gather the gifts for themselves. So too, our attempts to help the poor should involve them working in some way, if at all possible. Second, the *mitzva* was for the poor to collect actual produce, rather than the money the owner made by selling it. Similarly, today, it is proper for manufacturers to provide the poor with their products rather than give them money. Third, ideally the poor should be helped in ways which involve minimal expense for the wealthy and maximal benefit for the poor. The agricultural gifts accomplished this wise and worthy goal remarkably well. For example, let us say the pay rate for a fieldhand to harvest 100 kilograms of produce was 100 shekels. If the owner also had to hire someone to gather the produce that was dropped, forgotten, or incompletely formed, the owner would have had to pay significantly more. Therefore, it turns out that the poor, who had no other work, benefited significantly from gathering what was left in the field, while the owner lost only a little. Additionally, there was a certain advantage to the owner in having the poor remove the forgotten fruits, because it prevented pests from being attracted to the trees and damaging them. This was especially true for grapes, which tend to be particularly delicate. As for *pe'ah*, it is true the owner would not have needed to pay extra for fieldhands to harvest it. Nevertheless, because *pe'ah* was at the end of the field, it was convenient for the owner, tired from a hard day's work, to just leave it for the poor. Additionally, when dealing with fruits, *pe'ah* could be left from the highest fruits of the tree. These fruits would have been difficult for the fieldhands to reach, so it was convenient to leave them. The children of the poor could easily climb the trees and pick the fruits.

Nowadays, as we mentioned above, these agricultural gifts are no longer practical. Nevertheless, it would be advisable for our contemporary religious leaders to study modern economy and employment in depth, examine the plight of the poor and the causes of poverty, and derive principles from the original *mitzvot* to arrive at the best way to help the unfortunate of today. The goal would be to find a way in which the manufacturers of what people need – food, medicine, clothing, furniture, and housing – can involve the poor with their production and distribution. The efforts to help the poor would involve their being active participants, with a limited loss to the donors and a great benefit to the recipients.

5. The *Mitzva* of *Tzedaka*

In the past, there was a *mitzva* to give *tzedaka* (charity) when the agricultural gifts were not adequate to provide for a poor person's basic needs. The same applies today, when it is impossible for the poor to survive based on agricultural gifts. Thus, it is a *mitzva* to give *tzedaka* to a needy person who lacks what the vast majority of the population would consider basic necessities. The obligation applies first and foremost to the deprived person's family members. If they are unable or unwilling to help, it devolves upon his friends and neighbors. If they too are unable or unwilling to help, it devolves upon all residents of the city.

The more a recipient feels respected and less embarrassed, the better the *tzedaka* is. Therefore, the highest level of *tzedaka* is to help the poor find work, allowing them to support themselves and avoid asking for charity. This category also includes underwriting the poor's education, thus allowing them to study a profession and support their family with dignity. The unfortunate who are unable to work, should be given *tzedaka* in a way that does not damage their pride. Giving anonymously is a good example of this, as recipients are not embarrassed when they do not know who gave them the money. Besides money, the *mitzva* of *tzedaka* can also be fulfilled by giving food, clothing, or furniture to help the poor and bring them joy.

6. The Tithe for the Poor

As we mentioned above, one tenth of the agricultural produce was given to the needy in the third and sixth years of each seven-year cycle. While poor people's basic necessities were taken care of through the agricultural gifts (and supplemented with charity when necessary), this tithe was meant to give the indigent a couple of good years when they could enjoy relative comfort. This taste of plenty may have been meant to motivate those with the ability to work (or their children) to work harder and more efficiently in the subsequent lean years, allowing them to break the cycle of poverty and enjoy prosperity and financial independence. In contrast, had the poor been given a medium-sized handout every year, they would have gotten used to making ends meet with it. They would not have experienced the extra bit of joy, and they would not have developed the desire to improve their lot.

7. Prioritizing

If a number of poor people ask for help, but we do not have the means to help them all, three principles should guide us in deciding whom to help. These principles are derived from a verse: "If, however, there is a needy person among you, one of your kinsfolk in any of your settlements in the land that the Lord your God is giving you, do not harden your heart and shut your hand against your needy kinsfolk" (Deuteronomy 15:7).

The first principle is based on the word "needy." The destitute who are hungry, take precedence over those who simply need clothing or furniture, as their need is more acute.

The second principle is based on "one of your kinsfolk." One's family members take precedence, with closer relatives being given higher priority. Parents take precedence over grown children. Children take precedence over siblings. Siblings take precedence over uncles and aunts, and uncles and aunts take precedence over cousins and close friends.

The third principle is based on "any of your settlements." The impoverished of one's own city take precedence over the poor of another city. More precisely, one's immediate neighbors take precedence over the poor of the neighborhood; the needy of the neighborhood take precedence over the poor of the city; and the deprived of the city take precedence over the poor of another city.

When these three principles conflict, the first takes precedence over the second, and the second over the third.

Those who are in charge of community charity funds for a neighborhood or a city must deal with all the poor in their charge using the first principle, and giving precedence to those who are most needy.

When Jews live alongside non-Jews who are good neighbors, there is a *mitzva* to help the non-Jewish poor together with the Jewish poor.

8. Concentric Circles of Responsibility

We see from the prioritizing principles that the responsibility to help others spreads in ever-widening circles. This makes a lot of sense, because if every person were to be responsible for the whole world, or even for all of the people of his city, we would not be able to adequately help anyone. In contrast, if people are responsible for those closest to them, they can help with everything needed, such as finding work, providing food, educating the children, and marrying them off. Furthermore, those dealing with their immediate circle know the people well and know the truth about their situation, so the help can be more precisely and effectively dispensed. This is the efficient way to rescue people from the cycle of poverty, which also benefits society as a whole.

Therefore, the primary responsibility to assist is on the family. If the family members cannot do it alone, the neighbors must help. If the neighbors cannot manage either, the responsibility devolves upon the community. Accordingly, the custom has been for each Jewish community to appoint people to be in charge of charity distribution. They must be wise and righteous, with a good sense of how to distribute the necessary aid in the most dignified and effective ways.

9. Charity Distributors

When choosing a charity distributor, every effort should be made to find people who know the poor of the community well and are familiar with their situations. If the charity distributor does not know the recipients' families, their work situation, their debt situation, and their bank balance, it increases the likelihood the money will go to frauds or to the unworthy – gamblers, drug addicts, drunks, or just spendthrifts. Giving charity to the undeserving is not a *mitzva* but a sin. This is a risk even when the charity goes to those who are truly in need. When givers do not know the recipient well, it is possible they will make things worse, as they may be getting the poor person accustomed to accepting easy money rather than encouraging them to get a job. This is not doing the needy any favor, because it damages their self-respect and their family's respect for them. It also gets the children comfortable with indolence and may destroy their confidence in their ability to work and support themselves. Therefore, the proper way to support the poor is through wise and responsible charity distributors, who can clarify people's true needs and identify the best methods to provide for them. A state's welfare system should do its best to adopt these principles as well.

10. Giving Beggars

In the past some people were so hungry that they might starve to death if someone did not give them money to buy a piece of bread. Therefore, the Sages directed us to give any beggar enough to buy a piece of bread – but not more, in order to discourage frauds from begging. However, in the State of Israel today, it is hard to argue that beggars are actually starving. Therefore, there is no longer a *mitzva* to give to everyone who asks. Rather, they should be referred to welfare services or charity distributors.

11. The Mitzva in First World Countries

When a country has various state agencies to service the poor and other disadvantaged people, every citizen has the privilege of participating in the *mitzva* of *tzedaka*. However, at the same time, everyone should try to ensure that the rules and regulations encourage those in need to become independent, rather than supporting themselves through stipends (or, even worse, to file false reports in order to receive aid).

Everyone should also try to ensure that the welfare system does not relieve a poor person's relatives, friends, and neighbors of responsibility. This is both because the obligation to help begins with them, and because they are in a position to do the best job of helping. Since they know this needy person well, and for a longer period of time, they are in a good position to help them find work, save them from making bad financial decisions, and guide their children out of the cycle of poverty.

12. Giving a Tenth to Charity

Just as the Torah commanded us to take tithes from agricultural produce, the Sages mandated that we set aside a tenth (10%) of our income for charity and Torah institutions. The money set aside to fulfill this obligation is commonly referred to as *ma'aser* or *ma'aser* money. One who wishes to fulfill the *mitzva* maximally may donate up to a fifth (20%). However, people should not give away more than this unless they are extremely wealthy, as one cannot predict what the future may bring.

The *mitzva* of giving a tenth applies to all discretionary income. This includes take-home pay, interest on investments, gifts and inheritances, child allowances, and scholarships that can be used at the recipient's discretion. However, money given on condition it be used for a specific purpose is exempt from *ma'aser*. For example, money that parents give their children to buy a house, clothing, or anything else is exempt, as is scholarship money which covers tuition.

Those whose finances are very tight are exempt from giving *ma'aser*. However, people who make a reasonable amount of money but whose expenses are high due to purchasing an apartment or the like, may not assert that their financial situation is precarious. This claim can be made only by a person who objectively does not have the money, such as someone in a low-income bracket.

13. *Ma'aser* Recipients

The Torah-mandated tithes were meant to support the priests and Levites, who were in charge of Jewish education. Ideally, today too, the recipients of *ma'aser* money are those *yeshivot* that train the next generation of rabbis and educators. They will teach and guide the nation in the ways of Torah and *mitzvot*, morality and industriousness, work and study, family values and volunteering. Nevertheless, if there are many poor people who lack the basic necessities of food and clothing, most *ma'aser* money should be directed to them.

This order of priorities is very reasonable. In a healthy society, *ma'aser* to rabbinic colleges functions as preventive medicine. With proper Torah guidance, everyone will understand the values of education and work. People will do their work industriously and professionally, families will budget properly, blessing will proliferate, and very few people will be poor. Yet, if this preventive medicine fails and people become "sick" – meaning those who study Torah do not educate the community to work and to develop society, science, and the economy – then most *ma'aser* needs to be dedicated to those who are "sick," namely the poor and others in need.

In terms of orders of priorities within yeshiva donations, donors should give preference to those *yeshivot* whose worldview is most similar to their own. This way they become partners in forming a Torah world in accordance with their values.

When necessary, one may use *ma'aser* money to take care of other religious needs, such as building a synagogue. But *ma'aser* may not be used for obligations. For example, one may not use this money to buy *tefillin* (phylacteries) or *mezuzot*, or to pay synagogue dues. One may not use *ma'aser* to pay tuition either, since education is an obligation incumbent upon the parents.

14. *Ma'aser* and Wealth

The Sages tell us that one who gives *ma'aser* will be rewarded with wealth. The homiletical basis is the verse, "You shall set aside every year a tenth part (*aser te'aser*) of all the yield" (Deuteronomy 14:22). Based on the repetition in the Hebrew, they declare: "Give one tenth (*aser*) so that you may become wealthy (*titasher*)." As a rule, people may not perform a *mitzva* intending to test God, to see if He will help them as a reward for doing the *mitzva*. However, when it comes to charity, this is permissible. As it says, "Bring the full tithe . . . and thus put Me to the test – said the Lord of Hosts. I will surely open the floodgates of the sky for you and pour down blessings on you" (Malachi 3:10). This still does not mean that those who tithe will become wealthy in a miraculous fashion, but rather that God will bless the fruits of their labor. In the merit of their tithing, they will be successful at work, and will make wise business decisions. Still, if they are lazy and negligent, they will not become wealthy.

It should be noted that some rabbis tend to be lenient about tithing and exempt most people from the obligation, either because of their financial situation or because these rabbis allow tuition money to count as *ma'aser*. Nevertheless, the principle is what I have written above. Additionally, experience shows that people who follow it are indeed blessed with success and wealth.

15. Charity Boxes

Some people make sure to have a charity box at home. Every day, whether before praying or at some other point, they put some money in it. Periodically, they empty the box and donate the value of the coins collected to *yeshivot* or to the poor. Even though the primary fulfillment of the *mitzva* of charity is to give a tenth or a fifth every month from one's earnings, these people go beyond the call of duty, donating daily to accustom themselves to giving to good causes.

16. Lending Money

Offering interest-free loans is a *mitzva*. The purpose of the *mitzva* is to enable people to meet their basic expenses when they have temporary financial difficulty. Therefore, a borrower may not use a loan to buy luxury items unless the lender has agreed to this.

Lenders must document their loans, in order to avoid later unpleasantness about the amount or terms of the loan. The only person who is permitted to give an undocumented loan is someone who is ready to forgive a debt wholeheartedly if the borrower forgets about it.

Sometimes borrowers are unable to repay a loan. In such cases, it is forbidden to make their lives miserable, forcing them to go into debt or sell necessities in order to return the money. Thus we read, "Do not be like a moneylender" (Exodus 22:24). However, when it is known that a prospective borrower is irresponsible and there is a reasonable chance the borrower will not repay the loan, there is no *mitzva* to lend them money, since the *mitzva* to lend is meant to help responsible people who will make every effort to repay the loan.

17. Debt Relief

To help release poor people from their debts, the Torah ordained that all debts were wiped out once every seven years, at the end of the sabbatical year. Later, towards the end of the Second Temple period, times were very difficult, and many poor people were unable to repay their debts. Because of this, the rich stopped lending money to the poor, to avoid losing their money with the advent of the sabbatical year. Therefore, the Sages ordained that those who wanted to prevent their loans from being wiped out could lend the money out through the rabbinic courts, using a special document called a *prozbul*. This was a non-ideal solution though, dictated by an unfortunate necessity. Today's sages and leaders should think seriously about how debt relief might be applied in our times.

18. Interest-Free Loans

It is very common for Jewish communities to establish free loan societies, which offer interest-free loans to community members in need. The people in charge of these communal funds must be both wise and trustworthy. They should be able to check out each borrower, confirming both necessity and the ability to repay. They must also know how to deal with borrowers who are having difficulties repaying loans and decide when to insist on repayment and when to forgive the loan.

19. The Prohibition of Interest

It is a severe transgression to lend money with interest, as this involves taking advantage of someone else's hardship for personal gain. As a result of taking out loans with interest, people sometimes lose their homes and everything they own. In the past, this could even lead to someone being sold into slavery. Often, adversity which leads people to borrow is ongoing, and the interest keeps compounding until it utterly ruins borrowers and their families. Those who participate in lending with interest (the witnesses or guarantors) are guilty of being accessories. The borrower is sinning as well. Therefore, someone in a financial crisis must make every possible effort to get through it without taking out an interest-bearing loan.

20. *Heter Iska*

How can modern banks and businesses function if money cannot be lent or borrowed with interest? A rabbinic document called a *heter iska* (literally: business permission) addresses this problem. It structures business transactions as investments for which there is no interest but rather profit-sharing. One side provides the funds and the other puts in the time and effort that will make the investment grow. For example, a lending institution invests in a factory so that the factory owner can buy additional equipment. The factory's earnings will increase, and the two sides will share in the profits. To avoid complications, the percentage the investor will receive is agreed upon in advance. Similarly, young adults accepted to a training program for an in-demand profession, but do not have the money to pay tuition, can turn to a lending institution to invest in their studies using the *heter iska* framework. When they finish their studies and begin earning money, they return the investment along with part of the earnings. It is important that use of the *heter iska* does not cause us to forget the important *mitzva* of interest-free loans for those in need.

21. Overdraft

Even though Israeli banks allow a personal account to be overdrawn up to a pre-arranged limit, some maintain that Jewish law forbids a person to go into overdraft (if this is not done in the context of a business). This is because the *heter iska* for banks is designed for money-making investments. When money is withdrawn simply to cover ongoing expenses for food, clothing, and other necessities, the interest charged by the bank on the overdrawn account is prohibited. Others offer a variety of justifications to permit overdraft when truly necessary.

Everyone agrees that one may go into short-term overdraft to meet ongoing expenses, otherwise they would have to withdraw money early from a savings plan and suffer a penalty. The overdraft interest is viewed as a business expense in order to avoid a much greater loss.

22. A Source of Blessing for All Nations

The Jewish nation is meant to bring blessing upon all nations and societies. This was promised to all three patriarchs. (See 1:6 above.) Thus, the more resources the Jewish people have, the greater their *mitzva* to aid other nations. And the closer in spirit a nation is to the Jewish people, the greater the obligation.

As we have seen, the highest level of *tzedaka* is that which allows the poor to be self-sufficient. Similarly, aiding other nations should primarily involve helping them develop their own economy in all areas, including agriculture, manufacturing, education, and healthcare.

CHAPTER 7

The Justice System

1. The Torah's Justice System

It is natural for people to argue every so often. To resolve arguments justly, every city has a *mitzva* to appoint judges. Their job is to adjudicate and to punish those who harm others. There is also a *mitzva* to appoint police officers. Their job is to enforce the judges' rulings. As it says, "You shall appoint judges and officers in all your gates, which the Lord your God is giving you according to your tribes, and they shall govern the people with due justice" (Deuteronomy 16:18).

It is a *mitzva* to streamline the judicial process and to resolve disputes as quickly as possible, because the longer a dispute lasts, the stronger the mutual hatred becomes. The Torah specifies having judges at the gates of every city, so disputes can be ended within hours, or at most a day. If one side needs time to gather evidence or locate witnesses, a reasonable amount of time may be allotted for this.

2. The Judges

The judges should be "capable men who fear God, trustworthy men who spurn ill-gotten gains" (Exodus 18:21). The

Hebrew for "capable men" is *anshei ḥayil*, which can be translated more literally as "men of valor" or "heroes." This refers to judges who have the courage to decide justly, without regard to threats from criminals or the pressure of public opinion. Along the same lines, judges are admonished to fear no one, for judgment is God's" (Deuteronomy 1:17). "Trustworthy men" refers to judges who treat everyone equally and do not favor anyone. As we read, "You shall not render an unfair decision; do not favor the poor or show deference to the rich; judge your fellow with righteousness" (Leviticus 19:15). "Who spurn ill-gotten gains" refers to people who hate money gained dishonestly. This is to ensure that the judges will not be tempted to accept bribes. The Torah demands: "Do not take bribes, for bribes blind the clear-sighted and upset the pleas of those who are in the right" (Exodus 23:8).

3. The Witnesses

In a contested case, one of the primary ways to clarify what happened is to find witnesses. This allows the court to reach a reliable verdict. Therefore, if a person saw something which could help clarify an incident, the Torah obligates one to testify; it is a sin if one does not do so. (Leviticus 5:1). The judges must thoroughly examine witnesses to ensure there are no contradictions in their testimonies, and they have not extrapolated incorrectly based on what they saw. The Torah strongly exhorts against false testimony. This admonition is so important that it is the ninth of the Ten Commandments. Additionally, the Torah decrees fitting punishment for false witnesses: "If a man appears against another to testify maliciously . . . You shall do to him as he schemed to do to his fellow" (Deuteronomy 19:16-19).

4. Damages – "An Eye for an Eye"

The Torah states, "If anyone maims his fellow, as he has done so shall it be done to him: fracture for fracture, eye for eye, tooth for tooth" (Leviticus 24:19-20). The Sages explain that the offender needs to pay the victim the monetary value of the eye or tooth. (This is a good example of the relationship between the Oral Torah and Written Torah. The Written Torah lays down a principle – that the aggressor deserves to be punished measure for measure. The Oral Torah clarifies this in a precise and practical way.) The payment includes five elements:

- Damages – the monetary value of the eye or foot.
- Pain – compensation for the physical suffering.
- Medical – payment for the doctors and medicine.
- Unemployment – payment for the workdays missed.
- Embarrassment – compensation for the embarrassment of being beaten and degraded.

5. The Death Penalty

There are close to 30 sins which carry a death penalty in principle. These include committing murder, adultery, or incest, desecrating the Sabbath publicly, and kidnapping and selling a person into slavery. A court composed of 23 ordained judges had the authority to put someone to death. (The ordination required here was the original ordination granted by teacher to student in an unbroken chain that began with Moses.)

However, in contrast to other nations and religions of ancient times, it was very rare for the Jews to actually put anyone to death. In fact, one of the Sages asserted that a Sanhedrin that executed one person in seven years was considered to have deviated from the accepted norm and was called "brutal." Another Sage maintained that a court that executed even one person in 70 years was considered brutal. This is because the terms and conditions the *halakha* establishes for capital punishment are so restrictive that they are very difficult to meet. One of these conditions is there must be witnesses who explicitly told the perpetrator before sinning that the punishment is death if he commits this sin. Furthermore, it must be clear the sinner understood the warning and did it anyway. With the exception of people with severe anger management problems, no one would do such a thing. We see the Torah's death penalty is not meant to be put into practice. Rather, it is meant to achieve two things: 1) to make the gravity of the sins clear, and 2) to establish communal norms so no one would dare to commit these sins publicly.

In practice, on the rare occasion the death penalty was meted out, it was primarily to murderers. But before the destruction of the Second Temple, when the Jews were under Roman rule, society's moral levels declined, and murder abounded. The Sages saw the death penalty was no longer serving as a deterrent. If the courts had put Torah law into practice, they would have had to execute more than one person in seven years. It was decided the Sanhedrin would exile itself from its proper location near the Temple and move to a nearby street. This move meant the courts throughout the land no longer had the authority to adjudicate death penalty cases. Since the goal of punishment is deterrence (and the accompanying preservation of human lives), there was no reason to continue imposing it if it was not effective. We learn from this that the High Court had the authority whether or not to impose capital punishment depending on the circumstances; by moving, the Sanhedrin had effectively repealed the death penalty.

6. Fines Requiring Ordained Judges

The Torah establishes fines for certain offenses. For example, if a man seduced a young woman and she wanted to marry him, he was obligated to marry her. If she did not want to, he had to pay her a fine (Exodus 22:15-16). A thief who was caught was also fined and had to pay double what was stolen (*ibid.* 22:3). For judges to have the authority to impose fines, they needed the original ordination. Since this ordination could take place only in the Land of Israel, it ceased following the Temple's destruction and the nation's exile, and judges lost their authority to issue fines.

Ever since, judges have been merely agents of the earlier Sages, and their activities are limited in scope. They can still adjudicate matters critical to society's functioning. Fines though, which are meant to elevate us to the status of a nation of priests and a holy people, are in abeyance. Therefore, a rabbinic court can tell a thief to repay what was stolen, but not to pay double. Nevertheless, even today's rabbis who lack the original ordination have the responsibility to pass ordinances and impose fines when necessary, to ensure the smooth functioning of society.

7. Jewish Jurisprudence

It is unfortunate that the original ordination has lapsed, and the result has been a decrease in the authority of rabbinic judges. Furthermore, because our exile lasted so long, many areas of modern economy, society, and governance have not yet been fully elucidated by *halakha*. Nevertheless, there is still a *mitzva* to take any disagreements to a court that follows Jewish law. In the verse, "These are the rules that you shall set before them" (Exodus 21:1), "them" refers to the judges and rabbis who rule in accordance with Torah law.

When the State of Israel was founded, it should have

established a justice system of Jewish jurisprudence, combining the classic values of the Torah with the modern legal wisdom of developed nations. Unfortunately, because the founders were skeptical the Torah could make a positive contribution to a modern justice system, they decided that Jewish jurisprudence would be consulted only in cases in which secular jurisprudence failed to provide a resolution.

Since the modern Israeli justice system refuses to give proper weight to Jewish jurisprudence, it is not acceptable according to *halakha*. Therefore, if two Israeli citizens have a disagreement, they must take it to a court that follows *halakha*. Only if one side refuses to go to a rabbinic court may the other side resort to a secular court. Some contemporary rabbinic authorities say that as long as a person cannot realistically turn to Jewish jurisprudence, one may have the case heard by a secular court, because the community has the right to decide that it wants to use a justice system proven in enlightened countries. In any case, all rabbinic opinions agree that the Israeli justice system should give more weight to Jewish values. When it becomes primarily based on these values, the justice system will become acceptable according to *halakha*.

8. The Ideal Justice System

The vision of our redemption includes the return of the original ordination and the reestablishment of the Sanhedrin. The members of the Sanhedrin must be Torah scholars who are also knowledgeable in a variety of fields, particularly economics, sociology, and anthropology. (This is an interpretation of the traditional requirement for a Sanhedrin member to know "70 languages.") These sages will clarify Torah law in a way that fits contemporary economics and society, and they will gradually restore Torah law to its proper place. The Knesset's legislation and public policy will continue to apply, but the Sanhedrin will work together with elected officials to decide what needs to be refined and what needs to be replaced. At the same time, they will make sure to protect everyone's human rights, so that no one is harmed by the process of improving the justice system.

In the meantime, the more judges give weight to Torah values, and the more Torah scholars, jurists, and economists work to clarify what the Torah would ideally say, the more progress will be made toward the grand vision of a Torah justice system – a system which will uplift society and lead to truth and peace.

Family

Chapter 8: Marriage 118
Chapter 9: Nidda. 130
Chapter 10: Protecting Marriage 138
Chapter 11: The Wedding 154
Chapter 12: Parents and Children 166
Chapter 13: Family Celebrations 177
Chapter 14: Mourning 186

Marriage

1. The Value of Marriage

Marriage is an extremely important *mitzva*. It allows a person to put many values into practice: love and sanctity, unity and faith, loyalty and joy, life and blessing. A person fulfills two important *mitzvot* by getting married. The first is marriage itself, which includes the commitment of each partner to love their spouse and look after their wellbeing and happiness. The second is procreation, the *mitzva* to have children.

Some people mistakenly believe that procreation is the primary purpose of marriage. In truth though, marital love is more important. To understand this, we need to review some basic religious concepts:

God created an imperfect world, allowing humans to complete it. This enables us to be partners with God in everything good in the world and to enjoy it fully. The greatest deficiency in all of creation is division. The one God indeed created everything, but because He concealed His light, all creatures are disconnected from Him, and consequently from one another. Each creature looks out only for itself, thus leading to all the world's strife, discord, conflict, and war.

The goals of Jewish faith are to see beyond the surface separation, believe in the one God, and restore unity to the world. This is why the *mitzva* of "Love your fellow as yourself" is called a "major Torah principle." Its ultimate actualization is the marriage covenant between husband and wife, enabling two distinct individuals to unite completely, body and soul. Often, the body and the soul are in conflict. The soul longs for good while the body is attracted to evil. The soul longs for eternity while the body longs for temporary pleasure. Within marriage, the body and soul unite. Even carnal desires, which often lead a person to sin, are uplifted. The *mitzva* of marriage joins together the noble ideals of faithfulness and unity with the greatest pleasure. The moral value of total devotion joins with the greatest joy.

While the entire creation is God's handiwork and thus expresses unity, the union of a man and woman expresses an even more profound unity. We can see this clearly when we look at the story of the creation of Adam and Eve. According to the Talmud, they were originally connected back-to-back. God then separated them. When they chose to reunite of their own volition, their bond was stronger, loving, and procreational. As it says: "So the Lord God cast a deep sleep upon the man; and, while he slept, He took one of his sides and closed up the flesh at that spot. And the Lord God fashioned the side that He had taken from the man into a woman; and He brought her to the man. Then the man said, 'This one at last is bone of my bones and flesh of my flesh. This one shall be called Woman, for from man was she taken.' Hence a man leaves his father and mother and clings to his wife, so that they become one flesh" (Genesis 2:21-24). Singles all face the same challenge – to find their soulmate, and thus complete themselves and the world. It is from this starting point that a couple can move on to the second *mitzva* – procreation.

Being married is so important that the Sages tell us that a man who is not married "is not a man". They derive this homiletically from the verses, "This is the record of Adam's line . . . He made him in the likeness of God; male and female He created them. He blessed them and called them Man" (*ibid.* 5:1-2). Only when two people are a couple is the image of God within them fully revealed. This allows them to be blessed and to have children. As we read, "And God created man in His image, in the image of God He created him; male and female He created them. God blessed them and God said to them, 'Be fruitful and multiply'" (*ibid.* verses 27-28). The Sages add that anyone who is unmarried is left without joy, without blessing, without goodness, without Torah, without a [protective] wall, and without peace. Faithful marriages filled with love and joy bring down a flow of supernal light to the loving couple, adding life and blessing to the world. This is what Rabbi Akiva means when he states, "If husband and wife are worthy, the Divine Presence is with them; if they are not, fire consumes them" (*Sota* 17a).

We will first explain the value of marital love which expresses itself through the *mitzva* of *ona* (marital relations). This will be followed by an explanation of the *mitzva* of procreation. To fulfill these wonderful *mitzvot* in purity, the Torah also prescribes the *nidda* laws (as we will see in Chapter 9). To fulfill them with sanctity, the Torah prescribes laws of modesty, prohibits adultery, allows for divorce, and defines the couple's fiduciary responsibilities (as we will explain in Chapter 10). In Chapter 11 we will describe how a traditional Jewish wedding is conducted.

2. The Mitzva of *Ona*

The primary *mitzva* within marriage is that a couple unite lovingly. The full expression of this unity is through the *mitzva* of *ona*, which connects the couple completely, body and soul. Each wishes to pleasure his or her partner to the best of their ability until they reach orgasm. The word *ona* has two meanings: 1) Time and frequency, meaning this *mitzva* must be fulfilled at regular intervals. 2) Responsiveness and reciprocity. The couple must respond to one another with pleasure and joy.

Since the stamina of a male is limited (more so than that of a female), the frequency with which he can engage in sexual relations is limited. Thus, the required frequency is based on his capability. For healthy, young men who are on vacation and relaxed, the *mitzva* applies every night. For men who are working, it applies twice a week; for those whose work is particularly taxing, once a week. If the couple are uncertain as to what category they are in, it is preferable for them to fulfill the *mitzva* twice a week, which is the average frequency for most people for most of their lives. For the young, three times a week is better; for the elderly, once a week is enough. Additionally, on *mikveh* night and on the night before one member of the couple is traveling, it is obligatory to fulfill the *mitzva* of *ona*. All this is presuming the woman is ritually pure. However, during *nidda* time, even touching is prohibited.

The *mitzva* must be fulfilled with passion and ecstasy, the husband trying to bring his wife as much joy and pleasure as possible, and the wife trying to bring her husband as much joy and pleasure as possible. The husband should bring complete joy to his wife, to the point where her joy and pleasure climax in orgasm. Short of this, their sexual relations may result in frustration, for the lead-up to orgasm builds up physical and psychological tension that is blissfully released upon orgasm. If she does not experience orgasm, her tensions and frustration will generally remain.

The wife has a *mitzva* to be responsive and to actively participate in the *mitzva* as best she can, for without her desire and efforts to increase their mutual pleasure, it is impossible to fulfill the *mitzva*. However, if she is so exhausted or tense that it will be difficult for her to achieve orgasm, she may choose to forgo it and suffice with sexual union that brings sweet pleasure but not complete bliss. This too is a fulfillment of the *mitzva*. Nevertheless, it is best to try to ensure that it does not happen too frequently. The wife's orgasm need not take place during coitus itself; it is possible (and for most couples, it is best) for the husband to use manual stimulation to enable his wife to reach orgasm before him, and from this they proceed to the consummation of their sexual union.

The more a husband and wife give and receive pleasure at the set times (*onot*) of this *mitzva*, the better. This is also mandated by the *mitzva* of "Love your fellow as yourself" (Leviticus 19:18), which entails a spouse looking out for the good of the other to the best of their ability. Since the greatest physical and emotional pleasure is that shared by husband and wife, if a man deprives his wife of this enjoyable pleasure, he is being oppressive, since no other man can provide her with this joy.

The *mitzva* is also called *derekh eretz*, "the way of the world," since every healthy person yearns for pleasurable sexual union, the greatest palpable physical pleasure a person can experience in this world. If a husband or wife does not feel that yearning, they must try to heal themselves, so that their sexual union will be joyful for both of them.

3. Beyond the Set Times

As well as the set obligation of the *mitzva* of *ona*, which for most men is twice a week, it is a *mitzva* for every husband to have sexual relations with his wife when she desires him, as long as he is capable of consummating the union with the proper joy. Thus, the *mitzva* of *ona* has two aspects (corresponding to the two meanings of the word, as we said above).

First, there are set times, which provide a regular expression for the couple's bond and mutual desire. Second, when the desire of one spouse is aroused, it is a *mitzva* and a duty for the other spouse to be responsive to the best of their ability.

A question arises regarding the first component of the *mitzva*. Why must the Torah establish set times for a couple to express their love for each other? Why not leave the frequency of the *mitzva* up to them?

It often happens that life's demands grow as the years pass. Since sexual relations are no longer new and special as at first, the couple are liable to push it off, whether because of exhaustion, worry, aches and pains. However, each time they both agree to forgo the *mitzva*, their loving relationship is actually weakened. Deep in their hearts, each one is hurt that the other does not yearn for more intimacy, and when one does not initiate, the other also loses interest, deepening the sense of insult and the growing distance between them. Therefore, the *mitzva* of *ona* comes to instruct them to be intimate on a regular basis. Only on rare occasions, when they are especially tense, may they forgo the *mitzva* by mutual consent.

Another reason for the set times is that the *mitzva* must be done with full attentiveness, so the couple can truly enjoy themselves. The Sages assessed how frequently a couple can fulfill the *mitzva* of *ona* in a wholesome manner. If the husband goes too far beyond this frequency, there is concern it will become superficial for him, something he does just to satisfy his urges, without bringing proper pleasure to his wife. The unique joy of the *mitzva* would wane. Conversely, if the wife is interested in sexual relations more frequently than the husband is physically capable of, this may lead to trouble, emotional as well as physical.

Unfortunately, in modern society, marriage and intimacy are not a high priority, so many people live alone. In fact, some comprehensive studies have found that in large cities of the western world, most adults had not had sexual relations within the past year. Even among married people, many had not had relations more than once a month.

4. How to Fulfill This Important *Mitzva*

When a couple unite with love and joy, they connect with the very root of life. A spark of the divine rests upon them, and the entire world is blessed with life and joy. Therefore, our Sages tell us that people should sanctify themselves before engaging in this *mitzva*. This means each person should think about how to please their partner and put their partner's enjoyment before their own. The greater their mutual enjoyment, the greater their *mitzva* fulfillment. Other suggestions for how to fulfill this *mitzva* include complimenting one's spouse often, respecting them, and caring for them in all aspects of life.

5. Difficulties Fulfilling the *Mitzva*

Ona is such an essential expression of marriage that when one member of a couple is not willing to properly fulfill this *mitzva*, the other may demand a divorce. If this is an ongoing problem, it is even advisable to divorce. Therefore, when there are physical or emotional difficulties which prevent physical intimacy, a couple must get help. Whether they should consult a rabbi, a therapist, or a doctor depends on the nature and severity of the issue. Even when a couple are able to have relations but without enjoyment, it is advisable for them to make every effort to resolve the problem so they can fulfill the *mitzva* with pleasure and joy.

Some cases are so severe that, whether for physical or emotional reasons, one member of the couple is not able to enjoy the *mitzva*, despite counseling and other efforts. When the issue is with the wife, the marriage can continue as long as she agrees, out of love for her husband, to be intimate at the set times. When the issue is with the husband, the situation is more complex. On the one hand, if he is unable to have sexual relations, his wife is entitled to a divorce. On the other hand, if she loves him, she may decide to stay in the marriage despite this. He must then please her to the best of his ability.

6. Procreation

The biblical *mitzva* to be fruitful and multiply is extraordinarily important. Since it is fundamental to the continued existence of humanity, it is the first *mitzva* mentioned in the Torah. As it says, "God blessed them and God said to them, 'Be fruitful and multiply'" (Genesis 1:28). Procreating is following in the path of God Himself – just as God created the world and continues to maintain it, so too a person "creates" children and "maintains" them. This also makes people partners of God, as the Sages say, "There are three partners in the creation of a person: God, the father, and the mother" (*Nidda* 31a).

The Sages go so far as to consider procreating the first and foremost goal of creation, based on the verse: "He did not create it to be empty; He formed it to be inhabited" (Isaiah 45:18). The Talmud declares that whoever sustains one life is considered to have sustained an entire world. How much more admirable are the parents who give birth to children, raise them, and educate them. They truly sustain an entire world.

The *mitzva* of procreation is so imperative the Sages state that a person who refrains from procreation is comparable to a murderer and diminishes the manifestation of the Divine Presence in the world. This is because every person is unique, revealing an additional aspect of the divine image. Accordingly, refraining from bringing more people into the world reduces the revelation of the divine in the world.

7. The Parameters of the *Mitzva*

Procreation has three levels of obligation. The Torah requirement is to have a son and a daughter. The rabbinic obligation is to have four or five children. The ideal is to have as many children as one can handle.

The Torah requirement is to have a son and daughter who are themselves able to procreate. If either the son or daughter is infertile, the parents have not fulfilled the *mitzva*. Similarly, if either the son or daughter predeceases the parents and dies childless, the parents did not fulfill it. Only if each of the two children had a surviving child have the parents fulfilled the *mitzva*, since their line is carried on by the two grandchildren. If their son had 10 children but their daughter died childless, they have fulfilled the *mitzva* but not ideally, since only one child carries on the line.

The rabbinic obligation is to have four or five children. There are two primary reasons for this extension of the *mitzva*. First, life itself has tremendous value. Second, even parents blessed with a son and a daughter cannot be certain the family will continue through them. Perhaps one of them will die, be infertile, or never marry.

The ideal is to for people to have as many children as they can handle. Not only does this add life to the world, but it fulfills the blessings that God bestowed upon our ancestors, "I will make your descendants as numerous as the stars of heaven" (Genesis 26:4), and "Your descendants shall be as the dust of the earth" (*ibid.* 28:14). The Jewish people's inheritance of the Land, and redemption, also depend upon the fulfillment of this *mitzva*.

What is the practical ramification of having different levels of obligation? People must make all-out efforts to fulfill the Torah obligation. Singles must search out their partners, and married couples having trouble becoming pregnant are required to undergo whatever treatments are conventionally prescribed by doctors. However, all-out effort is not required in order to fulfill the rabbinic obligation. Therefore, if a couple are worried they will have unusual difficulty in raising and educating their children, they may stop after fulfilling the Torah mandate. A couple with no unusual problems should not hesitate. Rather, they should fulfill the rabbinic obligation of having four or five children.

When it comes to fulfilling the ideal, many other factors may come into play, including the couple's happiness, wellbeing, and self-fulfillment. In other words, even though the birth of each child fulfills a tremendous *mitzva*, a couple may choose not to have additional children if they feel this would be too stressful and would have a negative impact on their lives - robbing them of peace of mind and happiness, preventing them from making use of their talents as they had hoped, or holding them back in their professional life. Together, the couple should weigh all these factors; if they disagree, they must find a compromise, as they are partners in this together. If they are having trouble reaching a joint decision, they should consult with someone wise and insightful.

8. Birth Control

As a rule, a couple who have not fulfilled the Torah obligation may not use birth control. However, in cases of great necessity, birth control is permitted on a temporary basis. This must be done in a way that avoids wasting seed, by means of the pill or an IUD. When necessary, a diaphragm or spermicide (foam or vaginal suppository) may be used, but not a condom.

After each birth, it is permissible, and even advisable, to take a break for a year in order to allow the woman's body to recover. After the Torah obligation has been fulfilled, birth control may be used for two years following a birth. It is preferable not to wait longer than this. After the rabbinic obligation has been fulfilled, a couple may use the birth control methods mentioned above, for an unlimited time.

The Torah prohibits male castration. The Sages extend this, prohibiting a woman from rendering herself permanently infertile. If a pregnancy would endanger her, there are halakhic solutions which do not involve sterilization, and which also do not interfere with the couple's ability to engage in marital relations.

9. A Childless Couple

The suffering of the childless is intense. Despite this, they should believe that everything is for the best, and is meant to purify them and increase their joy in this world and in the next. In addition to undertaking fertility treatments, they must also pray. Sometimes, when a soul is particularly special, it has trouble descending to this world. Only through the couple's spiritual efforts – praying and increasing their Torah study and acts of kindness – can they prepare the world for the arrival of such a soul. This is why there are many cases of righteous men and women who were childless. Hannah, for example, gave birth to her son Samuel (the greatest of all prophets after Moses) only following her powerful prayer which pierced the heavens. (See I Samuel 2:1-10.)

If a couple have been married for 10 years with no children and doctors have told them that each of them might be able to have children with a different spouse, it is a *mitzva* for them to divorce and remarry others. Nevertheless, if they are very much in love, and divorcing would cause them immense suffering, they are permitted to remain together. Nowadays, some fertility challenges can be met with the help of a surrogate.

If a couple adopt a child, they are fulfilling a great *mitzva*. Our Sages state, "One who raises an orphaned boy or girl in his home is considered by the Torah as if he gave birth to them" (*Megilla* 13a). Alternatively, if the couple dedicate themselves to teaching Torah, *mitzvot*, and ethical behavior, in a sense their students can be considered their children. Donating to institutions that educate underprivileged children can also be considered a type of substitute for having children.

10. Consolation for the Childless

A couple that has not been blessed with children face a great challenge. Will they wallow in their pain, and lose their faith and *joie de vivre*? Or will they overcome their sorrow, increase their love for each other, fulfill the *mitzva* of *ona* with extra joy, and constantly think about how to bring goodness and joy into the lives of their families and friends? Though the couple have not been blessed with children, their intimacy still has great intrinsic value. This is reflected in the kabbalistic idea that each time a devoted couple unite sexually with love and passion, an abundance of life and blessing is added to this world. New souls are created in the supernal realms, which then descend to this world and are born to other people. There is a special purity in a childless couple's love, which is unconditional and independent of shared children. Their loving unity gives expression to divine unity.

CHAPTER 9

Nidda

1. *Nidda* Impurity and Purification

Uterine blood flow renders a woman halakhically impure. When she is impure, meaning from the day she sees blood until the day she immerses in a *mikveh* to purify herself, the couple may not be intimate, or even touch one another. During this time of menstrual impurity, she is referred to as a *nidda*, and the couple's state is commonly referred to as being in *nidda*. Clearly, it is a very challenging time. The separation is painful, and the longing grows stronger day by day. The prohibition of giving physical expression to their love means that the couple suffer. However, along with this suffering (which purifies their love), there is also anticipation which gets stronger and stronger until *mikveh* night. Then they can finally reunite in love and joy, breaking through all barriers separating them.

Although we cannot fully understand the reasons behind God's commandments, we do know that all the *mitzvot* are intended to benefit us in this world and the next. In this case, the painful abstinence strengthens, deepens, and fans the flame of love. Separating allows the couple to recreate, on a month-ly basis, the feelings they had for each other when they were first married. Meanwhile, during the separation time, they can deepen their conversations, or throw themselves into activities which mitigate the pain of separation.

Let us give a little background to the concept of impurity. As a rule, impurity is related to death. This is why the Sages designate a corpse the ultimate impurity. Similarly, when a woman has her period, it is a type of death, as it involves the loss of an egg and tissue that had the potential to become a life. This loss also reminds us that while we may wish to love and live endlessly, our ability to do so is severely limited. Any honest psychologist would agree that intermittent periods of abstinence are the best way to keep the flame of love burning bright. However, without feeling obligated by the Torah's commandment, people would not have the strength to actually do this.

Thanks to these two polar opposites – the *mitzva* to be intimate and the requirement to abstain – the couple preserve their love, which becomes purer every month. By the time they are older, with the wife approaching menopause, they have a deep understanding of how to please one another. Their love is so deep that they no longer need the separation periods. Earlier, while pregnant or nursing, a woman generally does not have her period and the couple need not separate. Perhaps, thanks to the life-giving work in which the couple are involved, their love then increases in vitality even without the aid of separation.

According to the original Torah law, the impurity of a menstruant lasts for seven days, including the days on which she bleeds. A *zava*, whose bleeding is abnormal and continues for three days beyond her regular period, must count seven clean days after she stops bleeding. According to rabbinic law and custom, though, all women count seven clean days after they stop bleeding, as the *zava* does.

2. The Process of Purification

Three stages of purification are necessary to end the status of *nidda*:

1) A *hefsek tahara* (see next section)
2) Seven clean days without blood
3) Immersion

Generally, a woman can begin counting seven clean days only after four days of bleeding. So, the couple must separate for at least 11 days – four days of bleeding and seven clean days. Often, a woman's period lasts five to seven days, in which case the separation is longer. If a woman has a short period and stops bleeding after one to three days, she may clean herself well internally, perform a *hefsek tahara* before sunset, and start counting seven clean days.

3. The *Hefsek Tahara*

In order to begin counting the seven clean days following her period, a woman must establish that she has indeed stopped bleeding, by conducting a thorough internal check (*bedika*). This check is known as the *hefsek tahara*. Even after she has stopped bleeding though, old blood may remain in the vagina. Therefore, before attempting a *hefsek*, a woman should take a soft cloth and wet it (to avoid hurting the sensitive skin), wrap it around her finger, and clean out any vestiges of blood. Sometimes she may need to repeat this a few times. Afterwards, she should use a small, clean white cloth to do a thorough internal check. If the cloth shows no shade of red or black, she has confirmed her period has ended. It is convenient to use pre-packaged *bedika* cloths (which can be bought at a *mikveh*) for both the pre-check cleaning and the checking itself.

According to Jewish law, the day starts with sunset, so the *hefsek tahara* should ideally be done in the last few hours before sunset (*shki'a*). It is also preferable to use a *mokh daĥuk*; this means in addition to the thorough check with the *bedika* cloth, it is also good to leave a *bedika* cloth in the vagina during twilight, which extends from sunset until the emergence of stars (*tzeit*). (These times can be found in some local Jewish calendars as well as on the MyZmanim website.) If a woman was not able to do a *hefsek* before sunset, she has forfeited the day, and cannot begin her seven-day count until sunset the next day. Therefore, if a woman is worried she will forget to do a *hefsek* close to sunset, she should do it earlier in the afternoon, or even in the morning.

4. The Seven Clean Days

To ensure there are seven complete days, we begin the first day at sunset and end the seventh day at *tzeit*. This means the seven clean days end on the same day of the week they started. During this week, a woman must make sure she remains free of blood. To do this, she checks herself internally every day with a *bedika* cloth. She also wears white underwear for the week. If she finds even a drop of blood on the cloth, or if she finds a stain of at least two centimeters diameter in her underwear, she must do a new *hefsek tahara* before sunset and start counting the seven clean days again.

If a woman knows that her period has ended, but she sometimes bleeds anyway (whether because of an IUD, hormonal pills, or vaginal cuts), she should check herself only twice during the seven clean days. She should also wear colored underwear, to avoid seeing stains that might cause halakhic difficulties.

5. Pure and Impure Blood

The blood which renders a woman impure is uterine blood, which flows regularly during her menstrual cycle or irregularly in the case of a *zava*. In contrast, blood from a cut or tear in the vagina or uterus does not cause impurity. Additionally, uterine secretions do not cause impurity if they do not contain blood. Therefore, if the secretions are brown or yellow, they do not cause impurity; if they are red or black, they do. In cases of doubt, a rabbi or rebbetzin should be consulted. If the husband is asking, a rabbi should be consulted; if the wife is asking, any rebbetzin or woman who knows the *halakha*.

6. *Mikveh* Preparation

For *mikveh* immersion to be kosher, there must be no barrier (*ḥatzitza*) separating the woman from the water. What is considered a barrier for these purposes? Whatever most women would not want stuck to their body or hair, such as lice or nits, dirt, and knots in hair. To get rid of knots, the hair must be shampooed and combed out well. Hair dye which still looks good does not need to be removed. If peeling skin, scabs, and calluses can be easily removed by soaking them in water, (and this will not cause bleeding), they should be removed. If it is difficult, they do not need to be removed. Creams which are absorbed by the skin are not a problem even if their effects can be felt on the skin.

A woman is not required to open her mouth during immersion, but it is permissible for her to do so. Therefore, there must not be any barrier there, such as a shred of meat caught between the teeth. A properly made filling, even a temporary one, is not a problem. However, if a woman is embarrassed to be seen with the temporary filling, it is a barrier.

Anything on the body that is tightly fitted should be removed so that the entire body can come into contact with the water. This includes rings, earrings, hair pins, necklaces, and bracelets. Anything stuck to the eyes or eyelashes, such as leftover makeup, should be removed. Many women cut their nails before immersing, as dirt can get underneath. If a woman likes to have long nails, she can immerse as long as she cleans beneath them very well. If she wants to immerse with her nails polished, she must make sure they look good and are unchipped. Finally, she should blow her nose.

All these preparations should be done calmly. Some women prepare in preparation rooms at the *mikveh*, while others do so at home.

7. Immersing in the *Mikveh*

Immersion is done at night after the completion of the seven clean days. A kosher immersion requires the entire body to be immersed at once. If a finger or even one hair is not in the water, the immersion is invalid. Since a woman cannot see herself, and there is a concern that some hair or part of her body might not go underwater, it is customary to have a *mikveh* attendant present to watch and make sure the immersion is done properly. The stance taken for immersion is meant to ensure that water will come into contact with all parts of the body – knees gently bent, feet apart, and hands stretched out in front of the body, with nothing scrunched up.

The widespread custom is for a woman to start by immersing once to wet her body. After doing so, she lifts her head out of the water and makes the following blessing: "Blessed are You, Lord our God, King of the Universe, Who sanctified us with His *mitzvot* and commanded us to immerse." She then immerses again and becomes pure.

8. *Nidda* Restrictions

During the days of menstrual impurity, a husband and wife are required to separate, as it says, "Do not come near a woman during her period of impurity to uncover her nakedness" (Leviticus 18:19). The Torah prohibition includes any hugging or touching, even with clothes on. In order to prevent couples from transgressing, the Sages added additional safeguards: the couple may not sleep in one bed; they must separate the beds to avoid touching each other even in their sleep; they may not hand anything to one another, lest they touch each other; and they may not eat alone without leaving something on the table to serve as a reminder she is a *nidda*. Additionally, a husband may not look at the parts of the body his wife usually keeps covered. The couple should make a point of avoiding anything likely to arouse either of them.

9. Separation Times in Anticipation of Her Period

The Sages ordained that a couple should avoid having relations on the day or night when the woman is likely to get her period. This is out of concern she might start bleeding while they are being intimate.

When a woman's period is not absolutely regular, there are three times the couple should separate. The first is called the *haflaga* (interval). The couple calculate how many days passed between her last two periods. For example, if they were 33 days apart, the couple count 33 days from the most recent period and separate then. The second time is the *beinonit* (standard), which is 30 days from the previous period. The third is the *ḥodesh* (month), meaning the couple chart which day of the Hebrew month she began her last period. They then separate on that day of the next Hebrew month. If the month is "long" (30 days), the *ḥodesh* time will be the day after the *beinonit* time. If it is a "short" month (29 days), the times coincide. If her most recent period began at night, the separation times for the upcoming month are at night; if it began by day (which is what happens most of the time), the separation times are by day.

If a woman has a very regular period (meaning her previous

three periods all started at the same interval, the standard 30-day interval, or the same day of the month), they do not need to separate at the three times, but only when she expects her period. If a woman usually has a very specific premenstrual symptom (such as a specific type of stomachache or headache) within a few hours of starting her period, they should separate when she experiences it, rather than at set times.

CHAPTER 10

Protecting Marriage

1. The Sexual Drive

At their root, our good and evil inclinations are one and the same. God has given us the choice of how to direct any given drive. The greater and more powerful a particular drive, the greater its potential to be a force for good or for evil. The most powerful of these desires is the sexual impulse. It can be positive, expressed with holiness and love, in a way that intensifies a couple's happiness and brings the next generation into being. Alternatively, it can be negative, expressed coarsely and destructively, in a way that devastates families through adultery and leads individuals to descend to the depths of depravity. Misdirecting this drive is so harmful that the prohibition of adultery is one of the Ten Commandments.

2. Sexual Prohibitions

As a general principle, love and sexual desire must be directed towards building a sacred relationship. It is forbidden to direct them anywhere else. The most common type of prohibited sexual behavior is adultery, defined by Jewish law as sex between a man and a married woman. This grave offense betrays the marriage covenant and destroys the wonderful, holy power of love.

Incest is another type of prohibited sexual behavior. It includes sex between a man and his close relatives: his mother, his aunt, his sister, his daughter, his brother's wife, or his father's wife. Additionally, once a man is married, his wife's close relatives are forbidden as well – her mother, sister, and daughter. Incest also includes sex between a woman and her close relatives or her husband's close relatives.

Male homosexual sex is prohibited. Bestiality is prohibited. These too are extremely grave transgressions.

Non-marital sex is prohibited. It does not matter whether the woman is single, widowed, or divorced. If she is also a *nidda*, the prohibition is more severe. Nevertheless, as long as there is neither incest nor betrayal through adultery, a child born as a result of such relationships is not a *mamzer*. (See the next section.)

Masturbation is also a sexual transgression. True, it is a less severe transgression than the others; many authorities consider it to be only rabbinically forbidden. It is still prohibited though. This is because the sexual drive is meant to be directed exclusively to the holy relationship of a husband and wife; it should not be wasted. For the same reason, it is prohibited for a woman to masturbate in a non-marital context. This prohibition includes lesbian sex (which Jewish law views as mutual masturbation).

3. *Mamzer*

A *mamzer* is a child who is the product of an adulterous or incestuous relationship. For most purposes, a *mamzer* has the same status as any other Jew. If he grows up to be righteous and knowledgeable in Torah, his status is higher than that of a High Priest who is not as righteous and knowledgeable.

However, one terrifying law applies to *mamzerim*. *Mamzerim* are not allowed to marry an ordinary Jew. If they do so and have a child, the child is also a *mamzer*. Although *mamzerim* are permitted to marry other *mamzerim* or converts, their children will still be *mamzerim*.

This law is one of the most difficult and painful in the Torah. Even though God's laws are beyond our comprehension and we can never fully understand their purpose, here it is clear that this drastic law has the important effect of protecting the holiness of marriage and the institution of the family. In certain cases, a rabbinic court can find ways to avoid declaring a child a *mamzer*. Therefore, someone dealing with a possible case of *mamzerut* should not make any decision before consulting a rabbinic judge with expertise in this area.

4. Marriage Restrictions

In addition to the prohibition of marrying a *mamzer*, there are marriage prohibitions binding upon all Jews, primarily the ban on marrying first-degree relatives.

If a married woman willingly had relations with someone other than her husband, she becomes prohibited to her husband and they must divorce. She also may not marry the man with whom she committed adultery. These laws are complex; sometimes it is possible to find ways to be lenient.

Intermarriage is a serious transgression. Not only that, it is also likely to lead to assimilation. If children are born as a result of such a relationship, their status follows that of the mother. If the mother is Jewish, so are the children; if she is non-Jewish, so are the children. However, if the children of a mixed marriage are interested in converting, they are encouraged to do so, since their father is Jewish.

Priests (men descended from Aaron) have additional restrictions, since they were consecrated to work in the Temple. A priest may not marry a convert, a divorcee, a woman who has undergone the *ḥalitza* ritual (a symbolic separation ritual performed when a man dies childless and his widow does not want to marry his brother), a woman who has committed incest, or a woman who has had relations with a non-Jew. If a priest married a woman forbidden to him, their daughter may not marry a priest, nor may the daughter of their male descendants. Yet a priest's daughter is not limited; any man who is permitted to marry a Jewish woman may marry a priest's daughter.

5. Laws of Modesty

The laws of sexual modesty are meant to prevent people from committing sexual transgressions, and to safeguard faithfulness in marriage. One of the most important of these rules is that men and women not married to each other may not hug, kiss, or touch each other affectionately. Touching in a non-affectionate way is permissible in cases of great necessity, such as for medical treatment. First-degree relatives are permitted to kiss one another. This applies to grandparents and grandchildren as well. A husband and wife may not touch when she is a *nidda* (9:8 above). Mixed dancing is forbidden.

Modesty also demands dressing modestly. Since men are naturally more inclined than women to notice the attractiveness of the opposite gender, more rules were laid down regarding women's clothing than men's. Recent authorities generally agree that modest dress for women means clothes that cover the body, including the upper arms and elbows, the thighs and knees. Married women are also required to cover their hair. Some authorities are more lenient and maintain that the modesty rules follow the norms accepted in a given place by most modest people.

6. Cross-Dressing and Protecting Sexual Identity

A man may not wear clothes clearly meant for women, nor may a woman wear clothes clearly designed for men. As it says, "A woman must not put on man's apparel, nor shall a man wear woman's clothing; for whoever does these things is abhorrent to the Lord your God" (Deuteronomy 22:5). There are two reasons for this prohibition. First, to prevent immodest behavior, which may lead to a rise in adultery and the weakening of the institution of the family. Second, so that we may preserve our unique identities. Clearly, it is forbidden to undergo sex reassignment surgery. Not only does that transgress the prohibition of cross-dressing, it transgresses the far more severe prohibition of sterilization (8:8 above).

7. Prohibited Seclusion

A man and a woman not married to each other are forbidden to be alone together in an isolated or inaccessible place. This is prohibited even if they are certain nothing inappropriate will happen. First, they can hope to be above temptation, but they cannot guarantee it. Second, people should not act in ways which will lead others to think they are sinning. Finally, even if these two people do not sin, there is a concern that others emulating their behavior may end up sinning.

Included in this prohibition are the cases of one man being isolated with two women (if neither is his wife or first-degree relative), or one woman being isolated with two men (if neither is her husband or first-degree relative). A person should avoid socializing with people who do not care about the laws pertaining to sexual modesty.

When colleagues of opposite genders share an office, they must make sure the door is never locked, and that it is likely other people will come in. If it is not likely, they should make sure to leave the door open so anyone passing by can see in. Similarly, when a repairman makes a house call and the wife is the only one home, or a consultant has a meeting with someone of the opposite gender, they must make sure people can see in. If not, they must leave the door open. Another way to avoid violating the prohibition of seclusion is by setting up a video camera with a live feed.

First-degree relatives such as parents and siblings (as well as grandparents) have no prohibition of being secluded together. A husband and wife during *nidda* are also allowed to be alone together, since they know at some point she will immerse and they will be permitted to one another. Nevertheless, since they are so close to each other and their desire can be easily aroused, the Sages established safeguards to help them protect themselves (9:8 above).

In addition to the prohibition of seclusion, men and women need to act modestly in each other's presence. A man should not speak about personal matters to women other than his wife, nor should they go out to eat together or the like. The same applies to a woman with men other than her husband. A single person should not speak about these matters with someone of the opposite gender, unless that person is a potential spouse. All these rules are to ensure sexual desire is channeled into faithful love within the holy framework of marriage.

8. Marital Obligations

When they get married, a couple commit themselves to joining their lives together with love and joy. Along with the love comes the responsibility to try to provide for each other's needs. Truly loving one's spouse includes making sure they lack for nothing – food, clothing, shelter, furniture, medicine, healthcare, and more.

The Sages ordained that upon marriage, the husband

presents his wife with the *ketuba*, a marriage contract in which he obligates himself to support her and take care of all her needs, in accordance with the accepted norms in their time and place. If he divorces her, he commits to pay her at least two hundred *zuz* (which back then was enough to support her for a year). If the bride has previously been divorced or widowed, he commits to at least a hundred *zuz*. (Generally, the amount written in the *ketuba* was higher, and took into account the husband's wealth, the wife's status, and whatever they mutually agreed.) When the wife comes into the marriage with assets, the *ketuba* takes them into account and provides for them to be returned to her upon divorce, generally with additional money. If the husband predeceases the wife, she receives her *ketuba* money from his heirs.

The reason the husband is obligated to support his wife financially (and provide the *ketuba* upon death or divorce) is because until modern times, making a living generally involved hard physical labor and was done by men. Women were in charge of the childcare and housework; it was very time-consuming, as everything needed to be done manually (including drawing water, making the food, and sewing the clothing). So, a husband needed to be held responsible for supporting his wife and family.

In exchange for the husband's obligating himself to provide his wife with everything she needs, the wife obligates herself to take care of all the housework and childcare. She also agrees that all her earnings and whatever assets she brought into the marriage will be controlled by her husband. Since the monetary terms in the *ketuba* are meant to benefit the wife, she can opt out of these terms if she wants by declaring, "I do not want him to support me, and I do not want my earnings going to him." This means the husband does not have to provide for her; all the money she brought into the marriage remains under her control, and anything she earns she keeps. Along these lines, if the couple are both agreeable, the wife can obligate herself to support the husband since any monetary arrangement they make becomes binding. However, if they make an agreement which exempts one of them from the set times of marital relations without mandating that their partner must agree fully each time, the marriage is dissolved, because the *mitzva* of *ona* is a fundamental part of marriage.

These principles of marital obligations generate many additional laws. All are meant to help a couple resolve disagreements. Still, in the past, couples were usually in harmony. The husband took care of providing for the family, while including the wife as a partner in his decisions. The more she understood about business, the greater her influence. There were even cases in which the wife ran the family business. Many communities had pre-marital contracts in which the couple agreed to run their business as full partners with full transparency. Nowadays, even without such a pre-marital contract, this is the recommended practice.

9. Two Marital Laws That Evolved

The requirement of having a *ketuba* was particularly important when people still followed the original Torah laws that allowed a man to marry more than one woman, and to divorce his wife against her will. Let us explain.

The Torah did permit polygamy; however, it also indicated its undesirability. Clearly, polygamy undermines the deep love that should exist between a husband and wife and causes tension in the family. This is why in the Garden of Eden, God created one male and one female. Furthermore, in all of the Torah's stories involving multiple wives, serious trouble results. Why then was it permitted? It was a matter of economic necessity, which is not trivial. When making a living was difficult

and exhausting, and many people died young due to malnu-
trition and disease, unmarried women were in an untenable
situation, lacking a means of support and protection. There
was good reason for the Torah's commandment to help the
widow, someone whose protector and provider was gone.
This is why a well-off man was permitted to marry more than
one woman, as long as he was able to properly support them
all, and to satisfy each of his wives in accordance with the
ona rules. However, going as far back as Talmudic times, it is
rare to find documentation of polygamous marriages. About
a thousand years ago, when survival had become a little easier
and family values had taken deeper root, the rule was official-
ly changed. The sages in Germany, led by Rabbeinu Gershom
("Light of the Exile"), prohibited polygamy. Gradually, this rule
was accepted in more and more communities. Today, it binds
the entire Jewish people.

Another marital law changed over time. According to the
letter of the law, a man was allowed to divorce his wife without her consent. It would seem that without this provision, it
would have been difficult to get men to commit to marriage.
In any case, given this law, the monetary payment of the *ketuba* was vital, because it could serve as a deterrent for a husband who might otherwise irresponsibly decide to end his
marriage. A thousand years ago, Rabbeinu Gershom required
a wife's consent to divorce, and this rule became accepted as
well. Since then, the amount in the *ketuba* has served as the
starting point for negotiations if a marriage breaks up, since
divorce is no longer possible without the wife's consent. Only
in very difficult cases can a man pay the *ketuba* and divorce
his wife even against her will. This is limited to when a rabbinic court deems it necessary for the couple to divorce but the
wife refuses, and the husband is able to persuade one hundred rabbis of the validity of his cause.

10. Marital Obligations Then and Now

As we have seen, when a couple decided to marry in the past, the husband was responsible for supporting the family, while the wife was responsible for the housework and childcare. Today, thanks to improvements in technology (which include running water and inexpensive store-bought food and clothing), housework takes up less time. Making use of the extra time, women have begun to work and support themselves. With the money they earn, they can afford to hire household help and pay for childcare. This frees up even more time, which they can dedicate to work. In parallel, the education system has improved, giving women the opportunity to train in many well-paying fields. Gradually women's earnings have gone up, to the point that some of them now earn more than their husbands.

Despite these significant changes in women's financial and social status, what the *ketuba* requires of the husband is still important today, for two reasons. First, most families are still structured so the husband bears more responsibility for supporting the family, and the wife bears more responsibility for taking care of the home and the children. Second, when the *ketuba* requires the husband to support his wife, that is also for the children's sake. If he does not commit to her, there is a concern he might try to evade his parental obligation. Modern life has largely freed wives from economic dependence on their husbands, and freed husbands from domestic dependence on their wives. But this has damaged the stability of the nuclear family. A sizable number of children in the West grow up in one-parent families; their mother heads the household, and their father is not a presence in their lives. For this reason, it is crucial for a husband to take on financial responsibility for his wife when they marry. Of course, another benefit of the father's presence is the education in family values, which is badly needed today, much more so than in the past.

Be that as it may, the change in women's status gives rise to new questions about who is obliged to support the family, raise the children, and do the housework. These questions apply to all married couples (as well as divorced ones). The guiding principle for a couple trying to answer these new questions is to find something reasonable that works for both parties. (If a couple cannot resolve these issues, divorce is permitted, but society must encourage people to fight for their marriages and avoid hasty divorces.) Finding stability and balance is challenging, and it seems that as a society we are undergoing a period of experimentation while resolving some of the questions. This is similar to the process during the Second Temple period with regard to the *ketuba*. It went through a number of stages before it reached its final, balanced form.

II. Divorce

Despite the sanctity of marriage, the Torah does provide for the possibility of divorce; in truly serious cases of dysfunction, it is even a *mitzva*. This is because the purpose of marriage is for the couple to live together lovingly, happily, and peacefully. When there is fighting and suffering instead, divorce is permitted. However, couples should invest every effort in saving their marriage.

Anyone considering divorce should be made aware of a few things. First, many of those who initiate divorce realize years later that they made a mistake. While fighting with their spouse, they were sure their lives would take a turn for the better after divorce, but the problems and frustrations actually stayed with them. Second, even in a second marriage, a relationship will run into trouble unless there is generosity of spirit, an investment in the relationship, and a willingness to yield. Perhaps if they had adopted these attitudes in the first marriage, they could have had a happy marriage. Third, divorce is generally hard on children. Therefore, if at all possible, a couple in crisis should do all in their power to repair the relationship.

12. A Lesson from *Sota*

The Torah presents a scenario in Numbers Chap. 5 about a *sota* (suspected adulteress). Let us say a married woman became very friendly with another man, friendly enough that her husband suspected she was cheating on him. He warned her not to seclude herself with the other man, but she did so nevertheless. The husband suspected that she cheated on him, and thus had become forbidden to him. (See section 4 above.) She maintained she did not commit adultery. What was to be done? For the sake of peace in the home, the Torah ordered them to go up to the Temple. There they would write the Torah's words about the *sota* – including the name of God – on parchment, and dissolve the ink into a cup of water which the wife drank. If she had cheated, she would be punished by heaven and die. If she had not cheated, her health would improve, and the couple were permitted to resume living together. Even though erasing the name of God is a serious transgression, God commanded it to be done for the sake of restoring the couple's relationship. If the holy name of God could be erased to make peace between husband and wife, how much more so must people be prepared to swallow their pride and make every effort towards that peace. To this end, it is a *mitzva* for the husband's parents to praise his wife; and for the wife's parents to praise her husband. All the more so, parents and parents-in-law must be careful to avoid causing disagreements.

13. The Process of Divorce

Divorce in Jewish law is performed by giving a *get*, a divorce document written for the couple by a scribe. Two witnesses must sign the document, and the husband must give it to his wife in front of two witnesses. As soon as the wife receives the *get*, she is divorced. Along with the giving of the *get*, the couple also must finish dividing up their assets, and the husband must pay the wife the amount of the *ketuba*. If she is at fault in the divorce, he does not need to pay it. The financial details are complicated and may need to be brought to a rabbinic court.

14. Reasons for Divorce

The strongest reasons for a divorce are adultery, or the refusal to follow the set times of marital relations. This refusal on the part of either spouse is referred to as "rebellion." Let us say that an elderly man has become impotent after many years of marriage. While his wife does have the right to demand a divorce, the court will advise her to be loyal to him and stay in the marriage.

If a husband stops supporting his family, the wife has the right to demand a divorce. However, if he is not at fault, there is room for negotiation. Other legitimate grounds for divorce are domestic abuse, violence, and truly repulsive behavior. However, if the situation can be corrected, the court tries to broker a reconciliation.

15. *Aguna*

There are two ways for a married woman to leave her marriage: upon the death of her husband or upon receipt of a *get*. Lacking either one of these, she is still married. Were she to remarry, *halakha* would not recognize it. Occasionally, a husband disappears, and it is not clear whether he is alive or dead. This leaves his wife an *aguna* (chained wife). In such a tragic case, extreme efforts are made to clarify his status. If it can be proved he is dead, she is free to remarry.

16. Forcing a *Get*

In modern times, there is another type of *aguna*. Sometimes a religious court concludes that a wife is correct in demanding a *get* (divorce document), but the husband is unwilling to issue it. The court has the right to beat him day after day until he "agrees" to give the *get*, meaning he states he is willingly giving it. However, there are authorities who do not allow using physical force to extract a *get*. Because rabbinic courts today are weak, it is difficult to extract a *get* when the husband is particularly intractable. The problem is intensified since beatings are not condoned by civil law. Nevertheless, efforts are made to find ways to enforce a court order of a *get*, and these efforts are almost always successful. The more the legislators and courts work together, the fewer cases of *get* refusal will remain. Eventually they will simply die out.

A wife can also be responsible for her husband being "chained," since he cannot remarry as long as she does not agree to accept a *get*. However, this problem is not as hard to solve as the "chaining" of a wife; as we wrote above (section 9), a husband can receive permission to remarry in special cases, through a long process involving the agreement of a hundred rabbis. However, for a variety of reasons, the courts are often slow to apply sanctions to these wives, and the husbands remain "chained" for extended periods.

17. A Wife's Four Disadvantages

There are four areas in which a married woman's position is weaker than that of a married man.

1) The child of a married woman and any man other than her husband is a *mamzer*. In contrast, the child of a married man and a single woman is not a *mamzer*.
2) A married woman who committed adultery is prohibited

both to her husband and her lover. (In practice, a rabbi should be consulted.) In contrast, a married man who committed adultery is not prohibited to his wife.

3) A woman whose husband has disappeared cannot marry again, because she is still married as long as he is alive. However, a man whose wife has disappeared may remarry after receiving special permission from a rabbinic court, since the original Torah law allowed a husband to have more than one wife.

4) For the same reason, if a woman refuses to accept a *get*, after a long process the husband is likely to be permitted to remarry even without divorcing his first wife. In contrast, if a man refuses to give his wife a *get*, there is no way to permit her to remarry. Nevertheless, as we mentioned in the previous section, there are solutions for these cases as well.

18. The Value of the Family

God's laws are beyond our comprehension, so we will never be able to understand them fully. However, here we can identify an underlying principle, namely that a woman knows who her children are, because she gives birth to them. In contrast, a man might have doubts if his children are his own, or (God forbid) another man's. If he is uncertain about paternity, he will not be motivated to work to support his wife and children. Feeling alienated from them, he will not want to invest in them or in their education. Furthermore, a mother is naturally more devoted to her children than a father. She carries them in her womb for nine months, delivers them, nurses them, and takes care of them; most often she is more closely connected to them. In contrast, a father's connection to his children is based less on nature and more on moral responsibility, devotion, and love. Due to the strict laws pertaining to a wife who cheats, and the law which does not allow a wife to remarry without a *get*, a husband can be more confident that his wife is faithful, and that the children are really his. He can dedicate his life to his wife and children without any doubts, and make sacrifices to support them and ensure their wellbeing.

In secular society today, these laws are ignored because they are considered archaic, based on an extreme version of equality. But the state of society would seem to prove their importance, as the nuclear family without these laws is unravelling. One could say that *halakha* is not interested in establishing equality per se, but rather in charting a course that is most helpful in benefiting all members of the family. This is why *halakha* is more demanding of women in the laws about personal status, while it is more demanding of men in the laws about financial support.

Now that we have finished exploring the tremendous value of marriage, the rules designed to strengthen a couple's love, and to protect the family from life's obstacles, the time has come to learn about the wonderful event that transforms a man and a woman into a married couple.

CHAPTER II

The Wedding

1. The Wedding Day

The wedding day is the most important day of a couple's life. On this day, they will begin to completely observe the major Torah principle of "Love your fellow as yourself," which can be fully actualized only within the framework of marriage. On this holy day, the image of God within them shines forth. They break through the barriers of their individuality and enter into a covenant of love and devotion, revealing a spark of the unity of God. They have the opportunity to bring new life into the world and to become partners with God in continuing the process of creation.

It is incredible when we think about the long and wonderful journey the bride and groom begin when they stand under the *ḥuppa* (marriage canopy) – a never-ending journey with peaks of love and depths of commitment. They will experience both happy times and challenging intervals, as well as many stretches of blessed routine. There will be times when their love will be expressed as physical passion and other occasions when it will be expressed as friendly affection, manifested in myriad loving gestures. It is because the journey is so valuable that the difficulties and obstacles are so formidable. The more the couple succeed in adhering to the Torah's *mitzvot* and the Rabbis' safeguards, the more easily they will be able to meet the challenges and continue to develop and deepen a wonderful relationship.

God willing, they will raise children and eventually accompany them to their own *ḥuppot*. The grown children will then begin their own wonderful journeys, which will provide their parents with grandchildren and then great-grandchildren, and so on until the end of time. Were the bride and groom able to envision all of this at the *ḥuppa*, they would certainly faint on the spot, for the mind is incapable of grasping holiness and responsibility of this magnitude.

The couple face their first test when planning the wedding. Will they aim for a glamorous and glorious wedding, which may well cause tension and arguments? Or will they aim for a humble and modest wedding, *mitzva*-oriented, and joyfully celebrated with friends and family?

The Sages tell us that all of the couple's sins are forgiven when they get married. This is because on their wedding day, they wish to bring each other joy with all their hearts, and to raise and educate their future children to be good people in the eyes of God and humankind. To take advantage of this great opportunity for forgiveness, the bride and groom should repent on their wedding day and pray to God to help them fulfill their aspirations. Toward this purpose, some have a custom for the bride and groom to fast that day. (In some of those communities, they fast all day; in others, only in the morning.)

2. The *Badeken*

During the wedding, a process takes place in which the groom leaves his parents' home, joins his bride, and clings to her. As it says, "Hence a man leaves his father and mother and clings to his wife, so that they become one flesh" (Genesis 2:24). It is customary to escort the bride and groom from place to place, as if they were a king and queen. These companions are referred to as *shushbinim* and are usually the parents. The wedding guests sing and dance around the bride and groom.

Immediately before the ceremony, there is an Ashkenazic custom called the *Badeken* (literally "covering"). It begins with the groom being escorted to the bride, who is sitting in a special chair reminiscent of a throne. The groom picks up her veil and covers her face with it. This expresses his willingness to assume the responsibility of taking care of her and making her happy. Then the groom is escorted to the *ḥuppa*. After his arrival, the bride is escorted there as well. In some Sephardic communities, the veiling is done a little later, during the ceremony. The groom walks out from under the *ḥuppa* to greet the bride. He then covers her face with the veil, and the two enter the *ḥuppa* together.

Following Ashkenazic custom, the bride (escorted by her mother and new mother-in-law) circles the groom seven times under the *ḥuppa*. This custom has deep kabbalistic significance, hinting at the high spiritual status of women, who are connected to the divine enveloping light.

Then we reach the *kiddushin*. The officiating Rabbi makes the blessing over the wine and the *kiddushin*, the groom and bride sip the wine and the groom sanctifies (*mekadesh*) the bride with a ring. To enable them to complete their union through marriage *(nissuin)*, the groom presents the bride with her *ketuba*.

3. Introduction to *Kiddushin* and *Nissuin*

Halakhically, the wedding is made up of two parts: *kiddushin* and *nissuin*. *Kiddushin*, when the groom gives the bride a ring, which creates a relationship between the two of them.

The next step is *nissuin*, which includes the *ĥuppa* ceremony and *yiĥud* (see below), and permits the couple to begin their married life together.

Long ago, people generally waited a year between *kiddushin* and *nissuin*. During this year, the couple prepared for marriage. The groom, with the help of his father, built a home, arranged for the furniture, and saved up for the wedding feast; at the same time, the bride, with the help of her mother, prepared her clothing and jewelry.

However, over the course of time it was decided it was better to have the *kiddushin* and *nissuin* at the same event. Firstly, because sometimes the bride's or groom's family were forced to flee their homes during the year between the two ceremonies. This left the couple tied to each other through *kiddushin*, but without the ability to proceed to *nissuin* or to divorce (which is required after *kiddushin*, if there is no *nissuin*). Secondly, sometimes the not-quite-fully-married couple did not abide by the laws of sexual modesty in between the *kiddushin* and *nissuin*. Thirdly, when the age of marriage rose to over twenty, it was understood that *nissuin* should not be further delayed, as it is preferable for people to get married by the age of twenty if possible. For all these reasons, it became customary to perform *kiddushin* and *nissuin* together on the wedding day.

It should be noted that in Rabbinic Hebrew, a synonym for *kiddushin* is *erusin*. In contrast, in Modern Hebrew, people generally use the word "*erusin*" to refer to the engagement and the engagement party. Nevertheless, in Jewish law the term "*erusin*" refers to the giving of the ring.

We will now present the laws pertaining to *kiddushin* and *nissuin*. Following that, we will explain other Jewish wedding customs.

4. Requirements of *Kiddushin*

The way *kiddushin* is usually conducted is that the groom gives a ring to the bride and says to her, "Behold, you are consecrated to me with this ring in accordance with the law of Moses and Israel." It must be clear to the bride and groom what *kiddushin* entails. The groom must understand he is committing himself to do his best to make his bride happy. This includes fulfilling the *mitzva* of *ona* and supporting her comfortably. The bride in turn must understand she is committing herself to doing her best to make her groom happy. In addition, accepting the ring also means she is now prohibited to all other men. Since nowadays it is forbidden for a man to marry more than one wife, *kiddushin* also means the groom is prohibited to all other women.

Actually, according to the letter of the law, *kiddushin* can be done by giving a *perutah* (the smallest coin in Talmudic times, equivalent to several cents today), or something of equal worth. The idea is that the bride receives something of value from the groom to become married. Her agreement to accept this item indicates her willingness to become his wife, with everything this entails. Nevertheless, as we mentioned above, a ring is used. This way, the wife can continue to wear it as a permanent reminder of her married status.

If the bride is under the impression the ring is worth a thousand dollars, but it is actually worth less, the validity of the *kiddushin* is called into question. Therefore, the custom is to use a plain gold or silver ring with no ornamentation, so there will be no mistake about its value. The ring must belong to the groom; he must either have paid for it himself or have been given it as an outright gift.

Without kosher witnesses, there is no *kiddushin*. Even if the husband and wife later swear they performed *kiddushin*, it does not take effect unless witnesses are present. The witnesses validate the *kiddushin* as representatives of the Jewish nation. They must be adult males who are not related to the bride, the groom, or each other. To be "kosher," the witnesses must identify with the values upon which *kiddushin* is based, which means they must be observant Jews. Some sins invalidate a person as a witness. These include adultery or incest, theft or fraud, and public desecration of the Sabbath.

The blessings recited during *kiddushin* and *nissuin* have the status of public prayer, so they require the presence of ten men.

5. *Kiddushin* - Step by Step

A cup of wine is filled to express joy, which can break through boundaries and reveal people's hidden depths. The rabbi officiating at the ceremony takes the cup and recites two blessings:

1) "Blessed are You, Lord our God, King of the Universe, Who creates the fruit of the vine."

2) "Blessed are You, Lord our God, King of the Universe, Who has made us holy through His commandments, and has commanded us concerning forbidden unions, forbidding us those who are betrothed, and permitting us those who are wedded to us through *ĥuppa* and *kiddushin*. Blessed are You, Lord, Who sanctifies His people Israel through *ĥuppa* and *kiddushin*."

After reciting the blessings, the rabbi gives the cup to the groom, who takes a sip. Since it is still early in the ceremony and the couple are not yet married, the widespread custom is for the groom to return the cup to the rabbi. The rabbi then gives the cup to the bride's mother, who gives it to the bride to sip. (The parents or other people should drink the remaining wine.)

Following the preparatory blessings and the drinking of the wine, we arrive at the *kiddushin*. The rabbi confirms the ring belongs to the groom and the witnesses are present, kosher, and able to see everything. He confirms the bride is willing to accept the ring, and requests she extend her finger. The groom then recites, "Behold, you are consecrated to me with this ring in accordance with the law of Moses and Israel." When he places the ring on the bride's finger, the *kiddushin* ceremony is complete.

6. Giving the *Ketuba*

The Sages ordained that before the *nissuin*, the husband-to-be must give his intended wife a *ketuba* (marriage contract). (See 10:8 above.) Therefore, at this stage of the ceremony, the groom gives the bride the already signed *ketuba*. In the *ketuba*, the groom obligates himself to pay a certain amount upon termination of the marriage due to death or divorce. He also confirms the commitments he is assuming upon marriage, which can be summarized as follows: he agrees to follow standard Jewish practice - working, honoring, and supporting his wife and living with her, as is the norm for married couples.

It is formulated as a contract in which the witnesses report that on such and such a date, in such and such a place, this groom married that bride and assumed his obligations.

To reinforce the seriousness of the commitment the groom is undertaking, it is customary before the *badeken* for him to symbolically acquire his obligations, using a standard procedure of halakhic acquisition. The rabbi, acting as the bride's agent, hands over an item (usually a handkerchief or a pen) to the groom. In exchange for this, the rabbi symbolically acquires - on the bride's behalf - all the rights expressed in her *ketuba*. The witnesses then sign the *ketuba*. In Israel, it is customary for the groom to sign it as well. In Israel a copy of the *ketuba*, which the witnesses and groom sign, is later deposited with the Rabbinate as a backup.

Because the text of the *ketuba* was drafted over two thousand years ago, it is in Aramaic, which was the language most Jews spoke at the time. Ideally, the bride and groom should understand the obligations set out in the *ketuba*. It is customary for the rabbi or another honorable guest to read the *ketuba* (or part of it) out loud under the *ḥuppa*, to impress upon the groom the seriousness of the commitment he is undertaking. Nevertheless, many do not read aloud the precise amount the groom has agreed to pay (in the event of death or divorce), because that is private.

The groom then hands the signed *ketuba* to the bride. She needs to make sure to keep it somewhere safe (such as her home or her parents' home).

7. *Nissuin* – *Sheva Berakhot* and Seclusion

Nissuin, the step that finalizes the marriage, takes place when the bride and groom stand under the *ḥuppa* (wedding canopy), and the rabbi and other honorees recite the seven blessings (*sheva berakhot*). Because *nissuin* is so important, an additional cup of wine is poured, which each honoree holds while reciting a blessing.

We begin the *sheva berakhot* with general praises of God relating to creation. We proceed with more specific praises of God, and finally we offer good wishes to the bride and groom. The first of the seven blessings is the standard blessing over the wine, which expresses the joy of the wedding. The second blessing praises God for creation in general. The third blessing relates to the creation of humanity. The fourth blessing specifies that God created the human being in His image and divided this being into male and female. Having originally been created as one allows them to reunite lovingly and build "a building for eternity," meaning to procreate. Before turning to the bride and groom, we cannot forget the Land of Israel. It is waiting for its exiles to return, like a lonely woman waiting for the return of her children. Therefore, the fifth blessing asks that just as God brings joy to the bride and groom, He should bring comfort and cheer to the Land of Israel by joyously gathering in its people. This leads into the sixth blessing, where we ask God to bring joy to the bride and groom, just as He did to Adam and Eve in the garden of Eden. In the seventh and longest blessing, we praise God for creating joy, and we pray for the redemption of the cities of Judea and Jerusalem. We ask that "the sounds of joy and gladness, the sounds of the bridegroom and bride, the joyous sounds of bridegrooms from their wedding canopy, and of young people at their feasts of song" be heard in these cities once more. This blessing concludes by returning to the couple: "Blessed are You, Lord, Who makes the bridegroom rejoice with the bride." The bride and groom then sip the wine. Saying *sheva berakhot* under the *ḥuppa* is the primary fulfillment of *nissuin*.

The conclusion of *nissuin* takes place when the newlyweds are alone with each other. This demonstrates they have begun their married life together. Ashkenazic custom is for the couple to be escorted immediately after the *ḥuppa* to a "*ḥeder yiḥud*" (seclusion room), where they are left alone for several minutes. They eat there, and then come out to celebrate with their guests. Sephardic custom is for the seclusion to wait until the couple go home after the wedding.

8. Remembering Jerusalem

On the day of their immense joy, the bride and groom must connect with the eternal values of the Jewish people. Their personal happiness must be accompanied by prayers for national joy, namely the ingathering of the exiles and the rebuilding of Jerusalem and the Holy Land. How can anyone Jewish experience complete exhiliration without recognizing the pain of the Divine Presence and the Land of Israel? They grieve as long as Jews still live in exile, parts of the Land are still empty of Jews, and the Temple is still in ruins. Therefore, it is precisely when the couple reach the high point of their wedding – under the ḥuppa after the sheva berakhot – that a glass is broken to commemorate the Temple's destruction, and they declare: "If I forget you, O Jerusalem, let my right hand wither; let my tongue stick to my palate if I cease to think of you, if I do not keep Jerusalem in memory even at my happiest hour" (Psalms 137:5-6).

Jerusalem here represents the pain of the Land, Jerusalem, and the Temple. In fact, this reminds us of all the sorrow in the world. For as long as the Jewish people do not properly rebuild the Land, Jerusalem, and the Temple, the rest of the world also lacks joy, blessing, and peace. By mentioning Jerusalem, the bride and groom transform their personal milestone into a vision of global redemption, and their wedding becomes a stage in the Jewish people's long route to repair and redeem the world.

In Israel, when the verse about remembering Jerusalem is recited, the newlyweds' parents are reminded of all the previous generations of Jews who could only dream about living in Israel. Their hearts are filled with gratitude for the tremendous privilege of living in Israel and escorting their children to the ḥuppa there. The parents might also feel as if they are at the threshold of a new reality. Until now, the bride and groom were primarily their children. Now they are leaving home and establishing their own home. However, it is a life-affirming separation which will hopefully lead to the growth of their family. This is why the tears parents often shed now are in fact tears of joy.

9. The Wedding Reception

It is a big *mitzva* to make a bride and groom happy, and it is a *mitzva* for their families to host a large, festive meal that includes meat and wine. The wedding feast is the most important of all *mitzva* meals, even more so than Shabbat and holiday meals. In recognition of this, and to enhance the festive atmosphere, the guests dress appropriately and make a point of keeping conversation lighthearted and cheerful. More importantly, the guests give the couple gifts as well as words of blessing and encouragement. To further contribute to the festive atmosphere, it is customary to have a band, singing, and dancing. The songs should praise God and compliment the bride.

The Sages state that anyone who brings joy to the bride and groom will be blessed with Torah. They compare this to offering a thanksgiving sacrifice on the Temple altar and rebuilding the ruins of Jerusalem. It seems reasonable to ask, "Why is it so important to make the bride and groom happy? Of course they're happy; they're getting married!" However, the point is to turn the couple's private joy into communal joy and help the bride and groom realize how important it is they are now starting a family.

10. The Week of Celebration

Just as the world was created in seven days, so too the happiness at starting a new family continues for seven days. The wedding day counts as the first day. Even if the ceremony starts shortly before sunset (the end of the day in Jewish law), those few minutes are considered the first day; if the ceremony takes place after sunset, there are seven full days. During this seven-day period, the bride and groom celebrate together with their families and friends. The couple should not go to work or do any business. It is customary for them to dress festively for the whole week, and to go everywhere together.

People often try to have a celebratory meal (*sheva berakhot*) for the couple each day and to recite the Grace after Meals and the seven wedding blessings afterwards. To do this, a *minyan* (quorum of ten adult males) is required. Included in this *minyan* must be at least one new person, meaning someone who has not yet participated in the couple's festivity. Having a fresh presence renews their joy. On Shabbat and holidays, it is not necessary for someone new to attend, as the sanctity of the day itself intensifies the joy.

It is customary for the groom to be called up to the Torah on Shabbat morning, either the week before the wedding (Ashkenazic custom) or the week after the wedding (Sephardic custom). This Shabbat is therefore called *Shabbat ḥatan* (the groom's Shabbat).

11. A Second Marriage

The ceremony for a second marriage is identical to that of a first marriage. There are two differences though. Following a second marriage, the post-wedding celebration continues for three days rather than a week. Furthermore, the recitation of the seven blessings takes place only at the wedding, not at the festive meals on the days that follow. When we speak of a second marriage, we are referring to a case in which both bride and groom have been previously married. However, if it is a first marriage for either of them, the celebration extends for the full week.

CHAPTER 12

Parents and Children

1. The Magnitude of Gratitude

Just as we must be grateful to God for providing us with so much, including life itself, so too we should be grateful to our parents for providing us with so much, including life itself. Indeed, we are taught that just as there is a *mitzva* to honor God, so there is a *mitzva* to honor one's parents: "Honor your father and your mother" (Exodus 20:12); and just as there is a *mitzva* to revere God, so too there is a *mitzva* to revere one's parents: "Each of you must revere your mother and father" (Leviticus 19:3). Just as the Torah commands us not to curse God, so too it commands us not to curse our parents. The Sages tell us, "There are three partners in the creation of a person: God, the father, and the mother. When a person honors his or her parents, God says, 'I consider it as if I dwelt among them and they honored Me'" (*Kiddushin* 30b). The tremendous importance of this *mitzva* is clear from its inclusion in the Ten Commandments (2:17 above).

2. A Link in an Eternal Chain

The Torah provides guidelines to govern the parent-child relationship. Children have duties toward their parents – to honor and revere them. Parents have duties toward their children – to educate them. Honoring parents allows children to learn and benefit from the wisdom and life experience of past generations. Educating children allows parents to bequeath to them (and through them to future generations) what they have learned, together with their personal perspective. By following these two imperatives, parents and children connect with all generations and become an important link in the chain. They are part of the process of improving the world and bringing it closer to redemption.

3. Children's Two Obligations to Parents

Children must relate to their parents with honor and reverence. In Jewish law, honor involves helping one's parents. (See the next section.) Reverence involves treating them with veneration. (See section 5.) These *mitzvot* apply equally to the mother and the father. To make this clear, the Torah mentions the father first when discussing honor: "Honor your father and your mother." This is because many children are naturally more inclined to help their mother. So here the Torah puts the father first, teaching us that he is to be helped just as much as the mother. However, the Torah mentions the mother first when discussing reverence: "Each of you must revere your mother and father." This is because many children are naturally more inclined to revere their father. So here the Torah puts the mother first, teaching us that she is to be revered just as much as the father.

4. Helping Parents

As we said above, honor involves helping one's parents when assistance is needed. This includes feeding them and dressing them if they are sick or elderly; supporting them when they walk, if they need it, and helping them clean the house and buy food and medicine, if they are infirm. Children are obligated to do all of this even when they have their own families. Even if the parents' needs are so time-consuming that meeting them will require the children to reduce their work hours and spend less time with their families, that is what they should do. However, they are not obligated to quit their jobs or risk their livelihood. While helping, the children should remain cheerful, because what parents need most in these situations is dignity and positivity.

Children are not required to pay for all their parents' needs. However, if parents do not have the money to cover basic needs, their children must pay for them. If the children do not have the means to do so, they must find charities that will.

Children who are still living at home are obligated to do their share in taking care of the home, even if their parents are well. As children grow up and can help more, their duty to help in the maintaince of the home increases.

5. Revering Parents

As mentioned, reverence involves treating one's parents with veneration. This includes not sitting in their seat, not calling them by their first name, listening respectfully to what they say, not arguing with them like with a friend, and even more so not arguing disrespectfully. Also included are not to cause parents pain and being extremely careful not to disturb their sleep. However, if parents ask to be woken up, it is a *mitzva* to do so.

Classical sources also require standing up for parents whenever they enter or leave a room. However, when parents do not teach their children to do so, it indicates they are willing to forego this honor, and thus the children are exempted from it. Parents should let their children know if there are particular occasions on which they feel the children should stand up to honor them. In any case, if a parent comes to a child's room to speak with the child, the child should stand until the parent sits down. Similarly, when parents come to visit their married children, the children should get up to greet them when they come in, and escort them out when they leave.

Hitting a parent is a very serious transgression. Someone who does so and draws blood (in the presence of witnesses, after being warned not to do so) is liable to death: "He who strikes his father or his mother shall be put to death" (Exodus 21:15). Cursing a parent is also a serious transgression. If a child does this (in front of witnesses who warned him about the consequences), he is liable to death: "He who curses his father or his mother shall be put to death" (Exodus 21:17). Someone who commits these terrible sins should repent immediately. This includes asking forgiveness and placating the parent who was hurt, and treating this parent with the utmost respect from that point on.

6. Living Near Parents

It is a *mitzva* for children to live near their parents. This makes it easier for the children to visit, which allows them to honor them and make them happy, and to help them when necessary. While living nearby is admirable, it is not an obligation. In cases of great necessity, children may choose to live at a distance. For example, children may move away if there is no suitable employment or educational frameworks near the parents; if a child cannot afford to buy a home near the parents; and certainly, if a child wants to move to Israel, a *mitzva* which is the equivalent of all the other *mitzvot* together. Additionally, a spouse's preference about where to live must be taken into account. In any event, children who live far away must visit their parents often, in accordance with the norm and the circumstances. If parents are in dire straits, children must commit themselves to help. If parents do not require help but ask their child to visit every day because they enjoy their company, the child is not obligated to do so. The *mitzva* obligates the children to provide the help the parents need, not to spend all their time making the parents happy. Nevertheless, they are required to visit regularly, following the norm for those in similar circumstances.

If parents need full-time help, it is a *mitzva* for a child to have the parents move in so that the child can take care of them. This is on condition the child's spouse is in full agreement. If the spouse objects, the child must either find a proper facility for the parents, hire a caregiver, or go every day to help them.

7. The Limits of Honor

If a parent instructs a child to transgress a prohibition, even a rabbinic one, the child may not obey, as parents too are obligated to observe the *mitzvot*. Therefore, if a parent demands that a child break off contact with a relative or neighbor with whom the parent is quarreling, the child may not listen, as that would involve transgressing the *mitzva* of loving your fellow as yourself. What about when a parent makes demands regarding the child's life, such as the choice of a spouse or profession? Although the child must listen carefully and seriously consider the parent's position, the final decision is up to the child. After all, it is the child's life and not the parent's life which is at stake.

8. Giving Parents the Benefit of the Doubt

Honor needs to be based on honest appreciation. Accordingly, the *mitzva* of honoring parents includes contemplating and learning from their good deeds and positive character traits. Even if others see the parents as ordinary people, it is a *mitzva* for the children to look for the good in them, until they can view them as people of sterling character.

Nevertheless, if the parents sin in certain areas, or have certain character flaws, the children should acknowledge that. If the children remain in denial, there is a risk they too will perpetuate this bad behavior. At the same time as recognizing their parents' flaws, it is a *mitzva* for children to give their parents the benefit of the doubt – perhaps their flaws are due to the circumstances of their lives, and they are only partially responsible. Since parents are their children's roots, when children focus on their parents' weaknesses, they are focusing on the roots of their own weaknesses. Conversely, when children emphasize their parents' strengths, they connect with the roots of their own strengths, reinforce their positive traits, and are inspired to act properly.

9. The Scope of the Requirement

When a person's parents are deserving of respect, commanding it is unnecessary since logic and natural morality promise it. What is innovative in the commandment is that even if parents are not clearly deserving of respect, such as when they are very difficult or have major character flaws, there is still a *mitzva* to respect them. The Sages tell us that even if a son was adorned in beautiful clothing and seated at the head table, and his parents came and tore his clothes, smacked his head, and spit in his face, he should still not embarrass them. Rather he should remain silent, thus showing his awe of the King of kings, Who commanded him to treat them reverentially.

Similarly, children whose parents are suffering from dementia should not embarrass them. The children should try to treat them with love and respect, to the extent possible under the circumstances, until God has mercy upon them. However, if they fight and get angry every time they get together, and the parents make unreasonable demands, it is best to minimize visits. Rather, the children should ask others to deal with them. If the parents need full-time help, the children should either hire someone to care for them or find a nursing home. If this is not possible and one of the children must become the caregiver, that child should do his or her best to stay calm and respectful.

Parents should make efforts not to become too much of a burden on their children, so as to avoid causing the children to sin by failing at the *mitzva* of honoring them. There is precedent for requiring parents to make efforts to avoid causing a child to sin. In the past, a Jewish court would punish a parent who hit an adult child, because the parent was likely to cause his child to become angry, and possibly even hit his parent back. It should be noted that even though there is a verse that states, "He who spares the rod hates his child" (Proverbs 13:24), and even though in the past parents thought that hitting children was a necessary part of education, corporal punishment should be avoided today.

10. Immoral Parents

Some maintain that the *mitzva* of honoring parents applies even if the parents are wicked, and that even a *mamzer* (10:3 above) is obligated to honor his parents. Others maintain that children do not have to honor parents who are truly immoral or corrupt. Nevertheless, all agree that causing parents embarrassment or pain is forbidden.

If a parent is a danger to the children, the children must be protected and kept away from that parent. The children should be reassured they are not to blame for the parent's bad behavior. Even in such a terrible and complex situation, the children should try to find a way to judge the bad parent favorably. Even though their parents' actions are absolutely reprehensible, the children should assume the bad parent is sick, whether physically or psychologically. The greater the children's understanding that their abusive parent is ill, the more readily they will be able to separate the terrible actions, and appreciate any positive interactions in which their parent acted normally. Throughout their lives, the children can come back to those golden moments, which can serve as a positive basis for them to build a good relationship with their own children.

11. Divorced Parents

Children of divorce are obligated to respect both parents. This is the case even if they are being raised primarily by their mother, and she demands they cut contact with their father because he has hurt her and she claims he is a bad person. They are not allowed to listen to her. However, when children are young, it is hard for them to hold their own. Thus, it is hard to blame them if they do not have a good relationship with their father. Nevertheless, once they grow up, they must have respectful relationships with both parents.

12. Adopted Children

On moral grounds, adopted children must honor their adoptive parents in the same way as biological children. The Sages speak at length about the rewards of people who take in abandoned children. They tell us that in the World to Come, God has treasure houses to reward the righteous, including a special treasure house to reward those who bring up such children.

Adopted children are exempt from honoring their biological parents. When the parents gave their children up for adoption, they also waived their rights to honor. (In general, Jewish law says that if parents choose to relinquish the honor due them, they may do so.) So, the children have no obligation to search for them or to honor them. Nevertheless, it is often a good idea for them to do so. First, if their parents gave them up when things were very difficult, they might regret having done so, and long for a connection with their children. Second, if the adopted children do not identify their parents, they could end up marrying a prohibited relative, such as a sibling. Third, even though there is no obligation to honor the biological parents, it is still the fulfillment of the *mitzva*.

However, if the adoptive parents would find it extremely painful for their children to undertake a search for their biological parents, it is preferable the children do not search. After all, adopted children are obligated to honor their adoptive parents and not their biological ones. Similarly, if finding their birth parents might lead the children to experience a psychological crisis, it is better they do not search. Adopted children who are uncertain about what to do should consult with someone who is wise, experienced, and God-fearing, and who knows them well.

13. Converts

People who convert to Judaism must continue to honor their biological parents. Even though converts are considered to be newly born (and thus no longer related to their parents), they have a moral obligation to honor their parents, who gave birth to them and raised them. Therefore, converts must help their parents when they need help, pray for them when they get sick, and say *Kaddish* for them when they die.

Sometimes, converts may run into a problem. On the one hand, they want to treat their parents properly. On the other hand, if the parents do not respect the children's new faith and life path, the converts may be afraid their own children will be attracted by their grandparents' religion. They must find a balance, continuing to honor their parents while keeping a certain distance to make sure the parents will not have a negative influence on their grandchildren.

14. Stepparents

Children are obligated to honor a parent's spouse, even if he or she is not their biological parent. Great care should be taken with this *mitzva*, because showing disrespect for a stepparent is showing disrespect for the parent as well. While the obligation does not extend to helping stepparents in all the ways one must help parents, they must still be treated very reventially.

15. Older Relatives

Children are commanded to honor their grandparents, although honoring parents takes precedence in cases of conflict. There is a *mitzva* to respect one's older siblings as well as aunts and uncles, but honoring grandparents takes precedence. People must also honor their in-laws, although this reverence is not comparable to the extent due their own parents. Rather, in-laws must be treated the way the elderly and esteemed are treated.

16. Parents Should Not Show Favoritism

When discussing inheritance, the Sages instruct parents not to show favoritism among their children. Even if children are disrespectful or non-observant, their children may do better. Discrimination against problematic children may further distance them from the family and its traditions, and lead them to deprive their own children of a proper education. Moreover, a father playing favorites in his will is likely to cause discord among the children, which can destroy the family. The children whom the father wishes to draw close may well end up feeling distanced from him. The parent-child relationship must be absolute and unconditional. If children feel their relationship with their father is contingent upon their being properly respectful or even sycophantic, they will remember him as petty and vengeful. Of course, the same considerations pertain to a mother; she should not show favoritism either. The only child who may be disinherited is one who has separated from the Jewish people.

In the past, only sons would inherit, because daughters were integrated financially into their husbands' families. Instead of an inheritance, parents would give a daughter ten percent of their assets when she got married. If times were difficult, they would give even more. Nowadays, the economy is structured differently, and the status of women has changed. Therefore, it is advisable for parents to write a will in which their assets are divided equally among all their children. If parents did not do so, the rabbinic court tries to persuade the children to divide everything equally.

CHAPTER 13

Family Celebrations

1. *Brit Mila*

Brit mila (circumcision) is an expression of the covenant God entered into with the Jewish nation, the nation destined to repair the world by infusing it with faith and holiness. The ritual is a minor procedure on a baby boy, in which the foreskin is removed from the part of the body, the function of which is to joyfully unite a couple and add life and blessing to the world. The *mitzva* of *brit* is also connected to the *mitzvot* of procreation and settling the Land. Thus, God said to our fore-father Abraham, "I will establish My covenant between Me and you, and I will make you exceedingly numerous. . . I will maintain My covenant between Me and you, and your offspring to come, as an everlasting covenant throughout the ages, to be God to you and to your offspring to come. I assign the land in which you sojourn to you and your offspring to come, all the land of Canaan, as an everlasting holding. I will be their God. . . Such shall be the covenant between Me and you and your offspring to follow which you shall keep: every male among you shall be circumcised" (Genesis 17:2-10).

The *mitzva* of *brit* teaches us that a Jew must be willing to give up his life and blood for the sake of the covenant with God. As part of the covenant, the Jewish nation accepted a mission – to show there is a Creator and Director even when the world is filled with darkness and heresy; to pursue charity and kindness even when surrounded by corrupt and murderous nations; to make every effort to live a life of purity and morality even in a world filled with dishonesty and hypocrisy. The road to carrying out this great and sublime mission is paved with difficulties and sacrifices. This is symbolized by the blood and pain involved in circumcision; the foreskin represents everything wrong with the world, and the *mila* represents its repair.

There is no equivalent *mitzva* for a baby girl. One can learn from this that, by nature, females are less in need of correction than males. Accordingly, girls' education can be gentler than boys'.

It is a father's responsibility to arrange the *brit mila*. If he is unable to do so, the responsibility devolves to the mother. If a boy was not circumcised at birth, he must arrange it for himself at the age of thirteen, when he attains Jewish adulthood. Despite the importance of circumcision, if a man is not circumcised it does not mean he is not Jewish. Rather, anyone born to a Jewish mother is automatically Jewish. However, a man who wants to convert to Judaism must undergo circumcision as part of the conversion process.

2. Laws of *Brit Mila*

The *brit* is performed eight days after birth. While the number seven symbolizes the creation of the universe in seven days, the number eight expresses that which is beyond this world. The *brit* allows the newborn baby to connect with something that transcends the worldly, namely Torah and *mitzvot*. With their help, he can act to repair the world.

Even if the eighth day following the birth is Shabbat or a

Jewish holiday (*Yom Tov*), the *brit* is normally performed then. However, if a *brit* needed to be delayed past the eighth day, it does not supersede Shabbat or *Yom Tov*. For example, a *brit* is delayed because the baby is sick or weak, and the doctors are concerned it might endanger him. In such a case, even if the go-ahead for the *brit* is given on Shabbat or a holiday, it is performed on the following weekday. (If a baby is systemically ill, the *brit* takes place only a week after the recovery.) Additionally, if a baby is born via Caesarian section, the *brit* does not supersede Shabbat or *Yom Tov*.

Brit mila is performed during the day, i.e., between sunrise and sunset. It is preferable to have a *minyan* present. A qualified, God-fearing, professional *mohel* (circumciser) should be chosen, who will instruct the parents about what they need to do before and after the *brit*. It is customary for the attendees to stand during the *brit* to honor the baby and the *mitzva*. It is also customary to dress for a celebration and to follow the ceremony with a festive *mitzva* meal. Since the *brit* repairs and enhances the body – by revealing all the good– it is appropriate to celebrate by fueling the body with fine food.

3. The Honorees at a *Brit*

Many have the custom of honoring four people, plus a married couple, by assigning them roles in the ceremony. It is advisable for the baby's parents to decide beforehand whom they wish to honor. The roles are:

1) *Kvatters* – The couple who carry the baby to the *brit*. (Having *kvatters* is not a universal custom.) The infant's mother gives him to the woman selected. She then passes the baby to her husband, who brings him to the father. After the *brit*, this sequence is reversed.

2) The Chair of Elijah (*Kisei shel Eliyahu*) – The person who

places the baby upon the special chair that reminds us of Elijah (the prophet whose spirit attends every *brit*), and who then carries the baby to the *sandak*.

3) The *Sandak* – The person who sits and holds the baby on his knees while the *brit* is performed. This is the most important of the honors, and is generally given either to a grandfather or the rabbi.

4) The One Who Blesses – The person who, after the *brit* is performed, recites blessings over the wine and over the *brit*, and then names the baby. This honor is generally given to a Torah scholar.

5) The Second *Sandak* – The person who holds the baby during the recitation of the blessings. Some do not designate a separate person for this, but simply leave the baby with the *sandak*.

4. The *Brit* – Step by Step

Once the *sandak* is holding the baby, the *mohel* recites the initial blessing: "Blessed are You, Lord our God, King of the universe, Who sanctified us with His *mitzvot* and commanded us concerning circumcision." Immediately after the recitation, the *mohel* cuts off the foreskin. Before he finishes removing the thin membrane, the baby's father begins reciting two blessings: "Blessed are You, Lord our God, King of the universe, Who sanctified us with His *mitzvot* and commanded us to bring him into the covenant of Abraham our forefather," and "Blessed are You, Lord our God, King of the universe, Who has given us life, sustained us, and brought us to this time."

After being circumcised, the baby is passed back to the *sandak* or the second *sandak*. A cup of wine is poured, and two more blessings are recited by the fourth honoree. First is the standard blessing over the wine, and second is: "Blessed are You, Lord our God, King of the universe, Who made the beloved one [Isaac] holy from the womb, marked the decree of circumcision in his flesh, and gave his descendants the seal and sign of the holy covenant. As a reward for this, the Living God, our Portion, our Rock, did order deliverance from destruction for the beloved of our flesh, for the sake of His covenant that He set in our flesh. Blessed are You, Lord, Who establishes the covenant." The same person follows this with a prayer for the wellbeing of the child, which includes the naming. He concludes with the wish, "Just as he has entered into the covenant, so may he enter into Torah, marriage, and good deeds."

5. Introduction to *Pidyon Ha-ben*

Pidyon ha-ben is the *mitzva* for a father to redeem his firstborn son on the thirtieth day following his birth, by giving money to a priest (*Kohen*). Why? During the last of the ten plagues, the slaying of the firstborn, God killed all the firstborn Egyptians but spared the firstborn Israelites. As a result, the firstborns were singled out to be priests. Thus, every tribe and every family would have holy people who would behave piously and serve as teachers and role models. Unfortunately, this plan failed, as the firstborns did not prevent the sin of the golden calf. It was clearly necessary to dedicate an entire tribe to the task of perpetuating sanctity among the people. All the members of this tribe would view this as their holy mission. God chose the tribe of Levi, since they had not participated in the sin of the golden calf. Nevertheless, since firstborns had originally been singled out to be priests, the Torah requires a father to redeem his firstborn son by paying money to a priest.

We can extrapolate from this *mitzva* that every firstborn starts off with sanctity, presumably because his birth begins the next generation. However, in practice it is difficult to actualize this sanctity, since the excessive responsibility often imposed on firstborns may incline them to be high-strung and arrogant. Therefore, the firstborn should be redeemed, enabling him to live a normal life in which he can find his own way with modesty and moderation.

6. Laws of *Pidyon Ha-ben*

It is a *mitzva* to have the *pidyon* on the thirtieth day after birth, meaning four weeks and two days later. So, if the birth was on a Sunday, the *pidyon* takes place on a Tuesday. If the birth was on Thursday, the *pidyon* would be on Shabbat. However, since a *pidyon* may not be performed on Shabbat, it is delayed to Sunday.

It is customary to use five pure silver coins, whose total weight should be 85 grams. The *pidyon* may also be performed with objects of an equal value to that much silver, but not with paper money. Since the price of silver changes, the price of the five coins does too. In recent years, the price in Israel has fluctuated between 150 and 300 shekels.

While it is the father's obligation to perform the *pidyon*, whether the baby is considered a firstborn is dependent upon the mother. For this purpose, firstborn is defined as "the first to open the womb." So even if the father already had children with someone else, a child requires redemption if he is his mother's firstborn. If a baby was born after a miscarriage or abortion, and the limbs of that fetus had taken shape (meaning forty days had passed since conception), the live baby is exempt from *pidyon*, as he is not considered the first of the womb. Similarly, a baby born by Caesarian section is not redeemed, since he did not pass through the womb in the normal way.

The firstborn child of a priest or Levite, and the firstborn child of the daughter of a priest or Levite, do not require a *pidyon*.

7. The *Pidyon Ha-ben* – Step by Step

It is a *mitzva* to have a festive meal in honor of this special *mitzva*. This is how a *pidyon* ceremony is customarily conducted: Everyone does the ritual hand washing and eats some bread. Immediately following this, the father and the priest stand up and the father hands his firstborn to the priest. The priest asks the father, "Which do you prefer: to give me your firstborn son, the first birth of his mother, or to redeem him for five *selas* as you are bound to do according to the Torah?" What the priest is really asking is, "Do you prefer that your son be limited to holy work, or would you rather redeem him so he can live a normal life?" The father replies, "I wish to redeem my son. I present you with the cost of his redemption which I am bound to give according to the Torah." He then recites two blessings: "Blessed are You, Lord our God, King of the universe, Who sanctified us with His *mitzvot* and commanded us concerning the redemption of a son," and "Blessed are You, Lord our God, King of the universe, Who has given us life, sustained us, and brought us to this time." The father then gives the coins to the priest. The priest recites the priestly blessing (Numbers 6:24-26) over the baby, as well as additional blessings, and returns him to the father. Finally, the priest picks up the wine cup, recites the blessing over it, and drinks, to express his joy in performing this *mitzva*. The meal then resumes.

Nowadays, priests do not actually serve in the Temple nor specifically serve as teachers. Accordingly, many priests return the money to the father. However, they are not obligated to do so.

8. The First Haircut

Some have a custom to have a party when a boy turns three, to celebrate his reaching the age where we can begin to educate him in Torah and *mitzvot*. In many communities, they used to teach boys to read at age three; in some communities that is still the case. At the party, the boy gets his first "grown up" haircut. The *peyot* (sidelocks), which may not be shaved off, are left uncut (25:4 below). Some have a rabbi cut a lock of the boy's hair and bless him with success in his Torah study. These are relatively new customs, and by no means universal.

9. Education

It is a *mitzva* incumbent upon parents to teach their children Torah and to train them to keep the *mitzvot*. The more a child's understanding develops, the more Torah we teach the child. With observance as well, we teach children to perform any *mitzva* they can understand. By around age six, a child can start to learn seriously, and this is why children start school at six. When dealing with prohibitions, the rules are different. Even before children can understand what is prohibited, the parents are not allowed to cause them to sin (for example, by feeding them non-kosher food).

It is a *mitzva* for parents to educate their children to live a life of Torah, develop positive character traits, and engage in considerate behavior. True, teachers can reinforce what the parents teach, but the overall responsibility for educating children remains with the parents.

Personal example is the foundation of all education. Children often emulate their parents, so it is important they see their parents are content with what they have; love Torah and care about *mitzvot*; contribute to the world; do not chase after luxuries or awards; are happy with their friends; help others, and are considerate and respectful of everyone. Parents should also listen to their children talk about anything bothering them, and teach them how to interact with their friends. Of course, parents must also project a very positive attitude towards school. They should send the children off to school happily, encourage them to study, follow their progress, and communicate with their teachers. Parents should also share their faith and the values by which they live their lives. This can instill the children with faith in God and in their special mission, so when they grow up, they will be able to choose the best path to utilize their talents and improve the world.

10. *Bat* and *Bar Mitzva*

When children reach halakhic maturity – age twelve for girls and thirteen for boys – they are considered adults. From then on, they are obligated to study Torah and keep all the *mitzvot*. True, their parents must continue to educate them as long as they are living at home, but the primary responsibility passes to the young adults themselves.

It is a tremendous privilege to be obligated in *mitzvot*. In the words of our Sages, "The Holy One, blessed be He, wanted to confer merit upon the Jews. That is why He gave them Torah and commandments in abundance" (*Mishna, Makkot* 3:16). For this reason, it is customary to have a party when a child becomes subject to the *mitzvot* – which is the meaning of the phrases *bat* and *bar mitzva*.

Ideally, the party should be held on the day of the birthday. If that is difficult, the celebration may be delayed by a few days. During the celebration, words of Torah should be shared, the family's traditions should be evoked, and the young adult should be given encouragement as he or she enters this new stage of life.

In preparation for the *bat* or *bar mitzva*, it has recently become customary for the young adult to take on a project that involves Torah study or *mitzva* performance. Each family should choose a project with which it most identifies.

CHAPTER 14

Mourning

1. "Blessed is the True Judge"

No other loss compares to death. An awful sadness fills the relatives' hearts as they try to make sense of what has happened. How can it be that this person, whom they loved and was so alive, is suddenly dead and gone? Questions abound: Why didn't God save my relative? Why is there death at all? What is the purpose of this life in which the righteous often suffer? When faced with these big questions, there is a *mitzva* to strengthen one's faith in God, Who has the whole world in His hand. He rules and judges with fairness and justice. Even though sometimes we cannot understand His behavior, we need to have total faith that all He does is just, and for the best. For this reason, the Sages instructed mourners to recite the blessing, "Blessed are You, Lord our God, King of the universe, the true Judge."

2. The Necessity of Death

"And the Lord God commanded Adam, saying, 'Of every tree of the garden you are free to eat; but as for the tree of knowledge of good and bad, you must not eat of it; for as soon as you eat of it, you shall die'" (Genesis 2:16-17). The purpose of this instruction was to prevent evil from penetrating people's bodies. Obedience would have meant immortality. Nevertheless, Adam and Eve ate the fruit of that tree and were punished. As it says, "To Adam He said . . . 'By the sweat of your brow shall you get bread to eat, until you return to the ground – for from it you were taken. For dust you are, and to dust you shall return'" (*ibid.* 3:17-19). As a consequence, the same evil which penetrated our bodies would cause those bodies to self-destruct, ultimately leading to death.

However, this punishment was also designed to be beneficial and to help us improve ourselves. Without death, there would be no end to the harm the wicked could perpetrate. The strong would endlessly oppress the weak, while pursuing every worldly desire. Instead, now that death is inevitable, the wicked eventually die, and the world is better off.

Death benefits the righteous too. For there is no completely righteous person on earth who always does what is right and never sins (Ecclesiastes 7:20). Accordingly, the righteous would find their lives very frustrating without death. They would feel suffocated by their accumulated sins, without being able to escape from them and redeem themselves. Death, in separating body and soul, also destroys the sins the body has accrued, thus allowing the soul to ascend to the world of souls and be purified. More precisely, it is the righteous whose souls ascend immediately to heaven, where they can bask in the glory of the Divine Presence. Ordinary people, who need to be purified of their sins, are sent to hell for as long as the purification takes. Then they too ascend to heaven and once more connect with God. "The dust returns to the ground as it was, and the soul returns to God, Who bestowed it" (*ibid.* 12:7).

Thus sins are eradicated when death separates body and soul. In this way, death repairs every individual and all of humanity. At the end of days, when the entire world has been repaired, the souls will be reborn and live once again, in new bodies God will provide when He resurrects the dead. (That is, except for those who were completely evil. When they die, their bodies rot and their souls burn, becoming ash beneath the feet of the righteous.)

Parallel to the body's burial, the soul begins its purification process and begins to shine. The mourners must bear this in mind. Remembering the good deeds of the deceased, they can help with the purification. The more the mourners improve themselves as a result of the deceased's good example, the higher the soul ascends. At the end of the purification process, the soul is on a higher level than before, the same way that penitents (who have been purified through suffering) are on a higher level than the completely righteous. Because sin entered the bodies of Adam and Eve, all their descendants struggle with sin. But all become penitents. First, they are purified through the suffering and death of their bodies, and then their souls are refined in fires on high. They reach the highest levels in the world of souls, until the world is completely repaired. When the dead are resurrected, the souls will be reborn and live a perfect life for all of eternity.

The laws of mourning all express acknowledgment of divine judgment, an acceptance combining sadness and faith. On the one hand, the pain is terrible, and therefore crying and grief are appropriate. On the other hand, mourners must not drown in despair or mourn excessively, as the sorrow and pain are meant to improve and cleanse. Therefore, the Torah commands that mourners must not self-harm, gouging skin or tearing out hair. As we said above, God governs the world with justice and goodness; excessive mourning indicates a lack of belief in this fundamental of faith.

3. The Seven Relatives Who Mourn

A family is a highly interconnected unit. When one member dies, a part of their relatives dies with them – that is, unless their legacy is kept alive. Therefore, first-degree relatives are obligated to mourn. If they mourn their relative in a way that honors his or her memory and inspires them to be better people, the deceased's soul will be preserved in the bonds of eternal life. This in turn gives them life as well. But if the relatives do not mourn properly, they are not helping the soul of the departed ascend in heaven, and hence a part of them dies as well.

The seven relatives who must mourn are mother and father, brother and sister, son and daughter, and spouse. Other relatives, such as grandchildren and nieces and nephews, do not have an obligation to sit *shiva*. Nevertheless, since they too experience some grief, they should be somber during the *shiva* (the one-week mourning period) and help provide the mourners with whatever they need.

4. *Onenim*

When first-degree relatives are informed of a death, they assume the status of *onenim*. This term refers to people whose entire being is consumed by grief. They must stop all other activities and focus their full attention on the deceased, arranging for the body to be properly cared for until the burial, and then taking care of the burial itself. For this reason, from the time of death until the end of the funeral, *onenim* are exempt from all positive *mitzvot*, such as reciting prayers and blessings and putting on *tefillin*. However, they are still required to avoid violating any prohibitions. For example, before they eat bread they must wash their hands ritually, as it is forbidden to eat bread with unwashed hands. At the same time, they do not recite the blessings on the handwashing and the bread. *Onenim* refrain from eating meat or drinking wine, as doing so makes people happy.

If relatives are notified about a death on Shabbat, they continue observing Shabbat as usual. They are only considered *onenim* once Shabbat is over.

5. Tearing Clothes

At the beginning of the funeral, the mourners stand and tear their shirts. If they did not recite the blessing of "the true Judge" at the time of the death or upon hearing of it, they recite the blessing at the funeral before tearing. The tear is started using a knife or scissors. The members of the burial society can help with this, but the mourners should continue tearing the fabric themselves until the tear is at least eight centimeters long. The tearing gives concrete expression to the mourning. Just as the garment is torn, so the life of the mourners has been torn. Part of them remains alive, and part of them has left with the deceased and gone to another world.

Mourners wear the ripped item of clothing during the whole week of *shiva*. Only when going to sleep may they change into untorn nightwear. If the torn clothing gets dirty, they may change, but they must tear the new clothing as well. Someone who was dressed in something very expensive before the funeral is allowed to change into something cheaper. (Not only does this preserve the expensive item, but it is also more appropriate to come to a funeral in simpler clothing.) Ideally, anyone present at the time of a person's passing should tear their clothing out of grief, but this is not the custom, possibly so as not to create a situation in which people avoid visiting the critically ill for fear of needing to tear their clothes.

6. Burial and the Dignity of the Deceased

There is a *mitzva* to bury the dead immediately, as it says, "You must bury him the same day" (Deuteronomy 21:23). Burial may be delayed only if there is a very good reason related to the dignity of the deceased. Those who participate in the funeral are fulfilling the *mitzva* of being kind to the family as well as the deceased; to the latter, the kindness is even greater because there will be no reciprocity. Therefore, all those who knew and valued the deceased and who live nearby should participate in the funeral.

It is a *mitzva* to bury the body in the ground ("for from it you were taken"), and it is a *mitzva* for the participants to help fill in the grave with dirt. Symbolically, burial covers the shame of death, caused by the sin of Adam and Eve. Burial in the ground also involves forgiveness, which is why during the burial we recite the verse "He is compassionate; He forgives iniquity" (Psalms 78:38).

It is customary to bury the dead in simple white shrouds, equalizing the rich and the poor. Even when burial is done in tiers, it is still considered burying in the ground. However, cremation does not fulfill the *mitzva* of burial. If the opportunity arises to donate organs to save lives, it is a *mitzva* to do so, and does not detract from the *mitzva* of burial.

Whether at a funeral or any other time, visitors to a cemetery should recite the following blessing upon seeing the graves, in order to properly focus their thoughts and feelings: "Blessed are You, Lord our God, King of the universe, Who created you justly, fed you justly, supported you justly, brought you to life justly, and gathered you in justly. He knows the numbers of all of you, and in the future, He will resurrect you justly for eternal life. Blessed are You, Lord, Who resurrects the dead" (Sephardic formulation). The blessing is recited if the visitor has not seen graves within thirty days.

7. Eulogies and Other Funeral Customs

There is a *mitzva* to eulogize the deceased. The purpose of eulogies is to acknowledge the value of the deceased's life, positive traits, and good deeds, so that people will emulate the person and keep his or her legacy alive. Eulogies are also meant to move people to cry and grieve. The Sages tell us that "All who cry over a good person are forgiven for all their sins" (*Shabbat* 105b). Since mourning a good person demonstrates what one considers to be important, it has tremendous corrective power that can atone for sin.

It is difficult to craft eulogies that precisely capture a person's positives; it is better to err on the side of overstating rather than understating. Nevertheless, one may not overdo this and lie when praising the deceased. If a person did not have any outstanding virtues, but did suffer in the course of his or her life or death, it is worth mentioning. Not only can suffering purify, but a person's greatness can be expressed in how he or she dealt with suffering. Additionally, hearing about suffering can move the attendees to feel sad and cry for the deceased.

When a funeral takes place on a holiday, the joy of the holiday takes precedence and eulogies are not delivered. If the deceased was a Torah scholar, he is eulogized briefly even on a holiday, so as to honor the Torah.

The funeral procession involves walking behind the body as it is carried to the grave. Those who participate must remain silent and certainly not speak of matters that do not relate to the dignity of the deceased. It is customary for the person conducting the funeral to recite these inspiring words from the Mishna: "Akavya ben Mahalallel said: Reflect on these three things and you will avoid sinning. Know where you came from, where you are going, and before Whom you will have to give an account and reckoning. 'Where you came from' – a putrid drop. 'Where you are going' – a place of dust, worms, and maggots. 'And before Whom you will have to give an account and reckoning' – the Supreme King of kings, the Holy One, blessed be He" (*Ethics of the Fathers* 3:1). It is also customary to recite

Psalm 91, which begins, "He who lives in the shelter of the Most High." Some recite this psalm only at a man's funeral, and at a woman's funeral they recite Proverbs 31 (starting from verse 10, "What a rare find is a capable wife").

At the conclusion of the gravesite ritual, the mourners recite *Kaddish* to elevate the soul of the departed. *Kaddish* continues through the month or year of mourning, as we will explain in section 14. If the deceased had no immediate relatives, someone else says *Kaddish*. The person conducting the funeral then recites the prayer that starts, "God full of mercy." This prayer asks God to mercifully accept the soul of the departed into heaven for eternal rest until the resurrection of the dead.

After the burial, the mourners remove their leather shoes, which signals the beginning of the *shiva*. (If they did not bring slippers with them and cannot walk barefoot, they should put some dirt in their shoes until they return home.) Those who have attended the burial now form two lines. The mourners pass between them and accept consolations. When departing the cemetery, it is customary for everyone to wash their hands ritually, as part of cleansing themselves from their encounter with death.

8. The Meal of Consolation

When the mourners return home following the funeral, it is a *mitzva* for their relatives or neighbors to make them the first meal, to help them recover from the intensity of the death and burial and to ease them back into life. This meal of consolation is referred to as *se'udat havra'a* (literally, the meal of recuperation). It would not be right for the mourners to need to worry about preparing a meal when the body of someone dear to them has just been laid in the grave. There is also a concern that some mourners would end up not eating and become weak as a result.

It is customary to serve round foods at this meal – eggs, lentils, pitta bread, or bagels – to remind the mourners that life is cyclical. Now they are at a low point, in mourning, but the wheel keeps turning, and they will experience happier times. Additionally, round foods have no "mouth" or opening, which hints at the desirability of silence at the upcoming *shiva*. During the week of *shiva* it is also common practice for friends and relatives to make things easier for the mourners by preparing food for them. However, if they do not do so, the mourners may cook for themselves.

9. Sitting *Shiva*

It is a *mitzva* for all the first-degree relatives to put their lives on hold for a week and mourn the deceased, to honor his or her memory and elevate the soul. This honor is expressed by the mourners showing they identify with the deceased, and it is as if a part of them has died too. Just as the deceased is lying in the ground, so too the mourners sit on or near the ground. The deceased does not work, bathe, or apply lotion, and neither do the mourners. This identification can also inspire them to emulate the deceased's good deeds, and this decision itself elevates the soul.

When possible, it is proper for the mourners to sit *shiva* together in the home of the deceased, to honor his or her memory. When necessary, they may sit together somewhere else, or divide up and sit in different places. The critical thing is that all the mourners sit *shiva*. When the primary *shiva* location is far from the home of one of the mourners, that mourner is permitted to spend part of the time sitting at home, so the neighbors there can offer comfort. It is customary to have a memorial candle lit for the entire seven-day mourning period.

The mourners may not leave the house. When it is difficult for a mourner to sleep where he is sitting *shiva*, he or she may discreetly travel back home to sleep. It is also permitted for a mourner to go home for Shabbat. (Sexual relations are forbidden during *shiva*.) If there is no *minyan* in the *shiva* house, the mourners may discreetly attend synagogue in order to say *Kaddish*.

We refer to people "sitting *shiva*" because the mourners sit on or near the ground. Even if they are sitting on mattresses or chairs less than three handsbreadths high (approximately 23 cm), they are considered to be sitting on the ground. Mourners with bad backs may sit on higher chairs or couches, but they should still try to sit lower than usual. Ideally, mourners should also sleep on mattresses on the floor, but they may sleep in bed if they find this difficult.

Mourners are not to go to work or engage in mundane activities during *shiva*, as they are meant to stay focused on the mourning. However, as we have mentioned above, they are allowed to make food for themselves and tidy up the house a bit. When necessary to avoid serious financial loss, they may speak discreetly and briefly about business matters.

Mourners should not greet people in the standard way as if everything was fine, nor should people greet them that way since clearly a mourner is not "fine." Some also do not shake hands.

Mourners are not allowed to study Torah, because studying Torah is a joyful activity, and it might also distract from the mourning. However, there is a *mitzva* to study Torah texts that relate to mourning, repentance, or moral instruction.

Mourners may not wash for pleasure (even a finger), but they may rinse away dirt. Someone who sweats heavily may wash his body with lukewarm water. A woman in mourning may not put on makeup during the *shiva*, unless it is necessary to avoid embarrassment. Mourners during *shiva* may not wash clothing or sheets, wear freshly laundered garments, or sleep on freshly laundered sheets. However, a stain on clothing may be removed with water. Mourners may change their underwear as needed. If they need to change clothing because of the smell, they can take a freshly laundered item and place it on the floor so it is considered dirty, and then wear it. Mourners may not use skin-care creams, but medicinal creams may be applied.

Mourners may not shave or get haircuts. This prohibition extends for thirty days. For those mourning a parent, the prohibition extends even longer. They may not get a haircut until their friends reproach them for having hair that is too long, and the time has come to have it cut.

Efforts should be made to hold the three-times daily prayer services in the *shiva* house, to elevate the soul of the departed. When possible, a Torah scroll should be borrowed from a synagogue so the Torah reading can take place on Monday and Thursday morning. Immediately before or after the services, it is customary to share words of moral instruction and Torah, especially *mishna* (as the Hebrew letters of *mishna* are the same as those of *neshama*, "soul"). On Shabbat, the custom is for the mourners to pray in the synagogue.

10. Counting the Seven Days

When it comes to determining the length of the *shiva*, part of a day is counted as a full day. Therefore, if the mourners begin sitting *shiva* a little before sunset, those few minutes are considered the first day of *shiva*. On the morning of the seventh day, the mourners are offered brief consolation and are then told the *shiva* is over. Some conclude with prayers of acceptance and consolation then, following which the mourners get up from *shiva*. Many mourners visit the grave on the day the *shiva* ends and recite Psalms there to elevate the soul of the departed. This is often done on the thirtieth day as well.

11. Shabbat and Holidays

Public mourning does not take place on Shabbat because of its sanctity. Therefore, with the approach of Shabbat, the mourners wash in lukewarm water, dress in Shabbat clothes, and go to synagogue. They also eat Shabbat meals as usual, including singing Shabbat songs, as they would do on any other Shabbat. However, private mourning practices stay in effect even on Shabbat. Therefore, sexual relations are still forbidden, as are washing and applying lotion for pleasure. Shabbat does count as one of the days of *shiva*, as Shabbat is the soul of the week. Even when the week is one of mourning, the Shabbat within it is a part of it, and elevates the week through its sanctity.

Holidays cancel *shiva*. Even though they are less holy than Shabbat, the aspect of rejoicing on them is more outstanding. Therefore, if the mourners sat *shiva* even for an hour before the start of a holiday, the onset of the holiday ends the *shiva*. The holidays which have this power are those mentioned in the Torah: Passover, Shavuot, Rosh Ha-shana, Yom Kippur, and Sukkot. By contrast, the holidays instituted by the rabbis – Ĥanuka, Purim, and Israeli Independence Day –do not cancel mourning. If a funeral takes place on the intermediary days of a holiday, the *shiva* is delayed until the holiday is over, at which point the mourners observe the seven days of mourning.

12. Comforting Mourners

There is a *mitzva* to comfort mourners, share their sorrow, and listen to them talk. The primary form of consolation is for the mourners and comforters to tell positive stories about the deceased. Ideally, these stories will inspire the listeners to repent and improve their behavior. Often people find out during the *shiva* that the deceased was a better person than they had thought. Most people are multifaceted, and in the day-to-day we often miss what is most important, namely the positive things that express the person's soul. These are what remain behind forever and are what we focus on during the *shiva*, to perpetuate the legacy and elevate the soul of the departed.

Those who come to the *shiva* to provide comfort are permitted to show interest in the deceased's life and activities. At the same time, they should be careful not to get sidetracked by discussions of work or other mundane matters; it is better to remain silent at a *shiva* than to engage in idle conversation. *Shiva* visitors need to be considerate. They should come at reasonable times and make sure not to stay too long when the mourners are tired. Talkative people must make efforts to restrain themselves so other visitors have their chance to comfort the mourners. If someone finds it difficult or impossible to visit the mourners in person, consolation may be offered by phone or letter.

It is a *mitzva* to connect the private sorrow of the mourners to the sorrow of the whole Jewish people. This makes the private sorrow more meaningful and can inspire repentance and self-improvement. Therefore, when leaving the *shiva*, the comforters part from the mourners by saying either "May you be comforted from heaven" (Sephardic custom), or "May the Lord comfort you among the other mourners of Zion and Jerusalem" (Ashkenazic custom; some add "And may you know no more sorrow").

13. The Month or Year of Mourning

Following the week of *shiva*, there is less intense mourning which lasts for thirty days after the funeral. This ends the mourning period for most relatives. However, for the death of a parent, the children are obligated to continue mourning for a full year.

During the thirty-day period, mourners may not get haircuts

or shave. They may not participate in weddings and other *mitzva* celebrations, and they certainly may not participate in secular celebrations. They may not listen to joyful music even in private or any music in public. They may not buy new clothing or furniture or make other joy-inducing purchases. When necessary, mourners may buy gifts for relatives. They may participate in a small meal with friends but may not host such a meal. They may not go on vacations or outings whose primary aim is enjoyment, but they may go on educational outings or quiet getaways. Children mourning a parent continue with these practices for a year, except for getting a haircut, which – as mentioned – is allowed once their friends tell them their hair is too long.

If the presence of the mourners is necessary at a wedding – that is, their absence would pain the bride or groom – they may join for the ceremony, but not for the meal. If the mourners are close relatives of the bride and groom, they may stay for the meal as long as they eat separately from the other guests. They may not stay in the hall for the music and dancing though, as that would be disrespectful to the departed. Mourners may be given an important job to do (such as seating the guests or serving the food) to permit them to remain in the hall even while music is playing. If a parent of the bride or groom is in mourning, they may participate fully in the wedding to avoid detracting from the couple's joy. Nevertheless, they may not dance, except when the bride or groom requests it, at which point they may do so briefly.

If a wedding date has already been set and then the bride or groom becomes a mourner, we do not postpone the wedding, even if the date is within the thirty-day mourning period.

14. Elevating the Soul and Saying *Kaddish*

During the year following a parent's death, the children should increase their Torah study, *mitzva* observance, and good deeds. The more they do so, the more helpful they are in saving their parent's soul from hell and elevating it in heaven. This applies even if the parent was righteous and certainly needs no help to merit reward in the afterlife. The soul enjoys and is elevated by the good deeds the children undertake in their parent's memory. It certainly applies if the parent was not righteous.

A son in mourning is required to say *Kaddish* in synagogue daily to elevate his parent's soul. If the son knows how to lead the weekday services and the congregation is agreeable, it is preferable for him to do so. It is customary to say *Kaddish* for only eleven months, stopping either a month or a week short of the full twelve months. This is because there is a tradition that the wicked spends a year in hell. If the son said *Kaddish* for the entire twelve months, it might imply that he thinks his parent was wicked. *Kaddish* is recited for the full year only if the deceased is halakhically considered wicked, such as someone who converted to another religion or someone who committed suicide (not due to mental health issues).

Even a son who is under the age of *bar mitzva* says *Kaddish* for his parents. What if there is no son to say *Kaddish*? If the deceased has a God-fearing father, grandson, or son-in-law, that relative may say *Kaddish* for him. If no male relative is available to recite *Kaddish*, the family should take money from the estate to hire a God-fearing person to say *Kaddish*.

An adopted child needs to say *Kaddish* for his adopted parents. It is proper for a convert to say *Kaddish* for his non-Jewish parents.

15. The Unveiling and Cemetery Customs

Some have a custom to have the tombstone put up (and "unveiled") by the thirtieth day following the funeral. It should include the name of the deceased, the name of the deceased's parents, and the dates of birth and death. Some praises of the deceased may also be included, though not exaggerated, as such exaggeration may cause the heavenly court to judge him or her more harshly.

When possible, a married couple should be buried together, so they are together in death as they were in life. This also makes things simpler for the children when they visit their parents' graves.

When visiting a grave, it is customary to place a pebble on the tombstone to show that someone was there. There is also a custom of non-Jewish origin to honor a grave by placing a wreath of flowers on it. Some Jews have adopted this custom. Even though there is no *mitzva* to do so, there is no prohibition either.

16. *Yahrzeit*

The anniversary of a death is called *yahrzeit* in Yiddish. The Sages tell us that each year, on this day, the deceased is once again judged by the heavenly court. This is because even after a person's life has ended, their influence has not. If it turns out the children they left behind are sinning, their soul should be punished for this, as they did not educate them properly. In contrast, if the children are elevating themselves by doing good deeds, the deceased must have educated them properly, and their memory continues to have a positive effect. The soul is uplifted and receives heavenly reward.

Therefore, on the *yahrzeit,* it is customary for children to study more Torah than usual, do good deeds, give charity, and say *Kaddish*. Some fast on this day as an expression of repentance. Those who find fasting difficult may give charity instead. There used to be a custom to light a 24-hour candle in the synagogue on a *yahrzeit,* to enhance the services by providing additional light for the prayers. Nowadays, when synagogues are illuminated with electric lights, there is not much point to this. Nevertheless, as a commemoration of the old custom, some light a *yahrzeit* candle at home. What is truly important though is to donate money to maintain the synagogue or to help the poor. When possible, the children should visit the grave on the *yahrzeit*. If it is not too difficult, other relatives should join them as well.

Faith, the People, & the Land

Chapter 15: Fundamentals of Faith 204
Chapter 16: Torah Study 228
Chapter 17: The Land and the People 247
Chapter 18: Conversion 277
Chapter 19: The Holy Temple 284

Fundamentals of Faith

1. Monotheism

The mitzva of *emuna*, faith, is to believe in the existence of the Creator, Who is the primary and sole source of the universe, including the dimension of time. God is one in that He is unified and unique. His exclusivity means there is none other after Him and He is not composed of multiple facets. He is infinite, has no form, and cannot be categorized or defined. All names and descriptions attributed to God in the Torah are God's revelation to us based on our limited human understanding, but they do not describe His essence.

Because God is one, we learn that all the distinct creatures are united at their core. Therefore, it is appropriate for people to exist with love for each other, and to reflect the harmony within creation by helping one another.

Because God is infinite, humanity continues to derive its endless aspiration to elevate and perfect itself.

Because God is unique and cannot be categorized, we learn that he reveals Himself in every category of creation from heaven above to earth below without exception. Every single thing is important because it contains a unique divine spark which animates it. People which were created in the image of God, should reveal this spark in its full glory.

Because God created time, we learn that the divine element is revealed at all times, with different times reflecting distinct aspects of the divine.

Due to the fundamental importance of faith, it is the subject of the first two of the Ten Commandments. The first is to believe in God, Who took us out of Egypt. The second is not to worship idols or make them.

2. Love and Reverence of God

It is a *mitzva* to love God and to revere Him, as it says, "You shall love the Lord your God" (Deuteronomy 6:5) and "You shall revere the Lord your God" (*ibid*. 10:20). To attain love and reverence of the Creator, we can observe creation and reflect on all its brilliance, power, majesty and beauty, from the vastness of space and its galaxies, to any tiny cell and its subatomic particles, including all that grows especially humans. We can look at the full range of human abilities and accomplishments – science and scholarship, literature and art, and above all, people's moral aspirations and ideals. Acknowledging all these can be the gateway to loving the Creator and feeling exalted before Him.

3. The Giving of the Torah

Since people are created in God's image, their deepest desire is to invest their lives and actions with meaning and enduring value. To address this need, God gave Israel the Torah, which contains divine guidance for living a good, blessed, and meaningful life. The Sages tell us that the world's existence is dependent upon the Torah. God created the world on the condition that the Jews would accept the Torah when it would be given. Should they refuse, the world would return to chaos. Without the Torah to reveal eternal, divine values, the world could not exist.

4. Faith and the Tendency Towards Idolatry

Faith is the birthright of all humanity. The human soul is connected to its divine source and draws life from it. As a result, it is natural for people to believe there is a higher, eternal power beyond the visible and that our lives are tied to the eternal. The value of our lives has meaning far beyond our routine ordinary existence on earth. That is why wherever people have settled we find that they established some kind of religious life. Based on this innate faith as a starting point, various human societies created religions for themselves which provided a framework for their faith and invested their lives with meaning. Generally, the founders of these religions imagined relatively abstract concepts of the gods. However, since abstract ideas are difficult to grasp, they created images and idols to give concrete expression to these higher powers. Presumably insightful people with depth understood that the idols and images were only symbols of the higher powers. However, most people believed the gods literally lived within their representations.

Since the gods were designed by people who sought to infuse their lives with faith, they personified everything their designers valued, such as life, the forces of nature, fertility, war, strength, victory, money, love, beauty, and so on. This created a destructive dynamic between the human desire for pleasure and honor and the heartfelt longing for faith. Rather than using faith to elevate people's aspirations by improving themselves and transforming their character for good, thereby increasing goodness and blessing in the world, faith degenerated into idolatry. Idol worship granted meaning and justification to the world that exists with its materialism and impulses. This blocked the path to the true faith in the one God, which would elevate and improve the world. For idolators, faith was reduced to a tool to promote their own desires and pleasures, with no interest in moral correction. To satisfy their own needs idolators were prepared to offer sacrifices, cast spells, or engage in magical practices to bring themselves wealth, defeat their enemies, and obtain whatever they wanted.

5. Were idols effective?

Were idols effective? How could people believe in idols made of wood and stone? They believed because it met their need to feel faith. Although this belief was false, idol worshipers lacked other options which would give expression to the faith so embedded in human life. When people expressed their belief in the idols, it gave them the confidence to accept that what they wanted was surely good and legitimate. Their aspirations and actions were justified since they were not acting only on their own behalf, but on behalf of powerful higher forces.

Furthermore, others explain that it is similar to the forces of nature that people can harness for their own needs. Just as there are spiritual forces referred to as angels and demons which control nature, humans could use magical means, to manipulate these forces of nature. In truth, all spiritual forces which activate nature are created by God and draw their energy from Him. However, idolators could connect to them and exploit them as detached from their divine source turning them into impure forces. This exploitation empowered people for a limited time but ultimately led to their destruction.

6. Integrating the First Two Commandments

Committing the sin of idolatry limits divine revelation to an exact idol or specific image. This reduces people's faith and awareness in all aspects of life to a narrow perspective. As a result, people become incapable of transcending their restricted environment with all its problems, and preventing them from actualizing moral solutions to improve their lot.

This idolatrous worldview led people to justify the actions of evil rulers who murdered, stole, and enslaved, since they were simply imitating the ways of the gods who protected them.

Therefore, the Torah absolutely forbids creating idols and images to concretize divine faith. By extension, it is prohibited to categorize God definitively, whether in intellectual or moral terms. Any definition limits God by favoring one value over others, thereby contradicting God's infinite nature, which is unlimited and undefined.

Since an idolatrous belief confines and reduces the divine, it is easily challenged by bringing up the values it excludes. Such questions without answers gradually increase until the believer is forced to deny it. However, since people are searching for some form of faith, they might replace it with a new idolatrous belief. Since this too is idolatry, the person will once again be disappointed, and ultimately reject it. Humanity waivers between acceptance and rejection of idolatry without ever acquiring peace of mind.

Only by decisively rejecting idolatry can people achieve pure faith in one God Who created everything - physical and metaphysical and who is beyond definition. This is faith in God's uniqueness. This pure faith does not foster questions that lead to denial. Rather, it motivates believers to continuously advance and elevate their service of God. Monotheism allows the Jewish people to accept the Torah and its commandments, whereby we can adhere to God's ways and add vitality to the world by working to improve it under God's sovereignty.

7. Prohibition of Idolatry

It is a serious transgression to worship idols. Those who do so are considered to have transgressed the entire Torah and detached themselves from the Jewish people. Included in this prohibition are bowing and sacrificing to an idol, lighting incense in front of it, and pouring wine libations for it. Also severely prohibited is following the specific mode of worship of any idolatrous sect (such as throwing a rock onto the pile consecrated to Mercury or defecating in front of Ba'al Pe'or). It is forbidden to sculpt an idol for someone else or to participate in building a temple for idolatry. This includes deriving benefit in any way from items used in idol worship or from its sale. A Jew in possession of an idol or any implement used in idolatry, may not sell it, melt it down, or make use of it in any way; rather, it must be destroyed. Only if a non-Jew had already nullified an idol's identity by breaking it, may a Jew use the broken pieces.

There is a *mitzva* to rid the Land of Israel of idolatry, to destroy idols, and demolish their altars, as it says, "You must destroy all the sites at which the nations you are to dispossess worshiped their god, whether on lofty mountains and on hills or under any luxuriant tree. Tear down their altars, smash their pillars, put their sacred posts to the fire, and cut down the images of their gods, obliterating their name from that site... Beware of being lured into their ways... Do not inquire about their gods... For they perform for their gods every abhorrent act that the Lord detests; they even offer up their sons and daughters in fire to their gods" (Deuteronomy 12:2-31). This *mitzva* does not apply to churches and mosques in Israel today. Although they contain an idolatrous element, there is no comparison to the abhorrent idolatry of ancient times, as long as the worshipers are good citizens and do not support murder and other evils.

It is forbidden to swear in the name of idolatry or to cause someone else to do so. Not only is it forbidden to enter a place where idols are worshiped, but it is forbidden to observe idolatry, read about it, or take an interest in them. Such activities are permitted only when necessary for Torah study, to teach people to distinguish between truth and falsehood.

8. Christianity and Islam

As a result of receiving the Torah, the Jewish people waged a prolonged battle against idol worship which was ultimately successful. The world progressed, and two large religions arose directly influenced by Judaism - Christianity and Islam. However, they still accommodated elements of idolatry. Their focus on defining certain attributes of God - kindness and love in Christianity; justice and strength in Islam - is still a form of idolatry.

It can be said that Christianity learned from Judaism the values of kindness and love which are powerful and creative forces. However, Christianity rejected the the values of justice and law, and consequently the unique mission of the Jews and their fulfillment of the commandments to improve the world. Therefore, it became impossible to actualize the idea of kindness within the reality of the world as it is. Christianity then became largely dismissive of this world, since perfecting it requires justice and law.

Christianity presents an additional problem by personifying God in the physical form of a human. This distortion of imagining God not as one, but as a trinity, defies the purity of God's exclusivity and monotheistic values. Over the course of history even the Christian value of love which it heralded became distorted. Often Christianity corrupted its central value of love by acting with zealous cruelty toward non-Christians.

Approximately five hundred years ago, the Protestant movement was founded to return Christianity to its biblical roots. Protestantism waged war to remove images and icons from its churches while they can still be found in Catholic and Orthodox churches. Yet even the Protestants have not internalized the change required to reject defining God as human.

Islam learned the values of divine strength and justice from Judaism. This includes obedience to God commands and willingness to keep His laws. However, its grand essential vision is incomplete. Since Islam came into existence well after Christianity, it succeeded in freeing itself from idols and images. Yet, since it did not preserve a direct link to the Torah of Israel, Islam contains an idolatrous element. It reduces the divine to dictates revealed to people from above and they be accepted with respect and submission, and imposed upon all humanity by force and coercion. Islam does not recognize the tremendous divine value of free choice and the range of human creativity in all its complexity. This creativity is actually divine revelation that is discovered and developed by humans who were created in God's image.[3]

9. The Righteous Among the Nations

Even among the pagans, some people were righteous and pious, and internalized the positive aspects of their belief system. Therefore, our Sages related respectfully to every non-Jew, even when they knew someone was an idolator. For an idolator might be pious, or may become pious at some future time. The Sages learned from the good deeds of the gentiles,

---

3   I would suggest that the difference between Christianity and Islam stems from the distinct lessons they learned from the Jews. Christianity developed in the period before the destruction of the Second Temple. On the one hand, it was inspired by the vision of the Jewish people living in its land with the Temple, a vision of great potential. On the other hand, it was struck by a sense of failure that the divine presence and observance of *mitzvot* failed to improve this world. As a result, Christianity adopted the attitude that humanity and the earth are fundamentally flawed and the only way to achieve forgiveness is to find refuge in the kingdom of heaven. In contrast, Islam developed several hundred years after the destruction of the Second Temple, during a time when the Jews were scattered in exile and had become more narrowly focused on studying Jewish law. Consequently, on the one hand, Islam was less inspired than Christianity by Judaism's vision, but on the other, it focused more on law and practical behavior, and did not personify God.

such as the act of honoring parents, from an idol-worshiping Roman officer.

The rabbis were even more open in their attitude toward believing Christians and Moslems. It is known that there have been pious and righteous gentiles among the faithful believers of Christianity and Islam. This attitude differed from that of many Christians and Moslems, who believed that one who does not accept their religion cannot be considered righteous or pious and will not be rewarded in the World to Come. We believe there are righteous people of different nationalities and religions, and their paths helped to elevate all nations and religions toward a more perfect faith.

10. Attitudes towards Different Religions

According to Jewish law, it is permissible for every nation to establish a religion for itself, which provides a framework appropriate to its character and culture. This is conditioned on being free of idolatry and connected to the pure faith in God revealed by the Jewish people. It must accept the fundamental values found in the Seven Noahide Laws (2:4 above), and not impose itself upon others by force.

In other words, the Jewish vision of redemption does not demand the obliteration of other religions. They may well have core values suited to perfect the characters of their adherents. The primary demand Judaism makes of other religions is to purge the evil idolatry within them that blocks the expression of perfect faith and leads to murderous conquest. As it says, "I will clean out the blood from its mouth, and the detestable things from between its teeth. Its survivors, too, shall belong to our God" (Zechariah 9:7).

11. Prohibited Magic and Sorcery

Included in the mitzva of faith is knowing that God created the world and the laws of nature by which it runs. He also created people in His image so they would protect and develop the world within these laws of nature. The more intensely people adhere to faith, morality and observe God's commandments, the more they will succeed in advancing and improving the world. When they turn their back on this mission, the result is more suffering and sorrow they will cause. Furthermore, the Creator determined that people will be rewarded or punished in the World to Come based on their choices. Sometimes people receive part of their divine reward or punishment revealed to them in this world. However, it is forbidden to rely on miracles or spiritual forces, since people are responsible to improve themselves and the world through diligence and integrity.

In contrast, idol worshipers are not interested in bettering the world. Rather, they are looking for the easy way to satisfy their desires and greed. Using knowledge of people's innate awareness of higher powers, the ancient sorcerers and magicians created various rituals and ceremonies to manipulate people into believing that these forces would bring people what they want, such as wealth, honor, revenge upon their enemies. People without knowledge of God were seduced by their promises, when in reality all these rituals and spells harmed those who relied on them. These practices actually distanced them from God and minimized their own sense of moral responsibility for their actions. This fostered negligence to correct their situation naturally through hard work. This is why the Torah commands the Jewish people: "When you enter the land that the Lord your God is giving you, you shall not learn to imitate the abhorrent practices of those nations. Let no one be found among you who consigns his son or daughter to the fire, or who is an augur, a soothsayer, a diviner, a sorcerer, one who casts spells, one who consults ghosts or familiar spirits, or one who inquires of the dead. For anyone who does such things is abhorrent to the Lord, and it is because of these abhorrent things that the Lord your God is dispossessing them before you. You must be wholehearted with the Lord your God" (Deuteronomy 18:9-13).

The Torah here prohibits calling upon mystical forces or engaging in strange practices or trickery in order to have a supernatural impact. The prohibition includes casting magic spells, creating illusions, and doing anything else impossible within the laws of nature. Similarly, fortune-telling is prohibited, whether by reading coffee ground (or tea leaves), making astrological calculations, or communicating with the dead. It is also a transgression to consult a magician, sorcerer, or fortune teller.

12. Contemporary Idolatry

While most societies have freed themselves from actually idolatrous rituals, the concept of idol worship still stands as a block to the world's elevation and redemption. Idolatry in its essence misdirects pure faith which strives for wholeness and corrupts it into faith in specific powers or limited values, claiming it will grant people the good life they seek.

There are two basic types of idolatrous beliefs. Some believe that if they manage to attain money or honor, or fulfill their various desires, they would truly be living the good life. These people are worshiping the idols of money, lust, and honor. In the short run, this "idolatry" provides great satisfaction to its adherents, energizing them to work hard to fulfill their dreams, but ultimately it fails. Even in cases when people fool themselves for years, feeling as if their dreams came true, they know in their hearts that all of their acquisitions in this world are hollow. King Solomon explains in Ecclesiastes that all earthly things that are considered good and beautiful but lack spiritual value are "vanity of vanities" and cannot provide true fulfillment.

A more elevated but still idolatrous belief is faith in values or ideologies that will supposedly make the world a better, more perfect place. These include love, truth, equality, nationalism, science, liberalism, and humanism. Similar to actual idolatry, striving for these concepts can make adherents' lives feel more meaningful, energizing them and helping them succeed during specific times because they are grounded in true values. Nevertheless, because each value or ideology is still narrow and limited, putting faith in it ultimately fails.

For example, those who put their faith in communism thought they would redeem the world by imposing economic equality. In the name of communism, they abandoned all other values, murdering millions of people and creating horrific suffering in many countries. Only after they recognized how much pain their belief cause did they abandon their "idolatry." Similarly, people today believe that liberalism will save the world imposing its ideology on society and trampling other values. To achieve this, they are willing to make great sacrifices - of other people. Ultimately, after humanity has suffered greatly, they will eventually understand that turning any ideology into the sole value is "idolatrous" and false.

Therefore, all specific values or ideologies are limited. As long as they are not connected to pure monotheism - which includes all the values - they are liable to become idolatrous. As a result, they cannot connect people to the all-inclusive God, nor can they improve people and the world. In addition, specific values and ideologies block the path to complete faith by providing a seemingly beneficial alternative, only shown to be false much later. It is important to note that it is dangerous to believe in a religious or social charismatic leader, even someone righteous, because such belief can be internalized as a type of idol worship.

Only the combination of faith in God and the rejection of

all idolatries of beliefs or ideologies, will elevate a person to a total faith connected to the divine source of life. This faith incorporates all the positive aspects of the other nations of the world. With the Torah's guidance, we can harmoniously integrate these different values to bring benefit and blessing to the individual and the world.

13. Faith Revealed Through the Exodus and Mount Sinai

It is not simple to maintain pure, idolatry-free monotheism, since it is difficult for people to believe in something entirely abstract. Therefore, our belief system does not rely solely on a deep philosophical approach to God, but rests primarily on God's revelation to the Israelites. This was an astonishing phenomenon that occurred to the world and Israel. The infinite God, Who defies categorization, revealed Himself to his nation, declaring: "I the Lord am your God Who brought you out of the land of Egypt, the house of bondage" (Exodus 20:2). This revelation did not address God defining Himself, but focused on God's leadership of his nation and the guidance found in the Torah. From then on, it became possible to connect to God without sinning through idolatry. Instead of concentrating on defining the essence of God which is beyond human comprehension, we focused on God's revelation to humanity according to our level of understanding. The higher we ascend spiritually, the more of the revelation we can absorb. While this ascension may be gradual, it has no upper limit.

It is Israel's destiny to reveal to the world faith in God and His leadership, which can be seen throughout Jewish history. The exodus from Egypt is the foundation of this faith since it heralded the birth of the Jewish nation. The vast miracles God performed clearly demonstrated God's mastery as if it was a re-creation of the world, conducted in full view of humanity.

Since then, until today when the Jews believe in God and His Torah, they merit blessing; when they betray their mission, curses descend upon them. In both cases, the world can clearly see God is in control. This is why multiple biblical passages deal with the Jews' sins and the resulting moral lessons.

It is the Jewish people's destiny and objective to reveal God's word to the world. God tasked them with this inescapable task. The only choice they face is whether to reveal God's word by serving as a positive example or a negative one. Even when they make the wrong choice and suffer as a result, this suffering ultimately serves a positive purpose as it leads people to recognize their sins and repent. Then God's word is revealed in a positive way which brings about repair and redemption.

14. Free Will

One of the foundations of faith is that God, the Creator of the universe and the One responsible for its continued existence, granted every human being free will. He decided that if people choose good, they bring life and blessing to themselves and the world; if they choose evil, they bring trouble and death. This is as it should be. For those who draw close to God by walking in the ways of truth and goodness are drawing closer to the source of life and blessing, thus meriting additional life and blessing. Those who distance themselves from God are distancing themselves from the source of life, so their lives are shortened by disease and suffering and tragedy overtakes them. Nevertheless, God wishes to benefit His creations, so that suffering and tragedy serve a purpose: to inspire people to repent and improve, to abandon sin and merit goodness. As it says, "Bear in mind that the Lord your God disciplines you just as a man disciplines his son" (Deuteronomy 8:5).

Free will is a manifestation of people being created in the

image of God with the awareness which enables them to choose between good and evil. Their choices affect not only themselves, but the entire world. They are able to choose to partner with God in order to settle and develop the world. As it says, "The Lord God took the man and placed him in the garden of Eden, to work it and tend it" (Genesis 2:15). "To work it" means to advance the world and improve it. "To tend it" means to protect it from harm. On the other hand, we are free to choose evil and destroy ourselves as experienced by the generation of the flood, whose sins against humanity caused God to wipe out all human and living creatures from the face of the earth.

15. Natural Order Required for Free Will

In order to enable people to freely choose their path, God set the world to operate according to the laws of nature, destiny, and probability. These laws apply equally to both righteous and the wicked. This is reflected in the various genes people carry and in the different environments they live. As a result, there are righteous people who have flawed genes and who die young from illness and wicked people who have healthy genes and live long pleasant lives. Similarly, the chances of people becoming rich or poor are largely dependent upon the circumstances of their upbringing.

Without such variables, free choice would be impossible. For if every sinner suffered an instant heart attack or financial loss, or if every person doing a *mitzva* received financial gain or other benefits, everyone would obey the divine commandments to avoid punishments and receive rewards. The unique attributes of humans who are created in the image of God would not be expressed. Only when people choose good for the 'sake of heaven' - to do what is truly good and not to receive instant reward, do they develop their positive character traits and deepen their understanding. This is what enables them to take part in repairing and improving the world. There-fore, most reward and punishment is not clearly revealed in this world. There are righteous people who suffer from hard-ship, and wicked people who enjoy the good life. This system offers every person a real choice.

16. Reward and Punishment in the World to Come

The completion of justice for the righteous and the wicked occurs in the World to Come, also called the World of Truth. In contrast to this world, where falsehood dominates, the true status of each person and the real worth of his or her deeds is clear in the World to Come.

The World to Come has two phases. The first phase begins with death, when each soul returns to the world of the souls. There, the righteous ascend to heaven to receive reward ac-cording to the value of their *mitzvot*, while the wicked de-scend to hell to receive punishment in accordance with their sins. As for those who were wicked but also made efforts to observe some *mitzvot*, they are still punished but ascend to heaven afterwards. The second phase of the World to Come will take place after the world is perfected. Then, with the resurrection of the dead, souls will permanently reunite with bodies, and soar to infinite heights (34:4-5 below).

17. Natural Reward and Punishment in This World

From a broader perspective we find that even within the natural order, those who choose good tend to benefit in this world too. Due to their goodness and loyalty, they succeed in establishing stable families and derive a lot of pleasure from them. Thanks to their diligence and honesty, they are trusted in business and achieve financial stability. Above all, they derive satisfaction and gratification from their virtuous deeds. When tragedy strikes, such people can find meaning in it, which further brings blessing to their lives.

In contrast, those who choose to sin tend to find that in the long term, their lives are not satisfying. Because they are not faithful, their relationships often fail and their families fall apart. Because sometimes they are not honest, people prefer not to do business with them or hire them. Because they are arrogant, they do not have true friends. Above all, they do not have true fulfillment, because their lack of values and faith creates a void in their lives. Even the pleasures of this world disappoint them with their emptiness. When tragedy strikes, these people have nowhere to turn for comfort and they are filled with anger and despair.

All humanity confronts this dilemma. The evil inclination wants people to look at the world superficially in the short-term to pursue money, honor, and pleasures. The good inclination stirs people to examine the world more profoundly over the long-term and to live a life filled with values, creativity, and blessing. Overall, even in this world over time the righteous are more likely to succeed while the wicked are more likely to fail, but freedom to choose remains intact.

18. Providence for the Individual

Within the natural order hides a divine providence that was established to direct every person specifically to where they belong. Generally, this results in rewarding the righteous and punishing the wicked. However, the way providence plays out is complex, and faces challenges that sometimes result in the suffering of the righteous and success of the wicked. While this intensifies our dilemma it preserves free will. The righteous who accept this strengthen their faith and ultimately acquire more blessing, while the wicked are confused by this and continue in their evil ways and are punished.

Seemingly this presents a difficulty, for the Torah explains in detail that God rewards the righteous and punishes the wicked in this world. Why do we see good people suffer and evil people prosper? Rather that the reward and punishment in this world described by the Torah is for the Jewish people as a collective, and not for each and every individual.

19. Reward and Punishment for the Jews in this World

The Jews are in a unique position as God's nation and whether in Israel or the diaspora, what happens to them reveals a message from God to the world. When the Jews choose righteousness, everyone can see they are blessed; when they choose evil, everyone can see they are punished. Because the moral condition of the Jews affects the whole world, the Jews as a whole are punished more severely for sinning than non-Jews. Conversely, the Jews as a whole receive greater reward than non-Jews for choosing virtue, since they are drawing down blessing for the entire world.

As it says, "If you follow My laws and faithfully observe My commandments, I will grant your rains in their season, so that the earth shall yield its produce and the trees of the field their fruit... I will grant peace in the land... You shall give chase to your enemies, and they shall fall before you by the sword... I will be ever present in your midst; I will be your God, and you shall be My people... But if you do not obey Me and do not observe all these commandments... I in turn will do this to you: I will wreak misery upon you – consumption and fever, which cause the eyes to pine and the body to languish. You shall sow your seed to no purpose, for your enemies shall eat it... I will lay your cities in ruin and make your sanctuaries desolate... And you I will scatter among the nations, and I will unsheathe the sword against you. Your land shall become a desolation... you shall perish among the nations; and the land of your enemies shall consume you" (Leviticus 26:3-38). "All nations will ask, 'Why did the Lord do thus to this land? Why that awful wrath?' They will be told, 'Because they forsook the covenant that the Lord, God of their fathers made with them when He freed them from the land of Egypt; they turned to the service of other gods and worshiped them... The Lord uprooted them from their soil in anger, fury, and great wrath, and cast them into another land, as is still the case" (Deuteronomy 29:23-27). Many other verses contain similar declarations. Since we are speaking of a nation, the arc of reward and punishment extends over a lengthy period, but it is visible to anyone who studies Jewish chronology in depth. Therefore, the history of the Jewish people is the history of the revelation of faith in this world.

The choices made by the Jewish people as a whole impact their lives in this world: "See, I set before you this day life and prosperity, death and adversity. For I command you this day to love the Lord your God, to walk in His ways, and to keep His commandments, His laws, and His rules, that you may thrive and increase, and that the Lord your God may bless you in the land that you are about to enter and possess. But if your heart turns away and you give no heed, and are lured into the worship and service of other gods, I declare to you this day that you shall certainly perish; you shall not long endure on the soil that you are crossing the Jordan to enter and possess" (Deuteronomy 30:15-18). God wants us to choose life as it says: "I call heaven and earth to witness against you this day: I have put before you life and death, blessing and curse. Choose life – if you and your offspring would live – by loving the Lord your God, heeding His commands, and holding fast to Him. For thereby you shall have life and shall long endure upon the soil that the Lord your God swore to your ancestors,

Abraham, Isaac, and Jacob, to give to them" (*ibid.* 19-20). Each and every individual Jew who chooses good adds blessing and life to the nation which appear even in this world.

20. The Status of Exile

When the Jews are punished with destruction and exile, God's direction of the world is deeply hidden. It appears as if God has abandoned the world, letting evil take over, whereby the wicked prosper and the righteous suffer. This was the case two thousand years ago when evil forces were strong enough to destroy the Temple sending the Jews into exile, and it remains the case today when the wicked prosper. Although it does not seem right that the righteous should suffer more, this is natural since they experience intense sorrow over the Jewish exile. They suffer heartache at this desecration of divine honor. From the depths of this pain and grief, the righteous merit bringing the redemption sooner, and they will be greatly rewarded for it.

21. God's Covenant with the Jews

According to the principles of justice, if the Jewish people choose evil it would call for God to destroy them along with the rest of the world (Heaven forbid). However, God chose His people and forged a covenant with them. Therefore, no matter how great their sins, God will not abandon them. Rather, He will afflict them terribly in order for them to repent. We are reminded of this aspect of the covenant each year on Yom Kippur (below 35:4). When justice applies to the Jewish people, it is not focused on whether they will continue to exist, but rather on how they will continue to exist: whether in peace and blessing or the opposite, Heaven forbid.

God also promised the Jews that redemption will ultimately arrive, and the world will be perfected. If the Jews as a whole repent, the redemption will come sooner, in peace and tranquility. If they do not repent, there will be a lengthy exile followed by terrible suffering and hardship. Ultimately, the Jewish people will return from exile, develop the Land, and continue to elevate themselves until redemption and complete repentance are achieved.

22. The Sins of the Golden Calf and the Spies

There were two fundamental sins committed by the generation which experienced the desert and received the Torah. The first was the sin of the golden calf which defied pure faith and belief in the Torah. The second was the sin of the spies which challenged the actualization of that vision of faith in the Land of Israel.

After the mass revelation at Sinai, Moses was called to ascend the mountain for forty days and forty nights to receive the Torah directly from the Almighty. The people expected Moses to descend on what they thought was the fortieth day. When he did not do so, they demanded that Aaron the High Priest make an idol that would represent the God, Who had redeemed them from Egypt. Aaron attempted to delay them but when they insisted, he took their gold jewelry and made a golden calf. He delayed the times of the sacrifice offerings until the next day, hoping that Moses would return in the interim. However, by the next morning, Moses still had not descended, and the people began sacrificing to the calf and celebrating. This evoked harsh heavenly judgment from God who sought to destroy the nation and start over with Moses and his descendants. Meanwhile, Moses descended bearing the Tablets of the Covenant. When he saw the golden calf, he was enraged and threw down the Tablets, which broke. He punished the sinners and began a process of repentance and repair. Moses prayed fervently on behalf of the people until God agreed to forgive the nation rather than destroy it.

About a year later, due to the nation's concerns about entering the Land, Moses sent spies to survey it. When they returned from their mission, they spoke so negatively about the Land that they weakened the nation's resolve. The spies reported that the Israelites would be unable to conquer the Land because its inhabitants were warriors and giants. "The whole community broke into loud cries, and the people wept that night [the night of Tisha Be-Av]. All the Israelites railed against Moses and Aaron. 'If only we had died in the land of Egypt,' the whole community shouted at them, 'or if only we might die in this wilderness! Why is the Lord taking us to that land to fall by the sword? Our wives and children will be carried off! It would be better for us to go back to Egypt!' And they said to one another, 'Let us head back to Egypt'" (Numbers 14:1-4). Due to this sin, the whole generation was doomed to die in the desert. It was only their children who would enter the Promised Land under the leadership of Joshua son of Nun. According to the Talmud, God said: You cried for nothing on this day, so I will cause this day to have something to cry about in future generations. If you do not rectify the sin of the spies, the Temple will be destroyed on this day. Since the people did not merit to amend this sin by settling the Land following the Torah's guidance, both Temples were later destroyed on Tisha Be-Av.

The people who sinned with the golden calf did have faith in God. However, they thought they needed the power of an intermediary and this impaired their pure faith and Torah belief. As a result, they lacked the fortitude to stand up to the spies, who sought to dissuade them from entering the Land. The people disdained the Land of Israel and betrayed their Torah mission. The Jewish nation did not fully rectify that sin with pure devotion and faith to be implemented in the Land of Israel. Therefore, generations later the First Temple was destroyed on Tisha Be-Av and later still, the Second Temple was destroyed then as well. (See 37:4 below about how our fasting on Tisha Be-Av is meant to rectify the sin of the spies.)

In every generation, the Jewish people are forced to cope with the challenge that could lead to the sin of the golden calf. Since the world is in a constant state of flux, at times it seems that the Torah's message is hidden and and there is no one to clarify it. There is a temptation to seek a "golden calf" such as a foreign ideology or excess piety or extreme austerity, which in reality, erode the delicate balance provided by the Torah's guidance.

Similarly, every generation is faced with challenges when fulfilling the *mitzva* of settling the Land, both in coping with external enemies and internal conflicts. To properly fulfill this *mitzva*, it is necessary to take spiritual concepts and *mitzvot* and "settle" them into the real world, with all its trials. People may complain that the concepts are too lofty or distant from reality or too difficult to put into practice. It falls on us to correct the sin of the spies by settling the Land according to the Torah's directive. We must demonstrate that specifically by following God's ways, the Land is settled with an abundance of blessing. (See 17:14 below about the sin of the spies in recent generations.)

The Jewish people's repentance and redemption as a whole are dependent upon rectifying these two sins. To rectify the sin of the golden calf, we must ensure that our pure faith remains free of any hint of idolatry (as we have explained in this chapter and will explain further in the next). To rectify the sin of the spies, we must devote ourselves to carrying out the mission of the Jewish people – to settle the Land in accordance with the Torah and to reveal the Divine Presence in all aspects of life. (This will be explained in Chapter 17, which focuses on the Land and the people).

CHAPTER 16

Torah Study

1. The Value of Torah Study

The *mitzva* of studying Torah is equivalent to all the other *mitzvot* altogether, and so is its reward. There are two reasons for this. First, it is impossible for Jews to properly observe the commandments and live a life of faith and morality without Torah knowledge. Second, since Torah study engages a person's noblest aspects – the mind and the soul – it ennobles the person and the world.

The Sages tell us that the Torah predates the world. God began by creating the Torah, which contains all ideals. Then, based on the blueprint embedded in the Torah, God created the world. The world's continued existence depends upon the Jewish people studying Torah day and night. The more in depth their Torah study, the greater insights they discover. These draw down blessing and life to the world, and ultimately perfect it.

The *mitzva* of Torah study applies to every Jew, even though Torah scholars alone have a profound enough understanding of its foundations to qualify them to dispense halakhic rulings. Studying Torah produces light – a light which uniquely reflects the soul of the person studying, and the time during which one studies. Torah study also contributes to the community, because directly or indirectly, every individual's Torah knowledge becomes part of the collective knowledge of Torah scholars.

2. The Parameters of the Mitzva

The great importance of Torah study can be seen in the existence of three independent *mitzvot* to study or teach Torah.

- First, parents have a *mitzva* to teach their children Torah, and to send them to schools where they will study Torah.
- Second, teachers and rabbis have a *mitzva* to teach Torah.
- Third, every Jew has an individual and personal *mitzva* to study Torah.

Thus, even if one was deprived of a Torah education as a child, one must find a way to study Torah later on in life.

Over two thousand years ago, a basic educational system was established to ensure Jewish children of all backgrounds would be able to study Torah. This included the provision that there be no more than twenty-five students in a classroom; if this number was exceeded, an assistant teacher was to be appointed. This model set a precedent for educational systems worldwide.

The insights of the Torah are infinite, and every letter can teach us something about law or lore. Nevertheless, the basic obligation to study Torah applies to the fundamentals. First and foremost, this means the Hebrew Bible (primarily the Pentateuch). People should also study works of *halakha*, faith, and morality necessary to help them discover how to live a virtuous life. There is no set curriculum for this. Every parent and every educational institution should design a course of study to teach their children these basics, as well as how to implement them on personal, family and global levels.

3. The Mitzva of Torah Study for Adults

Adults who studied Torah as children must constantly review what they learned. This prevents them from forgetting the basics and allows them to continue to broaden and deepen their Torah knowledge. Every additional understanding of Torah has a positive impact on one's soul, improves one's life (directly and indirectly), and adds goodness and blessing to the world. Therefore, it is important for every Jew to set aside time to study Torah every day, and even more time on Shabbat and holidays. Thus our Sages declare (*y. Shabbat* 15:3), "Shabbat and Yom Tov were given to us solely for the purpose of learning Torah."

Many important Torah works are available. Each one has its own outlook and emphasis. Everyone should choose the book right for them at that particular moment, which our Sages call "the area of Torah that one's heart desires." This means individuals should study the Torah topics and books that speak best to them. Nevertheless, it is a good idea to consult with a Torah scholar, because sometimes people might enjoy studying a certain book, but with only minimal gains.

4. How Much Time Must Be Dedicated to Torah Study?

Those people who are suited to become Torah scholars (by dint of talent, character, and drive) should devote the bulk of their day to Torah study. If necessary, they must make do financially with very little to dedicate themselves to their studies, succeed in them, and develop into excellent teachers. Most people do not aspire to this, so instead they should engage in developing the world through whatever work they do. While making a respectable living, they should set aside time daily to study Torah, and even more time on Shabbat and holidays. As for those who are retired or who do not need to work full time, and thus have free time on their hands, they should make sure not to waste the time frivolously. Rather, in addition to whatever productive things they normally do, they should also set aside a few solid hours to study Torah every day.

5. Men, Women, and Torah Study

The *mitzva* of Torah study includes two elements. The first is to know the Torah's teachings on faith, *halakha*, and morality. This knowledge is a prerequisite to living a Torah life, so all Jews are obligated by it, both men and women. The second element is to go further and study Torah in greater breadth and depth. Men are obligated in this type of study; women who wish to engage in it are performing a *mitzva*, but are not obligated to do so. The more free time a woman has, the more it behooves her to undertake this advanced Torah study as well.

For much of history, life was simpler and was lived locally, so practical *halakha* could be absorbed at home and only a minimal amount of formal study was necessary. Children would acquire the foundations of faith and morality through conversations with their parents and older family members. More recently, the world has become more complex, and all fields of study have expanded. The first element of Torah study has greatly expanded as well. Therefore, the difference between men's and women's obligations in Torah study today has narrowed significantly. In fact, many men and women do not manage to master the areas where everyone has the same requirement.

6. Writing a Torah Scroll and Buying Torah Books

Originally, it was incumbent upon every male Jew to write a kosher (valid) Torah scroll for himself, using ink and parchment. He was to study from this scroll throughout his life.

However, once it became permissible to write down the Oral Torah (see below), sacred Torah scrolls were no longer used for study. They were reserved for communal Torah reading, while books (first handwritten, then printed) were used for study. Therefore, nowadays people fulfill the *mitzva* of writing a Torah scroll by buying Torah books to guide them how to properly observe the *mitzvot*.

7. The Value of Secular Studies

Studying non-Torah subjects has a *mitzva* component, as every field of study expresses some type of divine wisdom. True, there is a fundamental difference between studying Torah and studying secular subjects: while all Jews are obligated to study Torah (because it makes them better people and is beneficial for the world), studying other disciplines is not compulsory. Nevertheless, studying them with the understanding they reflect divine wisdom does fulfill a *mitzva*. The more those secular studies are linked to a deeper understanding of Torah, the greater their value, because then studying them broadens and deepens one's understanding of the Torah.

The difference between the two types of wisdom was reflected in the Temple. Its inner chamber, the Holy of Holies, housed the Ark, which held the Torah and the Tablets. The outer chamber, the Holy, housed the Menora, which symbolized other disciplines (19:2-5 below). This teaches us that when other subjects are studied for the sake of heaven, they too possess holiness, though not as much as the Torah. Thus, the Sages referred to these disciplines as "external wisdom." This is in contrast to the wisdom of the Torah, which is meant to guide all knowledge. In general, people today often refer to non-Torah subjects as "secular studies," in contrast to the "sacred studies" of the Torah.

8. Integrating Secular Studies: The Debate

In the period of the Rishonim (about eight hundred years ago), studying secular studies was controversial. Many secular books at the time contained heretical beliefs. They attracted many young people, some of whom abandoned Judaism and assimilated. (Of course, the difficulties of the exile added to the temptation to assimilate.) This led many Torah giants to discourage students from studying secular studies; some discouraged adults as well.

About two hundred years ago, the problem became even more acute. The Enlightenment in Europe attracted many Jews who had faith that pure intellect was capable of solving all of humanity's problems. This premise led them to believe there was no further need for Torah and *mitzvot*. As a result, many Jews in Western Europe who studied secular disciplines abandoned their traditions and assimilated. In response, some rabbis prohibited studying secular studies. However, since most Torah giants recognized the great value of secular studies, they did not prohibit them, but rather advised caution when studying them.

Some Orthodox communities still avoid secular studies and do not teach them in their schools. (This is the position of most Ĥaredi schools in Israel.) Nevertheless, it is proper to integrate secular studies into the curriculum, as is the norm in Religious Zionist schools. There are a number of good reasons for this, as we will now explain.

First, secular studies are intrinsically worthwhile, as they allow people to better understand God's wisdom and recognize God's greatness. Second, studying them enables people to acquire professional skills, support themselves properly, and earn the respect of others. Third, learning secular studies opens the door for the Jews to contribute to humanity, thus sanctifying God's name. Above all, it would seem the integration of secular studies is more successful than the alternative in preserving Judaism in the long term.

At the same time, for this integration to succeed, religious studies must be given their due and taken very seriously. Parents must not only educate their children to the supreme value of Torah study, but also demonstrate it through personal example.

9. Supporting Torah Scholars

During Temple times, not only did the members of the tribe of Levi (priests and Levites) serve in the Temple and the justice system, they also filled many functions associated today with the rabbinate (teaching Torah, deciding *halakha*, and spiritual counseling). They were supported by Torah-mandated gifts from the nation, including tithes of produce, firstborn animals, and designated parts of the sacrifices. Other tribes generated impressive educators as well, who dedicated themselves to teaching without the support system. Sometimes they had rich family members who contributed to their sustenance, modeled on the partnership of Issachar and Zebulun. (The members of the tribe of Zebulun, who were often rich, supported the Torah scholars of the tribe of Issachar. They were considered equal partners, and reaped equal reward in heaven for the Torah study.)

With the destruction of the Temple and the subsequent exile, the priests and Levites no longer dedicated their lives to serving the public and teaching Torah. At the same time, the tithing obligations were minimized, and many Jews began to support themselves in ways other than agriculture. To ensure Torah study would continue, the Sages directed everyone to give ten percent of their earnings to support those of any tribe who were studying and teaching Torah. This charity is referred to as *ma'aser kesafim* (the monetary tithe) and still applies today. Those who wish to be more generous give twenty percent. *Ma'aser* money should also be devoted to providing basic necessities for the poor and needy (6:13 above).

Nowadays, the primary way in which we support Torah scholars is by contributing to *yeshivot* (religious academies) that train teachers, scholars, and community rabbis. In the past, individuals were entitled to decide on the recipients of their tithes. This policy motivated the priests and Levites to provide good service; those who did not make the effort, simply received less. Today as well, everyone can choose where to direct their charity. It makes sense to donate to *yeshivot* that reflect one's values, and thus increase their communal impact.

10. Honoring a Torah Scholar

Since the Torah is supreme and elevated above everything else, there is a *mitzva* to honor Torah scholars, who dedicate their lives to studying and teaching it. This honor helps inculcate a respectful attitude towards Torah and morality. A Torah scholar is on a higher level than even a high priest, if the high priest is not as learned as the scholar. This is true even if the scholar does not have notable lineage, and even if he is a *mamzer* (bastard). The Sages tell us to watch out for the children of the poor, because they often become great Torah sages. Rabbi Akiva, for example, was from a poor family of converts, yet he became one of the greatest Tanna'im. To express the great respect of the community for Torah scholars, people stand up for them when they enter or exit a room.

11. Funding Adult Yeshiva Students: The Debate

As we have seen, it is a *mitzva* for the Jewish people to support rabbis and teachers who devote their time to teaching Torah. If they had to find other work to support themselves, they would be unable to fulfil that function. A few hundred years ago, when the quantity of Torah material which needed to be mastered had greatly increased, a consensus grew that people should not only support scholars, but also students. After all, their studies in yeshiva were preparing them to serve the community. However, those studying Torah but not planning to serve the community may not accept donations or charity to fund their studies. As we said above, all Jews have an obligation to study Torah, and this study should be done for the sake of heaven, not for the sake of profit.

In our times, we face a new situation. Modern life presents our youth with great challenges. Many yeshiva high school graduates have not yet attained a level of Torah knowledge to allow them to live their lives by its light. Since the ideal is for every Jew to live a life of Torah and faith, we must enable all high school graduates to spend a few years in yeshiva after graduation. This provides them with a strong Torah foundation before they start a family and go out into the working world. It is legitimate to use *ma'aser* money to support the Torah studies of young people whose parents cannot afford the tuition. Similarly, there are penitents who have returned to Judaism and would like to acquire basic Torah knowledge. This is a legitimate need, so *ma'aser* money may be used to provide them with a stipend for a year or two of full-time Torah study. Once the young people or returnees have the basics under their belts, they are no longer allowed to accept money for learning Torah. They must learn a profession to support themselves, while continuing to set aside time for regular Torah study.

Despite this, in some circles, due to great concern of being influenced by the secular world, the permission to accept money to study Torah has been greatly extended and taken to an extreme. Those communities go so far as to encourage all young men who can study Torah to do so, while living off stipends from communal funds and donations. This approach is mistaken. As Maimonides writes (*Mishneh Torah*, Laws of Torah Study 3:10),

> *Anyone who decides that he will engage in Torah study, not work, and take charity to support himself is desecrating God's name, dishonoring the Torah, and dousing the light of the religion. He is also harming himself and losing his place in the World to Come, as it is forbidden to benefit from the words of Torah in this world. Thus our Sages state, "Anyone who benefits from the words of Torah loses his place in the World to Come" . . . and "All Torah study that is not accompanied by work is ultimately worthless." Such a person will end up robbing others.*

12. The Written Torah and the Oral Torah

The Written Torah consists of three parts. The five books of Moses (the Pentateuch), which Moses received through the highest level of prophecy, is the part of the Hebrew Bible called *Torah*. It contains all 613 *mitzvot* as well as the history of God's revelation of the fundamentals of faith and morality to the Israelites. Afterwards, over the course of a thousand years, there were countless prophets. God communicated with them and gave them prophesies for their time. What was relevant to later generations was incorporated into the part of the Bible called the Prophets (*Nevi'im*). There were also divinely inspired books that became incorporated into the part of the Bible called the Writings (*Ketuvim*). Thus, there are three component parts to *Tanakh*, which is the acronym for *Torah, Nevi'im, Ketuvim*. Of the three, it is the Torah given by Moses which is the primary source for normative Torah law.

The Oral Torah is the traditional explanation of the Written Torah. It starts with explanations for each *mitzva* God gave Moses orally at Sinai. It continues with the interpretations that sages throughout the ages have given for the *mitzvot*. Additionally, while the Written Torah is a heavenly presentation of general principles, the rabbis are empowered both to fill in details and to make protective limits and ordinances, measures which allow the Torah to be put into practice in the world in which we live.

13. Rabbinic Authority

The authority to make halakhic decisions and enactments was given to the Sanhedrin, the High Court of seventy-one Sages, which was located near the Temple. Once the Sanhedrin ruled in accordance with the majority of Sages, no individual sage was permitted to dissent. Not long before the destruction of the Second Temple, the Sanhedrin ceased to function. This means it is no longer possible to reach binding decisions when sages disagree, and rabbis cannot make enactments for the entire people. Only in cases of great necessity do rabbis make enactments to meet the needs of their time or place. Even then, the enactments become binding only if the majority of the community accepts them.

14. The Chain of Transmission

The Early Generations

God revealed the foundations of faith and the special mission of the Jewish people to our forefathers and mothers. Abraham was born in 1948 (according to the Jewish calendar, which counts from the creation of Adam and Eve). In 2238, his grandson Jacob, towards the end of his life, traveled with his children and grandchildren to Egypt, where his son Joseph was the vizier. After Joseph and his brothers died, the Egyptians enslaved the Israelites. The enslavement lasted about 120 years. Thanks to their faith that God would redeem them from Egypt and bring them to the good Land He had promised their ancestors, the Israelites preserved their identity, and were even fruitful. In fact, they grew to be a nation with six hundred thousand men in its army. (For more details, see ch. 2 above.)

Moses and the Giving of the Torah

In 2448, on the 15th of Nissan, God took the Israelites out of Egypt. Later that year, on the 7th of Sivan, they heard the Ten Commandments at Mount Sinai. Moses remained on the mountain for another forty days, while he received more of the Torah and the Tablets of the Covenant. During the forty years the Israelites wandered in the desert, Moses continued receiving the Torah from God and sharing it with his students and the rest of the nation. Towards the end of his life, Moses wrote out twelve copies of the completed Torah, one for each of the twelve tribes.

Joshua and the Elders

Following the death of Moses in 2489, his loyal disciple Joshua son of Nun became the leader. Under his leadership, the Israelites conquered the Land and divided it among the tribes. For almost four hundred years after Joshua died, the elders of each tribe continued transmitting the Torah from generation to generation. This was the period of the Judges, a turbulent time of highs and lows. Enemies would attack the Israelites and subjugate them; when the Israelites repented, God would provide them with a Judge who led them to victory against their enemies. The Judges included Othniel the son of Kenaz, Ehud son of Gera, Deborah the Prophet, Gideon, Jephthah, and Samson. During the period of the Judges, the Tabernacle was in Shiloh, in the tribal portion of Ephraim.

Samuel and the Monarchic Period

Four hundred years after the Exodus, a great prophet arose named Samuel. He judged the Israelites, increased the Torah's influence, and trained many students to become prophets. During his time, the people requested a king. In response, Samuel anointed Saul from the tribe of Benjamin. This was the beginning of the United Monarchy. Later, after King Saul sinned, Samuel anointed David from the tribe of Judah to rule in his stead. Samuel also presented David with the plans to build the Temple, which would be built by David's son Solomon.

Following King Solomon's death in 2965, the kingdom split in two. The Kingdom of Judah ruled over a minority of the tribes. It was under the rule of Davidic kings, with its capital in Jerusalem. The Kingdom of Israel ruled over most of the tribes. It had a variety of monarchs, and was based in Samaria. The splitting of the kingdom is seen as the first stage of the collapse of self-rule. Over two centuries later, it ultimately led to the destruction of the Kingdom of Israel at the hands of the Neo-Assyrian Empire in 3206. Over a century after that, the First Temple and the Kingdom of Judah were destroyed by the Neo-Babylonian Empire in 3339.

The Second Temple Period

The Judaeans were exiled to Babylonia, which became the Jewish center for approximately seventy years. Then, King Cyrus of Persia conquered Babylonia and permitted the Jews to return to the Land and build the Second Temple. Zerubbabel led the Jews who returned. However, few Jews took advantage of this opportunity, so the building of the Temple was delayed. (During the years of Persian rule, the Purim miracle took place in the Persian capital of Shushan; see 39:5 below.) Eventually, the returnees settled in and completed the building of the Second Temple.

Ezra the Scribe was active during this period, which saw the transition from the prophets to the Sages. He had a long-lasting impact on the nation, and was considered the most important leader after Moses. Ezra headed the Men of the Great Assembly, the court of 120 Sages which included the last of the prophets. They were responsible for deciding which books would be included in Tanakh. The Sages founded houses of study and trained many students. They also framed much of the Oral Law, putting safeguards and enactments in place to ensure the Torah's continuity.

In the middle of the Second Temple period, houses of study grew and study of the Oral Torah increased. This was largely in the wake of the successful Hasmonean rebellion (Maccabees). The Syrian-Greeks had made decrees against Judaism and defiled the Temple, which led the Hasmoneans to rebel. After their military victory, they wished to rededicate the Temple and light the *Menora*. However, they could find only one container of pure oil, which was enough to last for only a day. Miraculously though, the oil lasted for eight days. To commemorate the miracle of the oil, the purification of the Temple, and the miraculous victory of the Hasmoneans, the holiday of Ḥanuka was established in 3596 (164 BCE). For more about Ḥanuka, see ch. 38 below.

The Tanna'itic Period and the Writing of the Mishna

Originally, it was prohibited to write down the Oral Torah. While it was permissible for scholars to write brief notes for themselves, these were not collected into books to be shared with students. However, about 150 years after the destruction of the Temple in 3830 (70 CE), Rabbi Judah the Prince and the Sages of his time realized that not only were most of the Jews dispersed in exile, but the laws were increasing in volume and complexity and becoming difficult to remember. Therefore, they permitted writing down the Oral Torah. With the help of colleagues and students, Rabbi Judah the Prince redacted the six orders of the Mishna, a comprehensive outline of the Oral Torah at that time. It included the most important disagreements of the Tanna'im, the Sages who lived from the end of the Second Temple period until the redaction of the Mishna, and was completed in 3978 (218 CE).

The greatest Tanna'im included Hillel and Shammai, Rabban Yoĥanan ben Zakkai (who lived through the destruction of the Second Temple and enacted many laws meant to preserve the memory and values of the Temple), and Rabbi Akiva (who was martyred during the Bar Kokhba rebellion).

The Amora'ic Period and the Writing of the Talmud

With the completion of the Mishna, the period of the Amora'im began. These were the Sages who worked hard to analyze, explain, clarify, and expand upon the Mishna. Their teachings were collected in the Talmud (also known as Gemara) – first the Jerusalem Talmud, and later the Babylonian Talmud. The latter was finished about three hundred years after the Mishna, in 4260 (500 CE). Famous Amora'im included R. Yoĥanan and Resh Lakish; Rav and Shmuel; Abaye and Rava; and Ravina and Rav Ashi. During this period, Babylonia became the primary Torah center.

At the same time the Mishna and Talmud were being compiled, the Sages also composed commentaries on Tanakh. These commentaries, called "*midrashim*," include the halakhic works *Mekhilta*, *Sifra*, and *Sifrei*, and non-halakhic works such as *Midrash Rabba* and *Midrash Tanĥuma*. Other material was transmitted more discreetly and included the kabbalistic teachings which formed the basis of the *Zohar*.

The rabbis who lived from the Second Temple period through the Amora'ic period are referred to as "Sages." The standard Hebrew term for them is *Ĥazal*, an acronym that means "our Sages of blessed memory."

The Savora'im

The sages who followed the Amora'im were referred to as Savora'im, who were active until approximately 4349 (589 CE). This time period was one in which the Jews were constantly persecuted. The legacy of the Savora'im was the final redaction of the words of the Sages in the Babylonian Talmud and other rabbinic works.

Ge'onim

The following time period is referred to as the Ge'onic period. It lasted approximately 450 years, from 4349 to 4798 (539-1038 CE). During this time, Babylonia was still the center of Judaism, and the Torah leaders there – called Ge'onim – were the leaders of world Jewry. Jews from all over the world turned to them with their halakhic questions. (It was during this time that a serious, long-lasting dispute began between rabbinic Jews and Karaites. (The Karaites were Jews who did not accept the Oral Torah.) The Ge'onim produced responsa, halakhic rulings, and commentaries on the Talmud, although they were less prolific than those who came before and after them. Well-known Ge'onim included Rabbi Yehudai Gaon, Rabbi Saadia Gaon, Rabbi Sherira Gaon, and his son Rabbi Hai Gaon. The death of Rabbi Hai marked the end of the Ge'onic period.

The Rishonim

The next period also lasted about 450 years, from 4800 to 5252 (1040-1492 CE). During this time, the Jewish world continued to expand. Large communities could now be found in Spain, Ashkenaz (Germany and France), North Africa, and Yemen. The sages who lived during this medieval period are referred to as the Rishonim (the earlier ones). They wrote commentaries on both the written Torah and the Talmud. Rashi (an acronym for Rabbi Shlomo Yitzĥaki), who lived in northern France, wrote the most important commentaries on the Torah and the Talmud.

The Rishonim of Spain also wrote many important Torah books. The most important halakhic work was by Maimonides (known in Hebrew as Rambam, an acronym for Rabbi Moshe ben Maimon). This book, *Mishneh Torah*, organizes all the *mitzvot* and the laws pertaining to them, both theoretical and practical. A very influential work of Jewish thought, the *Kuzari*, was penned by Rabbi Yehuda Halevi, who was both a philosopher and a poet. Another great Spanish rabbi was Naĥmanides (known in Hebrew as Ramban, an acronym for Rabbi Moshe ben Naĥman). He immigrated to the Land of Israel in his old age, and his main disciple was Rashba (an acronym for Rabbi Shlomo ben Aderet).

During the time of the Rishonim, two halakhic schools of law and custom began to emerge: Sephardic and Ashkenazic. The Sephardic tradition is based largely on Rif (an acronym for Rabbi Yitzĥak Alfasi) and Rambam. The Ashkenazic tradition is based largely on *Tosafot* (a Talmudic commentary) and Rosh (an acronym for Rabbi Asher ben Yeĥiel).

Rabbi Yosef Karo served as a bridge between the Rishonim and the Aĥaronim. He was born in Spain and moved to the Land of Israel, where he died in Safed in 5335 (1575 CE). Rabbi Yosef Karo wrote the *Shulĥan Arukh*, summarizing all of practical *halakha*. After it was annotated by a Polish rabbi called Rema (an acronym for Rabbi Moshe Isserles), the *Shulĥan Arukh* became the central halakhic work for both Sephardim and Ashkenazim. Printing spread through Europe around this time, and the *Shulĥan Arukh* was one of the first major Jewish books to be printed.

The Aĥaronim

The subsequent rabbis are called the Aĥaronim (the later ones). During this time, spanning from the writing of the *Shulĥan Arukh* about 450 years ago through the present, tens of thousands of rabbinic works have been published in a variety of areas. These include biblical commentaries, commentaries on the Talmud and halakhic works, responsa, and books of Jewish thought, including Kabbala and Ĥasidut. Many rabbis are referred to by the names of their books. The rabbinic legalists who wrote commentaries on the *Shulĥan Arukh* include *Magen Avraham*, *Taz* (an acronym for *Turei Zahav*), *Shakh* (an acronym for *Siftei Kohen*), Ĥida (whose most important work is *Birkei Yosef*), and *Mishna Berura*. Authors of responsa include Radbaz, Noda Bi-Yehuda, and Ĥatam Sofer.

Towards the beginning of this period, an amazing individual named Rabbi Yitzĥak Luria revealed and explained many mystical matters. Known as the holy Ari, he died in Safed in 5332 (1572 CE). Other luminaries of Jewish thought and Kabbalah are Maharal (Rabbi Judah Loew), who was born in Poland and died in Prague in 5369 (1609 CE); Ohr HaĤayim (Rabbi Ĥayim ibn Attar), born in Morocco and died in Jerusalem in 5503 (1743 CE); Ramĥal (Rabbi Moshe Ĥayim Luzzatto), born in Italy and died in Acre in 5506 (1746 CE); Rashash (Rabbi Sar Shalom Sharabi), born in Yemen and died in Jerusalem in 5537 (1777 CE); and the Gaon (genius) of Vilna, a master of all areas of Torah study, who was born in Poland and died in Vilna in 5558 (1797 CE).

In the 1700s, Rabbi Israel Ba'al Shem Tov and his students started the Ĥasidut movement, which drew upon mysticism and succeeded in drawing the masses closer to tradition and reigniting their religious enthusiasm. (The Ba'al Shem Tov died in 5520, or 1760 CE.)

In Israel, the greatest sage of recent generations was Rabbi

Avraham Yitzchak HaKohen Kook, whose legacy includes many works of Jewish thought relating to the return of the Jewish people to the Land of Israel in modern times. (Rav Kook died in 5695, or 1935 CE.) Since the establishment of the State of Israel in 5648 (1948 CE), the center of Torah has returned from the diaspora to the Land of Israel.

CHAPTER 17

The Land and the People

1. The Land and God's Promises

God chose the Land of Israel, and the Divine Presence continues to be felt there. As it says, "For the Lord has chosen Zion; He has desired it for His seat" (Psalms 132:13), and "It is a land which the Lord your God looks after, on which the Lord your God always keep His eye, from year's beginning to year's end" (Deuteronomy 11:12). This means the Holy Land is the ideal place to live a religious Jewish life and to increase blessing in the world. This is why all three of the patriarchs had prophetic revelations in which God promised He would give the Land of Israel to their descendants (1:6 above).

When God redeemed the Israelites from Egypt, it was to bring them to the Land of Israel, as He made clear: "I have come down to rescue them from the Egyptians and to bring them out of that land to a good and spacious land, a land flowing with milk and honey" (Exodus 3:8). This is why the sin of the spies was so serious (Numbers ch. 13-14). How could the Jews have been afraid to fight for the Land, and how could they have refused to enter it? As a result of this sin, God decreed that the generation that had left Egypt would die in the desert. Only forty years later were their children able to conquer and settle the Land.

The history of the Jewish people in their Land demonstrates the revelation of faith in the world. This is seen throughout the Bible – when the Jews are faithful and observe the *mitzvot*, they are blessed; when they sin, they are punished. And if they do not repent, exile – the harshest of all punishments – befalls them. Multiple verses warn about this. For example: "You will soon perish from the good land that the Lord is assigning to you" (Deuteronomy 11:17); "You shall perish among the nations, and the land of your enemies shall consume you" (Leviticus 26:38); and "The Lord uprooted them from their soil in anger, fury, and great wrath, and cast them into another land, as is still the case" (Deuteronomy 29:27).

On the other hand, part of God's covenant with His people is His promise that He will never abandon them, even during their suffering in exile. Rather, the Divine Presence discreetly dwells among them; He watches over them and ensures they are not destroyed (Leviticus 26:44). Ultimately, each exile ends. God redeems the Jews and returns them to their Land, as it says, "Then the Lord your God will restore your fortunes and take you back in love. He will bring you together again from all the peoples where the Lord your God has scattered you. Even if your outcasts are at the ends of the world, from there the Lord your God will gather you, from there He will fetch you. And the Lord your God will bring you to the land that your fathers possessed, and you shall possess it; and He will make you more prosperous and more numerous than your fathers" (Deuteronomy 30:3-5).

At that point, it becomes clear the exile too has served a purpose. Being forced to deal with the challenges of exile and of exposure to different cultures has made it possible for us to clarify the Torah's spiritual and moral ideas. This helps us merit a return to the Land, which gives us the opportunity to put these values into practice as they are meant to be.

2. Expressing Monotheism in the Land

The Land of Israel is the place designated for the Jewish people to express monotheism. As we explained above (15:1), monotheism includes the idea that everything has a divine spark, so holiness is present in all areas of human endeavor. In the Land of Israel, this holiness can be accessed through the study of Torah and secular disciplines, and through working and participating in the economy. It can be found within the individual, the community, and the State.

In the diaspora, by contrast, Jews can only realize holiness in the abstract, and only within the limited context of their communities. Such sanctity is disconnected from the natural world and absent from communal and national life. In fact, the contributions diaspora Jews make in advancing knowledge and the economy are used by foreign nations in service of their own goals. Such contributions may even help these nations do terrible things. For example, Jews in Germany helped develop its economy, science, and society. In retrospect, the Jews indirectly paved the way for the Germans to initiate World War II and the Holocaust. Centuries earlier, Jews had a similar experience in medieval Christian Spain. There too, the Jews helped the country flourish, after which it turned against them through the Inquisition. In 20th century Russia, events followed a similar trajectory. Jews were central activists in the Russian Revolution, demanding justice, equality, and social welfare. Ultimately though, Russia became a totalitarian country infamous for its terrifying cruelty. While these are among the most blatant historical examples, to a lesser degree they are reflected in every exile.

To reiterate, truth and goodness are found only in the

abstract in the diaspora, pragmatically they are not feasible in the everyday plane or on the national level. This situation leaves the world in a state of disrepair and constitutes a terrible desecration of God's name. It deeply harms faith because it creates the impression that the word of God is relevant only in theory, while the real world can function satisfactorily (and possibly better) without it. This is why the Sages say that a Jew who lives in the diaspora is comparable to someone who worships idols. For neither person is practicing monotheism properly.

In contrast, monotheism can be expressed in the Land of Israel in ways both heavenly and earthly. It can be applied to a nation that includes a wide variety of people. Despite all the sins, difficulties, and complicated situations, the people can unite to reveal faith and divine values in all spheres of life. Such unity can serve as an inspiration to all nations to increase devotion, truth, and righteousness throughout the world. This is how it was in First and Second Temple times. With the help of God, it will happen again in the State of Israel when the Third Temple is rebuilt, may it be speedily and in our times.

3. The Uniqueness of the Land of Israel: Uniting Heaven and Earth

Many countries have natural water sources that allow them to easily cultivate crops and provide them with valuable produce. However, the agriculture of the Land of Israel is dependent upon rain: "But the land you are about to cross into . . . soaks up its water from the rains of heaven" (Deuteronomy 11:10-11). Therefore, in the natural course of events, the Land produces abundant quantities of fine fruits during rainy years but experiences famine during years of drought. As a result of the threat of drought, the Land's inhabitants face two challenges. The first is the spiritual (heavenly) challenge of having faith. Scarcity should inspire Jews to strengthen their faith, morals, and *mitzva* observance so they can merit God's compassion and blessed rain. The second is the mundane (earthly) challenge of taking responsibility. Drought should inspire the Jews to take up the challenge of finding long term solutions to food and rainwater storage, and to develop smart agriculture that uses a minimum of water.

Living up to this dual challenge is an example of what monotheism is about. It unites heaven and earth. It combines faith and action. A fundamental part of our belief is the idea that humanity, created in the image of God, is responsible for improving the world in all ways – agriculturally, economically, and socially. Therefore, in times of drought, we must respond on multiple levels. We are called upon to introspect, repent, and take responsibility for improving our commitment to Torah and *mitzvot* (those relating to God and those relating to people). And we are equally expected to comprehensively improve agriculture, the economy, and society.

God created the Land of Israel for these purposes. It is called the Holy Land because it is both heavenly ("holy") and earthly ("land"). It is designed for faith and divine values to be expressed within every sphere of life. It is there that faith and morality can be united with the will to become rich and enjoy all the pleasures of this world. If we follow the Torah's directives, everything in the Land is blessed. Heaven is no stranger to earth, nor is earth detaching itself from heaven. Rather, they enjoy an exceptional symbiotic relationship, which spreads blessing throughout the world.

4. Torah in the Land

The Torah can only be fully revealed in the Land of Israel, as it says, "For Torah shall come forth from Zion, the word of the Lord from Jerusalem" (Isaiah 2:3). This is why the Sanhedrin was located in the Land of Israel, right next to the Temple. This High Court had the authority to rule on any disagreements, pass enactments binding upon the entire Jewish people, and sanctify the months and institute leap years (thus determining the dates of the Jewish holidays). Furthermore, when prophecy existed, it was always connected to the Land of Israel: prophecy could take place only if the prophet was in the Land, or had begun to prophesy in the Land, or had prophesied about the Land.

5. The Primary Location for *Mitzva* Observance

God chose the Jewish people so they would observe the *mitzvot* in the Land. This idea applies not only to the *mitzvot* directly dependent upon the Land (see next section), but to all the *mitzvot*. As it says, "For you are about to cross the Jordan to enter and possess the land that the Lord your God is assigning to you. When you have occupied it and are settled in it, take care to observe all the laws and rules... These are the laws and rules that you must carefully observe in the land that the Lord, God of your fathers, is giving you to possess, as long as you live on earth" (Deuteronomy 11:31-12:1).

At first glance, it would seem there is no value to learning Torah and keeping *mitzvot* in the diaspora, where the Divine Presence does not dwell. Nevertheless, we are obligated to observe the *mitzvot* even in exile. For the covenant God made with His people includes the provision that He does not desert them even when they are suffering and persecuted in exile (Leviticus 26:44). Rather, the Divine Presence dwells discreetly among them. God also ascribes value to the Torah that people study and the *mitzvot* they perform in exile. First, this observance helps them survive and prevents assimilation. Second, it ensures they do not forget how to perform the *mitzvot*, and thus will be able to observe them properly upon their return to the Land.

6. *Mitzvot* Dependent Upon the Land

The *mitzvot* dependent upon the Land are first and foremost *mitzvot* that are national in scope: the *mitzva* to establish Jewish sovereignty in the Land and to settle it; the *mitzva* to form an army to defend the nation and the Land, and the *mitzva* to establish a government which can improve society and the economy. Other national *mitzvot* are the *mitzva* to build the Temple and the many *mitzvot* connected to Temple ritual, such as the *mitzvot* pertaining to the priests and Levites, the cities of refuge, the laws of purity and impurity, and many others.

Another *mitzva* of national importance is to establish a complete system of justice in the Land of Israel, including a High Court of seventy-one sages, courts of twenty-three, and courts of three in every city and neighborhood. A police force to enforce the law is an intrinsic part of the justice system. Only the High Court located in the Land is authorized to sanctify the months and intercalate the years, thus establishing the dates of the Jewish holidays. Additionally, only ordained judges have the authority to judge cases in all areas of Jewish law, and this ordination can take place only in the Land of Israel. Nevertheless, even in exile there is a *mitzva* to establish a basic judicial system, to the extent necessary to keep the Jewish community functioning.

7. Tithes

One of the *mitzvot* that applies only in the Land is tithing produce. In the past, the Torah obligated field owners to give about two percent (*teruma*) of their produce to the priests and ten percent (*ma'aser*) to the Levites, to enable them to study Torah and serve the community in the positions of educators, advisors, and halakhic adjudicators. An additional tithe was given to the poor during the third and sixth years of each seven-year cycle. During the other years, the "second tithe" was for the owners to bring to Jerusalem and eat in purity. This connected the whole nation to the Temple. However, when the majority of the Jews are not living in the Land, these *mitzvot* have only rabbinic force. Additionally, since the destruction of the Temple, priests can no longer eat *teruma* with the required sanctity. Accordingly, today tithing is a rabbinic obligation which serves to remind us of the original *mitzva*. (For more details about tithing, see 6:12-14 above and 24:4-5 below.)

8. The Sabbatical and the Jubilee

Another currently rabbinic *mitzva* is to have the land lie fallow every seventh year. Originally, the Torah promised that those who observe this law would be blessed during the preceding years, which would allow them to comfortably make it through the seventh year (*shmita*). In addition to this heavenly blessing, observing the sabbatical year also encouraged Jews to set aside grain, oil, and wine during the first six years to carry them through the seventh year. This was a useful lesson in deferring gratification and saving, not only to survive but to invest. Letting the land lie fallow had other benefits as well. During the sabbatical year, the farmers were freed up to study Torah and spend time with their family. They could recharge their spiritual energy and plan to improve and upgrade during the next six years. (See 6:17 above for the sabbatical year's debt relief, which applied even outside the Land.)

After seven cycles of *shmita*, the Torah commanded making the fiftieth year a Jubilee (*yovel*), when all land was not only left fallow but also returned to its original owners (5:3 above).

The *mitzvot* of *shmita* and *yovel* have biblical force only when the Jewish people are living in the Land according to their tribal allotments. When this is the case, everyone is on sabbatical at the same time, and they can help each other out. They do not need to compete with non-Jews in the Land who continue working. However, when the majority of the Jews are not living in the Land of Israel, as is currently the situation, the sabbatical year is only rabbinic (and the Jubilee is not observed at all). Therefore, today's rabbis have the power to circumvent the obligation of leaving the land fallow, when working the land is necessary to allow the Israeli agricultural sector to survive. The Chief Rabbis accomplish this by temporarily selling the land to a non-Jew. This is called the *heter mekhira* (permission through selling).

9. When These *Mitzvot* Apply

Let us summarize the history of the *mitzvot* whose status depends upon Jewish presence in the Land of Israel. After forty years in the desert, the Jews fulfilled the *mitzva* of conquering the Land. Once they divided the Land among the twelve tribes in 2503 (1258 BCE), they became obligated in all the agricultural *mitzvot*, including tithing, the sabbatical year, and the Jubilee.

However, it took many years for the Jews to complete the conquest and settle in the Land. In the interim, there was no Temple and no judicial system. Instead, the Tabernacle was in Shiloh, and various judges led the people for short periods of time. After about four hundred years of this, Samuel the Prophet became the judge. As a result of his activities, the judicial system was established, and the Jews began to fulfill the *mitzva* of establishing a government. Not long afterwards, the Davidic dynasty was inaugurated. David's son King Solomon fulfilled the *mitzva* to build the Temple in 2929 (832 BCE).

The First Temple stood for 410 years before the Babylonians destroyed it. As a result of the destruction of the First Temple and the exile of the Jewish people, the *mitzvot* of tithes, the sabbatical year, and the Jubilee could no longer be observed.

After seventy years of exile in Babylonia, the Jews began the process of returning to the Land and building the Second Temple. They established the Great Assembly, a high court of 120 Sages, with Ezra the Scribe at its head. The Men of the Great Assembly established the texts of blessings and prayer services, reestablished the justice system, and reinstituted the obligations of tithing, the sabbatical year, and *ḥalla* (24:6 below). However, since most of the Jews remained in exile, these *mitzvot* were only rabbinically binding, as is still the case today.

10. How Many Jews Are There?

Tithing will once again become a biblical obligation when the majority of Jews live in the Land of Israel. The sabbatical year and the Jubilee will be biblically mandated when the Land is redivided among the tribes. This raises the question of how we should count the Jews today to determine where the majority are living.

Some say the count should be based upon the number of people who identify as Jewish. This would make it approximately fifteen million today. However, it seems more reasonable to include those whose parents assimilated in the last few generations due to persecutions, revolutions, or the Holocaust. As long as documents or other evidence can prove that someone is matrilineally Jewish, it would seem they should be considered Jewish even if they do not identify as such. (As we said above in 10:4, Jewishness in *halakha* is determined by the mother's status.) If we do include them, we can estimate the number of Jews today to be between twenty and thirty million.

Perhaps we should even count descendants of Jews who assimilated hundreds of years ago due to the terrible hardship of exile, as long as they are descended from a direct line of Jewish mothers. The Sages, basing themselves on biblical prophecies about the future redemption, tell us that Elijah the Prophet will return lost Jews to the fold. Today, this group includes at least a hundred million people, maybe more, since millions of Jews were forced to stop practicing Judaism in the course of the long exile, with all the wars, persecutions, and anti-religious decrees. Furthermore, since Jewish law does not recognize conversions to other religions, forcibly converted Jews are still Jewish. It is reasonable to assume the number of those matrilineally descended from forced converts grew at the same rate as the non-Jews surrounding them. Based on this, some estimate that today, at least ten percent of Western Europeans, and ten percent of North and South Americans of Western European descent, should be considered Jewish. There are also matrilineally descended Jews in North Africa, Western Africa, and Eastern Europe. If this is the case, it could be a long time before the majority of the Jews are in the Land.

Ultimately though, the question of who is a Jew can be decided only by the High Court. Its members will include scholars who are experts in the social sciences as well as in Torah. They, together with community representatives, will determine how many Jews there are. They will also rule on how to redivide the Land among the various tribes.

11. The *Mitzva* of Settling the Land

We have seen that monotheism, Torah, and *mitzvot* are best put into practice when the Jewish people are living in the Land of Israel. Hence the great value assigned to the *mitzva* of settling the Land. The Sages go so far as to tell us that living in the Land is the equivalent of keeping all the *mitzvot* of the

Torah. Included in this *mitzva* is Jewish settlement and Jewish sovereignty. The Land may not be left desolate or in the hands of another nation. As it says, "And you shall take possession of the land and settle in it, for I have assigned the land to you to possess. You shall divide up the land..." (Numbers 33:53-54).

Since the Land is holy and there is a *mitzva* to settle it, anyone who contributes to Israel's development and advancement is fulfilling the *mitzva* of settling the Land. This includes all those involved in improving agriculture, building homes, paving roads, developing industry and business, doing academic research, beautifying the cities, cleaning the streets, and cultivating the gardens. It also includes those involved in Israel's educational system, the justice system, the welfare system, the healthcare system, and the arts. All are important participants in the *mitzva* of settling the Land. This *mitzva* is unique in imbuing all aspects of human life with value and elevating them to *mitzva* status.

12. Fighting for the Land

The Israelites were commanded to conquer the Land in order to settle it. This is even though people are usually exempt from performing a *mitzva* which would endanger themselves. Fighting for the Land is an exception to the rule because there is no war without danger and without casualties. Indeed, the Jews fought to conquer the Land in the time of Joshua. Later, in the time of Ezra, they were willing to sacrifice to settle the Land despite suffering enemy harassment. Later still, the Hasmoneans fought to the best of their ability to gain sovereignty.

If a nation is not prepared to make sacrifices to defend its land – such as endangering its youth by sending them to fight – sooner or later it will be wiped out and many of its young people will be killed in any case. In this light, the *mitzva* to fight and sacrifice for the Land is consistent with the supreme value of saving lives.

13. Returning to the Land

During the long exile, anyone who wished to immigrate to the Land of Israel faced immense difficulties. This prevented the Jewish people from moving en masse and establishing communities. Consequently, it was certainly not relevant to form an army to protect the Jewish residents and free the Land from foreign rule.

In modern times though, God has begun to fulfill His biblical promises. Divine providence, working through historical processes, has inspired a broad spectrum of Jews from all parts of society to act for the Land and redeem the nation. In the late 1800s, with genuine self-sacrifice, Jews began immigrating to the Land and settling it. They established the Zionist movement and began setting up Jewish settlements, communal institutions, and armed forces. Finally on the fifth of Iyar, 5708 (May 14, 1948), the State of Israel was declared. After two thousand years of exile, the Jewish people regained self-rule over parts of the Land of Israel and fulfilled the *mitzva* of settling the Land. Once there was an independent Jewish State, mass Jewish immigration began, and moves were made to settle all parts of the Land.

Even before the establishment of the State, any Jew living in the Land was fulfilling the *mitzva* to settle it on the individual level. Nevertheless, such a Jew could not fulfill the primary *mitzva*, namely for the Land to be under Jewish rule. Even when many Jews lived in the Land, the fundamental collective *mitzva* could not be fulfilled because it was under foreign rule. (See section 15 below.)

14. The Modern Version of the Sin of the Spies

About 120 years ago, when the Zionist movement was founded, there were approximately eleven million Jews in the world. (Actually, Religious Zionism had gotten off the ground fifty years earlier, through the work of Rabbi Zvi Hirsch Kalischer and Rabbi Judah Alkalai.) Over five million Arabs lived within the boundaries of the biblical Land of Israel (including parts of today's Lebanon, Syria, and Iraq), and another half-million lived on both sides of the River Jordan. The early part of the 20th century was an opportunity for the Jewish people to return and populate the Land. (This was called the Second Aliyah.)

However, the majority of Jews were afraid to uproot themselves and move to Israel, to fulfill our destiny as the Torah requires. Admittedly, immigrating to Israel then involved great hardship, so asking people to do so was a true test of religious commitment. Nevertheless, the failure to fulfill the *mitzva* of settling the Land when it was possible to do so can be described as the modern version of the sin of the spies. And just as the consequences were dire for the original version of the sin (section 1 above), we have paid a terrible price for the modern version of the sin. We have suffered the Holocaust, communist suppression, and assimilation.

Currently, about fifteen million Jews identify as such, with seven million of them in the Land of Israel. In contrast, the Arabs who surround the Land of Israel have reaped the benefits of the Industrial Revolution and advances in food production and medicine, and they now number over eighty million.[4] These numbers clearly show the severity of the sin of the spies – the sin of being afraid to move to Israel, conquer

---

4   If we include all the Arabs who lived in Egypt and the Maghreb (northwest Africa) 120 years ago, there were approximately twenty-two million, only double the Jewish population. Today they number approximately 270 million.

it, and settle it. As a result of the first sin, the generation that left Egypt had to die in the desert. Furthermore, God warned the Jews that if they didn't rectify the sin, it would lead to the Destruction of both Temples, for which we mourn on Tisha Be-Av (37:4 below). As a result of the second sin, most of the Jews who stayed in exile assimilated, were oppressed and even murdered.

How fortunate were the Jews who did choose to immigrate and settle the Land. Thanks to their efforts, the Jewish people succeeded in rebuilding after all these catastrophes. Imagine what the Jewish world would look like now if millions of Jews had immigrated to Israel before the Holocaust. We would number fifty million, and scholars of general and Torah studies would be dedicating themselves to perfecting the world under God's sovereignty. It is not too late. We can still correct the problem. In the words of the Bible (Jeremiah 31:5-6): "Come, let us go up to Zion, to the Lord our God! For thus said the Lord: Cry out in joy for Jacob, shout at the crossroads of the nations! Sing aloud in praise, and say: Save, O Lord, Your people, the remnant of Israel!"

15. The *Mitzva* of Living in the Land

Let us further clarify the *mitzva* of settling the Land, which is critical to our national existence, and which allows us to actualize our mission as a people. First and foremost, this is a communal *mitzva* which requires the Land to be under Jewish rule and the home of the majority of the Jewish people. Additionally, there is an individual *mitzva* incumbent upon every Jew to live in Israel. The Sages tell us, "One should always live in the Land of Israel, even in a city that is mostly non-Jewish; one should not live outside the Land, even in a city that is mostly Jewish" (*Ketubot* 110b).

A number of laws give concrete expression to the value of

this *mitzva*. First, if a married couple disagree about whether to move to Israel, the one who does not want to go must concede. If that spouse refuses, it is considered grounds for divorce. Not only that, if the husband refuses to go, he must pay his wife the *ketuba* money; if the wife refuses to go, she forfeits the *ketuba* money.

Second, children who want to immigrate to Israel do not have to obey if their parents ask them to remain in the diaspora. (If the parents need full-time help, the children may consider remaining with them for a few years to provide the care.)

Third, it is also prohibited to leave the Land of Israel and move abroad. If it is necessary to do so to study Torah, get married, or earn a living, it is permitted, but only for a short time. Some maintain it is forbidden to leave Israel even for a short trip. Others, myself included, say this is permissible.

16. Loving the Land

It is appropriate to praise and love the Land of Israel, following the example of the Torah, which calls it "the land of milk and honey" fifteen times. The verses elaborate: "For the Lord your God is bringing you into a good land, a land with streams and springs and fountains issuing from plain and hill; a land of wheat and barley, of vines, figs, and pomegranates, a land of olive trees and honey; a land where food will not be scarce, and you will lack nothing; a land whose rocks are iron, and from whose hills you can mine copper. When you have eaten your fill, give thanks to the Lord your God for the good land which He has given you" (Deuteronomy 8:7-10).

The Talmud tells us about Sages who left Babylonia for the Land of Israel. Upon reaching the boundaries of Israel, they kissed its stones and rolled in its dirt. This was an expression of their great love of the Land and a fulfillment of the verse, "Your servants take delight in its stones and cherish its dust"

(Psalms 102:15). Throughout history, kissing the ground was common among new immigrants to Israel. The love and longing for the Land were also reflected in the poems and songs that Jews in the diaspora wrote, expressing yearning for the Land. We will cite here just a few lines from two of the many poems of longing written by Rabbi Yehuda Halevi, who lived in medieval Spain:

> *O Zion, won't you ask how your captives are – the exiles who seek your welfare, who are the remnant of your flocks?... When I dream of your exiles' return, I am a lute for your songs... If only I could roam through those places where God was revealed to your prophets and heralds! Who will give me wings, so that I may wander far away? I would carry the pieces of my broken heart over your rugged mountains. I would bow down, my face on your ground; I would love your stones; your dust would move me to pity ("Ode to Zion," translated by T. Carmi).*

> *For you my soul is longing from limits of the west... O that I might fly on eagles' wings, that I might water your dust with my tears until they mingle together. Shall I not be tender to your stones and kiss them, and the taste of your soil be sweeter than honey to me? ("Beautiful of Elevation," translated by Nina Salaman).*

17. The Israeli Army

People who serve in the Israel Defense Forces are fulfilling two tremendous *mitzvot*, each of which is the equivalent of all the other *mitzvot* put together. The first *mitzva* is saving the Jews from their enemies. Since a person who saves one life is considered to have saved an entire world, imagine what an accomplishment it is to help save the entire Jewish people! The second *mitzva* is settling the Land. Without an army to defend the Land, it would be impossible to retain Jewish sovereignty. These two *mitzvot* are the values which motivated King David's soldiers as they prepared for war: "Let us be strong and resolute for the sake of our people and the land of our God" (II Samuel 10:12).

One who serves in the Israeli army, is expressing the part of oneself which is holy by virtue of being part of a holy nation. Most of the time we fulfill mitzvot as individuals. However, an individual who serves in the army takes on the elevated status of the nation, in which the Divine Presence dwells. Soldiers are fulfilling their army *mitzvot* as soon as they are drafted and start training. This is because the fact that we have a well-trained army serves as a deterrent in itself. Our enemies are afraid of us because they know we have a strong army. Therefore, even a soldier killed during training exercises is considered to have fallen in the service of God, the nation, and the Land.

Relying on an army is not an indication of a lack of faith in God. On the contrary, it involves using human strength (the physical) in the service of revealing God's word (the spiritual). This is what our great leaders did. Joshua and King David fought bravely to settle the Jews securely in their Land. In other words, it is ideal for the Jewish nation to fulfill the *mitzva* of settling God's Land by using the human abilities God gave us as a gift. Then, if it is necessary to fight, we can vanquish our enemies without relying on a miracle.

This physical-spiritual combination enables the world to move in the right direction. Eventually, the non-Jews will recognize the Jews' rights to their Land. The nations will coexist, with each one being assigned its most appropriate location. The prophecy of Isaiah will be fulfilled:

In the days to come, the Mount of the Lord's house shall stand firm above the mountains and tower above the hills; and all the nations shall gaze on it with joy. And the many peoples shall go and say: "Come, let us go up to the Mount of the Lord, to the House of the God of Jacob; that He may instruct us in His ways, and that we may walk in His paths." For Torah shall come forth from Zion, the word of the Lord from Jerusalem. Thus He will judge among the nations and arbitrate for the many peoples, and they shall beat their swords into plowshares and their spears into pruning hooks. Nation shall not take up sword against nation; they shall never again know war (Isaiah 2:2-4).

18. War and Fear

The moment soldiers enter a war, there is a *mitzva* to strengthen their faith and rely upon the Lord, God of Israel. They should be aware they are fighting to save God's people, the Jews. When they enter a battle, they should not be afraid at all, but confident God will help him emerge victorious. The soul of a Jewish soldier killed in war is bound in the bond of eternal life, in heaven, together with the most righteous people.

In biblical times, to encourage the soldiers, the priests and Levites went to war with them, carrying an ark containing a Torah scroll. There was also a *mitzva* for the priest to blow silver trumpets to strengthen faith. There was even a specially anointed priest who would give the soldiers a motivational talk: "Hear, O Israel! You are about to join battle with your enemy. Let not your courage falter. Do not be in fear, panic, or dread of them. For it is the Lord your God who marches with you to do battle for you against your enemy, to bring you victory" (Deuteronomy 20:3-4). At the same time, the police (who were generally Levites) were instructed to exempt certain people from the army if there were extenuating circumstances, and to punish deserters if there were not. Nowadays, the military's rabbinate, adjutancy, and police carry out these functions in the Israeli army.

19. Drafting Yeshiva Students

The *mitzva* to study Torah does not override the *mitzva* to serve in the army, so it is a *mitzva* for yeshiva students to enlist. Indeed, there is a tradition of this happening in the times of Joshua and King David.

However, there may be a few particularly talented individuals who have the potential to truly serve the nation through their exceptional Torah study. Such individuals should defer their service, as long as the army does not need to draft them, while greatly honoring soldiers who put their lives on the line to fulfill the *mitzva* of defending the people and the Land. They must study prodigiously to prepare themselves to serve the community as teachers and rabbis. In this way, they will contribute directly to the state's religious life, and indirectly to its security and development.

20. Maintaining Holiness in the Army

"Sanctity of the camp" is a special *mitzva* for soldiers to maintain their moral standards during their service. As it says, "When you go out as a troop against your enemies, be on your guard against anything untoward. . . Since the Lord your God moves about in your camp to protect you and to deliver your enemies to you, let your camp be holy; let Him not find anything unseemly among you and turn away from you" (Deuteronomy 23:10-15).

This *mitzva* includes avoiding gossip and anything else that might damage morale. It also includes maintaining standards of modesty (described above in 10:5-7). It is common knowledge that soldiers, under psychological pressure, often seek relief through cursing, speaking vulgarly, and acting crudely. To combat these tendencies, the Torah commands soldiers not to relax their moral standards. By preserving the holiness of the camp, they will accrue merit which will help them succeed in wartime and bring blessing in peacetime. It should be noted that maintaining modesty is not only an excuse given by the Ĥaredim for not serving in the army but also the primary challenge faced by halakhically observant soldiers during their service.

21. Women Serving

Women are also commanded to save lives and settle the Land. Nevertheless, according to Jewish tradition, women do not serve in the army. There are two explanations for this. First, the Sages tell us it is not the way of women to fight and conquer. Even at times of war, the nation needs to strike a balance. While the men are needed to risk their lives on the front lines, the women are needed to keep things as normal as possible on the home front. Second, the fraternizing of men and women in the army poses a threat to standards of modesty, as well as a dangerous distraction for the soldiers. As we mentioned in the previous section, the holiness of the camp demands a higher standard of modesty.

Although some maintain that women should enlist, serve in auxiliary roles, and even go into combat in cases of emergency, this is a minority opinion among Orthodox rabbis. Ĥaredi rabbis feel it is a serious transgression for women to serve. Most Religious Zionist rabbis feel that while there is no intrinsic prohibition, it is preferable for women not to serve, because of the modesty issues mentioned above. Additionally, experience shows that serving in the army leads some women to become less religious. Thus, the negatives outweigh the positives. Nevertheless, a religious woman soldier who contributes to the security of the State while sanctifying the name of God is fulfilling a *mitzva*.

22. The Ethics of War

The Torah commands the army to act as morally as possible, even during wartime. Therefore, before going to war with even our worst enemy – Amalek – there is a *mitzva* to first offer peace. As it says, "When you approach a town to attack it, you shall offer it terms of peace" (Deuteronomy 20:10). This means offering the enemy dignified terms of surrender, in which they have an autonomous state under Jewish rule, paying taxes and observing the seven Noahide laws. We only go to war if they reject peace.

Our objective in war is to achieve a resounding victory which will quash any further enemy desires to engage in battle. Therefore in biblical times, when the norms of war were (at the least) to kill all the enemy's men, the Jews were commanded to do this too, as it says, "When the Lord your God delivers it into your hand, you shall put all its males to the sword" (Deuteronomy 20:13). For had they not done so, there would definitely be additional fighting, and perhaps a Jewish defeat. In addition, had the Jews not followed the standard practice, the surrounding nations would have concluded that if they wanted to go to war against someone, the Jews were the best target. Winning against the Jews would be the worthwhile, but losing would have no major consequences.

Thus, Jewish war ethics demand two things. First, offer peace. Second, after victory, do not harm the enemy except as necessary and in accordance with the accepted norms. In biblical times, it was known that Jewish kings were kind. Some accommodated their enemies too much and ultimately succumbed to them (I Kings, ch. 20). Others, such as King David, followed the Torah's guidance to strike a balance between might and mercy. Such kings led the Jews to many glorious victories and a long period of peace.

Today as well, the army should strive for resounding victory and the total submission of our enemies, while being careful not to go beyond what is necessary and accepted. Thank God, due to the influence of the Bible, great rabbis, and righteous gentiles, the world has advanced morally. It is now generally agreed upon that soldiers are not to be killed outside of battle, and civilians are not to be harmed unless they are protecting an enemy. At the same time, victory must be overwhelming, so it will serve as a long-term deterrent to our enemies, and so there will be a degree of measure-for-measure punishment. We simply do to them what they tried to do to us. In an extreme case, when there is a group of truly evil people who dedicate their lives to terror and destruction, we should fight them to the death, as the Torah instructs regarding Amalek (39:3 below).

23. The Boundaries of the Land

Theoretically, the *mitzva* to settle the Land applies to a vast area, within the boundaries God promised to Abraham. As it says, "On that day the Lord made a covenant with Abram, saying, 'To your offspring I assign this land, from the river of Egypt [the Nile] to the great river, the river Euphrates'" (Genesis 15:18; see also Exodus 23:31 and Deuteronomy 1:7-8). However, in practice, the *mitzva* needs to be applied gradually, based on what the Jewish people is able to do. This is why God's instructions were to begin by conquering the land to the west of the Jordan River (the land with the most sanctity), and only afterwards to broaden out gradually to the east of the Jordan and the rest of the promised area. It was only because Kings Sihon and Og refused the Israelites' offer of peace, and instead waged war against them, that their land to the east of the Jordan was conquered. There are degrees of sanctity within the Land to the west: Judea and Samaria are the holiest, as this was where the patriarchs and matriarchs walked and prophesied. This was also the location of the Tabernacle (in Shiloh) and the Temple (in Jerusalem).

24. Non-Jews in the Land

Our vision of the future is for the Land to be settled by the Jewish people, for the Temple to stand on the Temple Mount in Jerusalem, and for all national institutions to be run in holy and moral ways, in accordance with the Torah's guidance. The Jews will then serve as a light to the nations. All this is in the prophecy of Isaiah we cited above (section 17).

To realize this vision, the entire Land must be populated by Jews, and non-Jews who have the status of *ger toshav*. A *ger toshav* is someone who accepts Jewish sovereignty over the Land, recognizes the Jews' special mission, and observes the seven Noahide laws. These laws reflect natural law (2:4 above). The prohibition of allowing non-Noahides to remain in the Land is mentioned many times in the Torah. For example: "They shall not remain in your land, lest they cause you to sin against Me: for you will serve their gods – and it will prove a snare to you" (Exodus 23:33); "Make no covenant with them and show no favor to them" (Deuteronomy 7:2); and "If you do not dispossess the inhabitants of the land, those whom you allow to remain shall be stings in your eyes and thorns in your sides, and they shall harass you in the land in which you live" (Numbers 33:55). In the context of war with non-Noahides, the enemy is to be expelled from the Land. In the context of peace, emigration is to be encouraged, with fair payment to be made for property and belongings left behind.

About eighty years ago, at the end of World War II, and

with the approval of the world powers, there were mass population transfers of tens of millions of people in Europe and elsewhere to avoid internecine fighting. Nowadays though, the international community no longer accepts this solution, and the State of Israel's economic and security situation does not allow it to ignore this position. Furthermore, thanks to the Torah's moral influence, the nations of the world have recently undertaken to protect minority rights, and we should agree this is a step in the right direction. Accordingly, the expulsion of non-Noahides is no longer practical.

Nevertheless, the Torah's vision of the future remains in place. Therefore, within the accepted moral framework of the times, Israel should attempt to develop a socio-economic policy that encourages emigration on the part of non-Jews who do not identify with Jewish values. One possibility would be requiring everyone to enlist in the army, and penalizing those who refuse to serve on nationalistic grounds. It is also possible that the next time Jewish-Arab tension leads to crisis or war, Israel will be able to take advantage of the opportunity to expel hostile non-Jews from our Land, as was necessary during the War of Independence.

In the meantime, it is not practical to expel non-Noahides. Besides, we do not know who among the non-Jewish residents are enemies, and who are loyal to the State (and could have the status of a *ger toshav*). Accordingly, our default is to follow the basic value of respecting all people. Perhaps this situation is divinely orchestrated so many of the non-Jews who live in the Land will eventually recognize the good in the Jewish return to Zion and the fulfillment of the prophecies. Instead of hating us, they will become trusted partners in the vision of the redemption of the Jews and the repair of the world.

25. Monarchy and Democracy

The Torah imposes many rules and restrictions upon a Jewish king. He may not have too many wives, nor accumulate horses, silver, or gold (beyond what is needed). He is required to write a Torah scroll for himself and take it with him when he travels. This is to ensure he remembers his monarchy is subject to the laws of the Torah and he must act in accordance with them. It is also to make sure he does not become too arrogant. Rather, he is expected to treat his subjects respectfully, and always keep in mind that it's the king's job to serve the nation.

Nevertheless, there is no explicit commandment to crown a king. This teaches us the primary *mitzva* is to have some system of government, based on what is best for the nation in a given time period. This system may be a monarchy or a democracy. The key is for the government to be subordinate to the Torah's laws and morals, and for it to take care of the people and help them realize their vision. For without proper leadership, with the authority and ability to enforce laws, an effective justice system cannot be established, an army cannot be maintained, and the Temple cannot be built to help realize our holy vision.

26. Governmental Authority

A basic principle in *halakha* states, "The law of the land is the law," which means it is binding. Anywhere in the world that Jews live, the government has the authority to make laws, pass ordinances, and levy taxes, and all the country's citizens must comply. This is because everyone understands the government has the authority to rule to protect people's lives and property. Lacking this, the world would descend into chaos. Thus the Sages tell us, "Pray for the welfare of the government. For if not for fear of it, people would eat each other alive" (*Ethics of the Fathers* 3:2).

However, the obligation to pay taxes and be law-abiding citizens assumes the government is one of law. Conversely, if a king or other leader issues decrees contrary to reason and morality as generally understood, the laws have no validity. Nevertheless, this exception is only where there is glaring injustice that can be traced to the very heart of the government. The commonplace corruption and occasional discrimination that plague almost every ruling body do not negate the principle that "The law of the land is the law."

Since a country's laws are binding, those who cheat on their taxes are transgressing the Torah's prohibition on stealing, as they are stealing from the community. This applies even in the case of a dictatorship, and it certainly applies in the case of a democratic government, which rules with broad-based public support. It also applies even in the case of a non-Jewish government, and it certainly applies in the case of a Jewish government, whose sovereignty allows us to fulfill the *mitzva* of settling the Land. Therefore, paying taxes in Israel should be looked at as an obligation we are pleased to fulfill. It allows us to be partners in helping the Jewish people lead a full life in their Land.

There is one more caveat though, pertaining to the obligation to keep the laws of the country. If a law obligates a Jew to transgress the Torah, such as to desecrate the Sabbath, it is not binding. This is what Joshua was told when he took up his role as leader – his orders would be binding as long as they did not contradict the Torah.

27. Separation of Powers

The idea of separation of powers is found in the Bible, which describes four authorities that balance one another. The first authority was the monarchy, in charge of governmental activity. The second was the justice system, which included courts in every neighborhood and city. The highest of them all, the

Great Sanhedrin, was located in Jerusalem near the Temple, and its sages were even empowered to judge a king and to confirm the appointment of a new king. The third authority was the priesthood, headed by the High Priest. The priests' job was to serve in the Temple, and – together with the Levites – to teach Torah and decide halakhic matters throughout the Land. The fourth authority was prophecy, in which God sent messages through prophets to elevate, guide, and rebuke the nation. Sometimes the prophets rebuked the king, the judges, or the priests. This last authority was not institutional, as it depended on a divine decision as to who was wise and righteous enough to receive prophecy. God also determined when a prophecy was needed and for what purpose.

These four authorities needed to work together. The king would appoint police officers, both to carry out the decisions of the courts and to protect the Temple. The priests would support the government, and indeed many police officers were priests or Levites. If the king deviated from his responsibility to follow the law of the Torah, he would be criticized by the sages, priests, and prophets. Sometimes this led to a transition of power, whether peaceful or through revolt.

Many western nations, such as the United States and the United Kingdom, were inspired by the Bible when it came to building a state. At the time, the Jews were in exile. Now we have been given the privilege of returning to our Land and establishing the State of Israel. We must examine the different types of government, identify each one's strengths and weaknesses from organizational and moral perspectives, and draw guidance from the Torah. By doing so, we can establish the best system of rule for the State of Israel.

28. The Future Messiah

As we have said, part of our mission is to build up the Land and the national spirit with the guidance of Torah and *mitzvot*.

This brings us closer to full redemption and the fulfillment of biblical prophecies about the Messiah. For example:

> *"A shoot shall grow out of the stump of Jesse, a twig shall spout from his stock. The spirit of the Lord shall alight upon him: a spirit of wisdom and insight, a spirit of counsel and valor, a spirit of devotion and reverence for the Lord... Thus he shall judge the poor with equity and decide with justice for the lowly of the land. He shall strike down a land with the rod of his mouth and slay the wicked with the breath of his lips. Justice shall be the girdle of his loins, and faithfulness the girdle of his waist. The wolf shall dwell with the lamb, the leopard lie down with the kid... In all of My sacred Mount, nothing evil or vile shall be done. For the land shall be filled with devotion to the Lord as water covers the sea"* (Isaiah 11:1-9).

Even though we do not know exactly what will occur, it is clear messianic rule will not harm the morals and values of liberal, democratic rule. Rather, it will elevate them so all moral values will come to harmonious expression. Perhaps this is what the Sages had in mind when they projected that *mitzvot* will be abrogated in the messianic era, i.e., the Jews will choose to keep them without needing to be commanded to do so. In any case, before all the promises of redemption can be fulfilled, there are prerequisites: the ingathering of the exiles, the settling of the Land, and the building of the Temple.

Our vision of the future redemption is not a static one, so that when achieved, we will have nothing to strive for. On the contrary, the repaired and perfected world will be a world of people constantly ascending and progressing to a more meaningful life, with greater understanding and more divine enlightenment. The resulting gratification will be experienced in all areas of life, and will be continuously renewed and endlessly elevated.

CHAPTER 18

Conversion

1. Loving the Convert

Non-Jews who wish to convert to Judaism may do so. This reflects the fundamental Jewish belief that people have the potential to transform themselves (unlike some belief systems, which maintain that people cannot change). Therefore, anyone who wants to join the Jewish people may do so. Following conversion, a convert is fully Jewish, and there is a *mitzva* to treat him or her with even more respect than other Jews. For even a minor slight is likely to be very hurtful. Therefore, the Torah demands that we be very careful about this.

Someone who hurts the feelings of a convert is transgressing three separate prohibitions. First is the prohibition of hurting any Jew. Additionally, two more admonitions pertain to a "stranger," which the Sages understand to mean a convert: "You shall not wrong a stranger or oppress him, for you were strangers in the land of Egypt" (Exodus 22:20), and "When a stranger resides with you in your land, you shall not wrong him . . ." (Leviticus 19:33-34). Similarly, loving a convert is mandated by two positive commandments. Besides the *mitzva* to love every Jew (Leviticus 19:18), there is a specific *mitzva* to love a convert: "You too must befriend the stranger, for you were strangers in the land of Egypt" (Deuteronomy 10:19). Converts deserve to be doubly loved, since they left their people and homeland of their own free will and chose to join the Jewish people.

As a direct result of welcoming converts, the Jews have been blessed. For example, Moses married the convert Zipporah. Later, when her father Jethro wanted to convert, he was happily accepted. As a result, he offered excellent advice, which is recorded in the Torah portion named for him. Boaz married the convert Ruth; as a reward, their great-grandchild was the righteous and heroic founder of the Jewish royal dynasty, King David. Rabbi Akiva too, one of the great Tanna'im, was a descendant of converts.

2. Our Complex Relationship to Conversion Candidates

In practice though, our relationship to potential converts is complicated. On the one hand, converts are beloved and desired if they truly wish to convert to join the Jewish people and be a partner in our grand mission to perfect the world under the sovereignty of God. On the other hand, if their motives are not pure, our Sages tell us that those who convert them will be punished, because they will not be interested in truly integrating into Judaism and this will cause difficulties. Therefore, rabbis who perform conversions are faced with a challenging dilemma. If they accept an insincere convert, they sin, and if they discourage a sincere convert, they also sin. The Sages tell us our forefathers refused to accept Timna as a convert. As a result, she joined Esau's tribe and gave birth to Amalek, archenemy of the Jews.

There are also cases when converts have mixed motives. Because their motivation is not totally pure, their conversion causes trouble in the short term. However, since there is also an element of sincerity in the wish to convert, they ultimately succeed in integrating and becoming a blessing for the Jewish people.

3. A Convert's Sincerity

As we said, a convert should not be accepted if he or she is insincere. This includes those who wish to convert to be eligible for financial benefits, to receive Israeli citizenship, or to marry a Jew. Nevertheless, if an Orthodox rabbinic court made the mistake of converting someone insincere, the conversion is valid since it was done in accordance with Jewish law.

In recent generations, in the wake of turmoil, wars, and spiritual upheavals, religious authority has weakened. Masses of Jews have moved away from tradition, and many have intermarried. As a result, we are now confronted with difficult questions. For example, what is to be done when prospective converts are children or grandchildren of Jews, but their mothers are not Jewish? On the one hand, it would seem that without the family connection, they would not be interested in converting. In other words, the primary motivator for their conversion is not identification with the Jewish people's spiritual mission. On the other hand, since they are of Jewish descent, they already have a deep connection to the Jewish nation, and likely have righteous ancestors, so it seems right to make efforts to return them to their people.

The question also arises as how to treat a Jewish man whose partner is a non-Jewish woman. If she converts, the couple can marry and live together according to Jewish law, but if she does not, their children are likely to assimilate and be lost to us.

In practice, the accepted ruling is as long as such conversion candidates are prepared to accept Torah and *mitzva* observance, we should convert them.

4. The Conversion Process

When a prospective convert approaches a rabbi about conversion, the rabbi is required to challenge the convert: "Why do you want to convert? Don't you know the Jews have always suffered and been persecuted by enemies who want to destroy them? The Holocaust was relatively recent, and there were countless pogroms before it. Even now there are enemies who threaten to wipe us out. All of this, because we are Jews. If you wish to draw closer to God and be a righteous person, you should know that a non-Jew can be a righteous gentile and can even be divinely inspired." When candidates remain adamant that they wish to convert despite all of this, we begin to teach them the basics of faith and Torah.

In the past, when most Jews lived in close-knit communities, prospective converts who were willing to accept Torah and *mitzva* observance would be taught a few *mitzvot* and then would convert and join the local community. After the conversion, they would continue to study and become used to keeping the *mitzvot*. They were not taught all the *mitzvot* before conversion, because even those with the purest of motives might be intimidated and withdraw if they were told about all of the *mitzvot* at once.

Nowadays though, most communities are not as cohesive, and (as we said in the previous section) a convert's primary motivation is often family connection. Under these circumstances, we are afraid if we do not teach converts extensively before conversion, they will not continue studying following the conversion, and will not advance in Torah and *mitzvot*. Therefore, the conversion process today commonly extends for about a year. Prospective converts study and become used to observing the *mitzvot* before converting. This way, when they tell the conversion court they are prepared to keep the *mitzvot*, there is good reason to believe them.

5. The Stages of Conversion

Converts become part of the Jewish people in the same way the Israelites did when they entered into their covenant with God after leaving Egypt: through circumcision, immersion, and acceptance of Torah and *mitzvot*.

Once potential converts have studied the basics of faith and the commandments, they must stand before a court of three rabbis (acting as the representatives of God and the Jewish people) and declare they accept the Torah and *mitzvot* upon themselves, the way the Jewish people did collectively at Mount Sinai. If the convert is male, he must then undergo the ritual of circumcision. Finally, the convert must immerse in a *mikveh*. (Before immersing, the convert again declares acceptance of Torah and *mitzvot*.) Emerging from the *mikveh*, the conversion complete, the individual has joined the Jewish people.

6. Accepting the *Mitzvot*

The essence of conversion is the convert's acceptance of the Jewish people's grand vision –actualized through Torah and *mitzvot* –and the wish to be a part of it. Therefore, if potential converts say they are unwilling to accept a particular *mitzva* as a matter of principle, we do not convert them. If someone converts them anyway, the conversion is invalid. Since the Reform and Conservative movements do not believe all the *mitzvot* must be observed, conversions performed under their auspices are not valid. One practical consequence is that if a man converted through one of these movements, married a Jewish woman and then left her, she may remarry even without obtaining a *get*.

In contrast, when converts fundamentally accept Torah and *mitzvot* upon themselves, their conversion is valid even if they are still unaware of many of the *mitzvot*, because they are prepared to keep everything. Furthermore, even if they are worried during conversion that they may not be able to keep all the *mitzvot* – whether because temptation might be overwhelming, or because they might have to work on the Shabbat in order to make a living – the conversion is valid, since fundamentally they want to observe the *mitzvot*. Of course, if a potential convert has no intention of keeping the *mitzvot* and lies to the court, the conversion is invalid.

The question arises as to the status of someone who wishes to convert with the intention of living a traditional lifestyle of partial observance, rather than an Orthodox lifestyle of complete observance. Many authorities are strict and maintain that such a person should not be converted; only someone who is planning to keep all the *mitzvot* – including Shabbat, the laws of family purity, the laws of kashrut, and the recitation of prayers and blessings – may be converted. (Even according to this opinion, if converts sincerely accepted all the *mitzvot* and a court agreed to convert them, but after the conversion their commitment weakened and they ceased being observant, they are still considered Jewish. Just as a non-observant Jew remains Jewish, so too a convert who converted properly and then stopped being observant remains Jewish.)

Others are more lenient and argue that if converts intend to live a traditional lifestyle, as long as their general approach to Torah and *mitzvot* is positive, they should be accepted. First, they are interested in observing some *mitzvot*, so there is a chance that over the course of time they will begin to observe them all. Second, they do intend to keep many *mitzvot*, which shows they do sincerely want to take part in the Jewish people's mission. Traditional Jews often observe interpersonal *mitzvot*; the laws of *kashrut*, and the rites of circumcision, marriage, burial, and mourning. So even if converts do not intend to observe Shabbat fully, they may be planning to take time off from work, to light Shabbat candles and recite *Kiddush*, and to celebrate the holidays. Converts planning to serve in the IDF, will also be observing the *mitzvot* connected to settling and defending the Land, which the Sages tell us are the equivalent of all the other *mitzvot* put together.

In practice, if a conversion court decides to follow the lenient opinion and accept a traditional-minded convert, the conversion is valid even according to the strict opinion.

CHAPTER 19

The Holy Temple

1. The *Mitzva* to Build a Tabernacle and Temple

The Jewish people have a *mitzva* to build a Temple on the Temple Mount in Jerusalem to house the Divine Presence. The Temple gives expression to a broad range of divine values and provides the Jewish people and the entire world with inspiration. As it says, "Let them make Me a sanctuary, that I may dwell among them" (Exodus 25:8).

First, the Jews built a temporary Tabernacle, which traveled with them through the desert. When they reached the Land of Israel, they set it up in Shiloh. However, God had commanded them to build something more permanent once they had established themselves in the Land and defeated their enemies (Deuteronomy 12:9-11). And this is what happened. After King David's conquests, his son Solomon built the Temple in Jerusalem, which stood for 410 years. Unfortunately, on account of our sins, the Babylonians destroyed the First Temple . About seventy years later, the Jews returned to the Land and built the Second Temple. It stood for 420 years. Unfortunately, since most of the Jews remained in exile, the Divine Presence was not manifested as clearly in the Second Temple as it had been in the First. Due to our sins, the Second Temple too was destroyed, at the hands of the Romans. We pray daily for the rebuilding of the Temple, speedily and in our days.

2. The Holy of Holies

The Temple Sanctuary was divided into two parts. The inner chamber (one third of the structure) was called the Holy of Holies, and the outer chamber (two thirds of the structure) was called the Holy. The Holy of Holies was the place dedicated to the revelation of the covenant between God and the Jews. Because it was so holy, only the High Priest was allowed to enter it, and even he could enter only once a year, on Yom Kippur.

Since the covenant is expressed through the Torah, the Ark of the Covenant – containing a Torah scroll and the Tablets of the Covenant Moses received at Sinai – was housed in the Holy of Holies. The Ark had a golden cover upon which were two cherubs in the form of a loving couple, a male and a female, symbolizing the loving relationship between God and His people Israel. As it says, "As a bridegroom rejoices over his bride, so will your God rejoice over you" (Isaiah 62:5). The presence of this form in the Holy of Holies also expressed the great sanctity of marriage. Not only can joyous love shared by husband and wife bring life to the world, but their monogamy can serve as a reminder of monotheism. This may be hinted at in the Sages' statement that if a husband and wife are blessed with true love, the Divine Presence is with them (8:1 above).

Thus, the Holy of Holies was the place for the revelation of the covenant between God and the Jews, a covenant all about faith in God and the sanctity of the Jewish people. These exalted values continue to be expressed through the Torah and through marriage.

3. The Three Vessels of the Holy

Holiness was represented in the three vessels located in the Holy: the table, the Menora, and the incense altar. The table represented working and making a living, the Menora represented secular studies, and the incense altar represented prayer. A curtain separated the Holy from the Holy of Holies to make it clear there are degrees of sanctity; the sanctity of the Holy derives from the Holy of Holies. Thus, these three types of sanctity – which can be expressed through working, studying, and praying – all stem from the sanctity of the covenant between God and His people, expressed through the Torah and through marriage.

4. The Table

The twelve "showbread" loaves, corresponding to the twelve tribes of Israel, were placed on the table in the Holy. This bread represented the sacred value of all the work people do to advance the world and increase its blessing and goodness. Through working, a person becomes a partner with God in developing the world and ensuring its continued existence. In particular, working in the Land of Israel is especially meritorious, as it fulfills the *mitzva* of settling the Land. It is comparable to working in the Garden of Eden. The table also served as a reminder of the importance of people's obligation to support their family.

5. The *Menora*

The golden *Menora* (candelabrum) represented all of the world's arts and sciences. Its seven ornate branches corresponded to the ancient idea that there are seven branches of wisdom. This conveyed the message that secular studies are ultimately divine, because their purpose is to help us understand the world God created. In practice, this message is expressed by the blessing we make upon seeing a great scholar in any discipline: "Who has given of His wisdom to human beings" (23:19 below).

Because Torah study is connected to the Holy of Holies, it is referred to as "internal wisdom"; because other disciplines are connected to the Holy, they are referred to as "external wisdom." When people study other subjects for the sake of heaven and tap into the Holy of Holies, they draw sanctity into the world and grow spiritually.

6. The Incense Altar

Incense was offered twice a day, morning and evening, on the incense altar (also known as the golden altar or inner altar). The incense represented the worship of the heart, which is what prayer is all about. As we read, "Take my prayer as an offering of incense" (Psalms 141:2).

The burning of incense also represented another fundamental value, namely repentance. When we repent, we "burn up" our sins and cling to God, ascending higher and higher like the incense smoke.

7. The Outer Altar and Sacrifice

The vessels found in the Holy and Holy of Holies would seem to represent all of the most important divine values. Why then were we also commanded to build a large altar in the Temple courtyard, with a perpetual fire burning for the sacrifices? To show the importance of dedication and self-sacrifice.

No beautiful, lofty values can endure without a willingness to sacrifice for them. One cannot master Torah without the willingness to sacrifice one's free time to study diligently. One cannot build an enduring marriage without mutual devotion and the willingness to concede and compromise. One cannot succeed at work without dedication and the willingness to put in extra time when necessary. A scientist will not succeed in discovering the secrets of nature without dedication and persistence in his or her research. Above all, the Jewish people cannot survive without soldiers willing to sacrifice themselves for the Land and the people. Therefore, the holiness of the outer altar (which derives from the Holy of Holies and the covenant between God and His people) can be said to extend everywhere Israeli soldiers stand guard to defend their Land and their people.

When we are deserving, this dedication and self-sacrifice can be expressed in multiple ways: when we tithe to support Torah scholars and the poor; when we are prepared to stand by family and friends who need help at any time of day or night; when we diligently study Torah even when we are tired; and when we undergo exhausting training exercises and wearying guard duty in the Israeli army.

Sometimes though, periods are so difficult that if we want to retain our connection to eternal values, we must be prepared to give up our very lives. Without an altar, there cannot be a Temple, nor can any of the sacred values survive. As the world progresses, there will be less need for people to sacrifice their lives for their nation and their eternal values. This may be what the Sages mean when they say that in the future all sacrifices will be discontinued, except for the thanksgiving offering (which expresses closeness to God in a heartwarming and joyful way).

8. The Basin and the Women's Mirrors

Another object in the Temple courtyard was the basin, made out of mirrors the women had donated. The Sages provide the following fascinating back story.

When our ancestors were slaves, the Egyptians wanted to prevent the men from reproducing, in order to wipe out the Israelites. To that end, they weighed them down with backbreaking labor from dawn to dusk and forced them to sleep in the fields instead of returning home. To the Israelite men, the situation seemed hopeless; their wives would give up on them and instead cling to their Egyptian masters. How could a husband look his wife in the eye? He was supposed to shelter her, protect her from tyrants and oppressors, support her and defend her honor, and be a role model for their children. Instead, he was a lowly slave under his master's heel. To spare himself further humiliation, he preferred not to attempt to approach his wife. He stifled his will to live. He did not want children, because he could not provide them with a decent future. When his wife approached him, he backed away, because he was afraid she would want to leave him soon anyway. Under such circumstances, most women would feel slighted and try to become the second wives of their Egyptian masters. And the people of Israel would have faced extinction.

Something else took place instead. The Sages recount:

> In the merit of the righteous women of that generation, Israel was redeemed from Egypt. When the women went to draw water, the Holy One arranged for small fish to enter their pitchers, so they drew up pitchers half-full of water and half-full of fish. They then set two pots on the fire, one for hot water and the other for the fish. Then they carried these to their husbands in the fields, where they bathed them, massaged them with oil, and gave them food and drink. Then they coupled with them among the sheepfolds (Sota 11b).

It was as if each woman said to her husband, "Although you are a contemptible slave in the eyes of the Egyptians, in my eyes you are precious and important. Just as I would greet you happily if you returned home from a respectable job, so I happily greet you now. I have come to the field to wash your feet, aching after a hard day's work, and to massage your body, bruised from beatings, because you are my husband and my love."

A *midrash* relates similarly:

> *While they ate and drank, the women held up mirrors and looked into them together with their husbands. She would say, "I am more beautiful than you," and he would respond, "I am better looking than you." This stimulated their desire, and they would procreate; the Holy One would ensure immediate conception... "The Israelites were fertile and prolific; they multiplied and increased very greatly" (Exodus 1:7) ... And all this proliferation was thanks to the mirrors (Tanhuma, Pekudei §9).*

After the Israelites left Egypt, received the Torah, and were commanded to erect the Tabernacle, every Jew donated gold, silver, copper, expensive fabrics, and precious gems for its construction. The same women who had given birth in the fields (and who were now old) asked themselves, "Do we have anything to contribute toward the building of the Tabernacle?" They went home and returned carrying the same mirrors they had used to beautify themselves. Even though they treasured these mirrors, they volunteered to donate them out of their intense passion for sanctity. But Moshe was disgusted, because he felt the whole point of mirrors was to arouse the evil inclination. God responded to Moshe, "You disdain these mirrors?! These mirrors produced these multitudes in Egypt! Accept them, because they are more beloved to Me than all other donations. Take them and use them to make the copper basin and its base, with which the priests will sanctify themselves for the divine service" (*Ibid.*).

We learn something wonderful from this story: there is nothing more pure and holy than unconditional, life-giving love. That is why these mirrors were specifically used to make the basin from which the priests purified and sanctified themselves in preparation for the Temple service.

9. The Daily Offering and the Incense

The daily offering was a lamb offered by the priests every morning and evening on the outer altar. It was the most important of the sacrifices. Offered in the name of the entire nation, it connected all created beings to their Source.

The cycle of life involves birth, growth, and ultimately death. People die every day, as do animal and plants. The burning question is: "What is the meaning of all this?" The daily offering imbued the cycle of life with meaning. Every living being aspires to perfect itself, partly through growth and development. When a being's world narrows to the point where continued growth is no longer possible, the spirit separates from the body. The soul then ascends – like a sacrifice – and returns to its Source. The daily offering served as a reminder that the end of life is associated with a return to God.

Incense was also offered daily, morning and evening. But while the daily offering expressed the obvious relationship of the Jews and God (and therefore offered on the outer altar), the incense with its lovely aroma expressed the inner dimension of that relationship (and therefore offered on the inner altar).

The incense was composed of eleven spices and herbs. Of these, ten had a pleasant aroma. These ten corresponded to the ten levels of holiness used in creating the world. The eleventh essential component of the incense, the galbanum, had an unpleasant smell. Nevertheless, the incense (which mixed it with the other spices and herbs) smelled good. This teaches us that if sinners (who are problematic as individuals) are connected to the community, they are part of its sanctity. This is transformative and improves everyone. The incense gave symbolic expression to Jewish unity.

This unity is also reflected in the prayers the Sages composed. Almost all the prayers are formulated in the plural and recited on behalf of the entire community. At the same time, each individual can use them as a jumping-off point, following them up with personalized petitions, such as asking to be blessed and to be able to do his or her part to help improve the world.

10. The Spiritual Center

The Temple served as a spiritual center, with Jews gathering there on the three pilgrimage festivals (Passover, Shavuot, and Sukkot). Anyone who wanted could come at other times too.

One of the *mitzvot* that strengthened the Jews' connection to the Temple was the second tithe. The second tithe was separated in the first, second, fourth, and fifth years of the seven-year cycle. This tithe – roughly 9% of the agricultural produce – was for the owners. They were obligated to eat this produce (or redeem it and eat other food bought with the money) in a state of purity in Jerusalem.

The Jews' connection to the Temple was also reinforced by the *mitzva* of the animal tithe. This involved setting aside one animal out of ten, bringing it to Jerusalem, offering it as a sacrifice, and eating it as part of a festive *mitzva* meal.

These *mitzvot* provided people with a spiritual vacation near the Temple, where they could enjoy *mitzva* meals and attend classes from the Torah giants of Jerusalem. The greater a family's material blessings, the longer they could remain in Jerusalem, benefiting from the divine presence and inviting the poor to share meals with them. If the family's children liked studying Torah, they could continue studying Torah in Jerusalem and live off their family's second tithe.

11. First Fruits

During Temple times, there was a *mitzva* to bring the first fruits (*bikurim*) to the priests in the Temple. Any Jew who owned property in the Land of Israel and grew any of the seven species (wheat, barley, grapes, figs, pomegranates, olives, and dates) would mark the fruits that were first to bud and declare: "These are first fruits." Once they ripened, the owner picked them, placed them in a pretty container, and took them with great fanfare to Jerusalem. When the first fruits were presented to a priest in the Temple, the owner recited the biblical text known as *mikra bikurim* (avowal verses, Deuteronomy 26:3-10), which summarizes the story and vision of the Jewish people. One would leave after bowing down to God. Then the family had a festive meal before God, making sure to include the needy in this spread.

Just as there is a *mitzva* to set aside (and present) the first of the produce, there is a *mitzva* to set aside (and sacrifice) the firstborn of the animals. Furthermore, the *mitzva* to sanctify and redeem one's firstborn son (*pidyon ha-ben*, 13:5 above) is so important that the Torah passage that mentions it is one of the four passages found in *tefillin* (20:8 below). The idea behind all of these sanctified "firsts" is everything should begin with a sacred ideal, which elicits inspiration and blessing upon all that follows. Similarly, whenever a person is faced with an important decision (such as whom to marry, what profession to train in, where to work, or where to live), the primary consideration must be value-based: Will a given choice help me become a better person and improve the world more effectively? With this as the frame of reference, all other considerations can be properly weighed, and the decision reached will be a source of blessing and success.

12. Inspiration from the Temple

Some people think the more one reveres the Temple, the more one must consider the rest of the world to be devoid of holiness. They are mistaken. The purpose of the Temple is to uplift and sanctify the whole world. A world with a Temple is a world sanctified by the divine values it contains.

This sheds light on the Sages' statement that people who leave the five agricultural gifts for the poor as the Torah mandates (6:2 above), it is as if they have built the Temple and offered sacrifices there. A farmer who puts in an honest day of hard work is importing the Temple's holiness into his field. Similarly, people who put in an honest day of hard work, doing their best to help others and playing their part in developing the economy and improving the world, are importing the Temple's holiness into the workplace. Going above and beyond to help humanity is the equivalent of building an altar and offering a sacrifice to God.

13. Inspiration from the Temple Service

The way the priests approached their Temple service can also serve as an example for how people should relate to their jobs. The priests prepared themselves and took special care not to become impure, which would have disqualified them from serving. Similarly, everyone should properly prepare themselves for their work and find meaning and holiness in it. Whatever their profession – teacher, doctor, engineer, salesperson, or anything else – people should try to get enough sleep so they can do their job well. Rather than being complacent, they should always look to become more knowledgeable about their job or more skilled at it and have in mind that through their work, they are making the world a better place.

A few outstanding individuals can be compared to the High Priest who entered the Holy of Holies to atone for the nation on Yom Kippur. Because their work is so holy, they must sometimes even sacrifice their families. For example, if a doctor with extraordinary life-saving skills gets a call from the hospital, he or she must drop whatever they may be doing and go, even if the call comes in the middle of their daughter's wedding. When the doctor takes leave of family and guests, all they can do is pray he or she succeeds in saving the critically ill patient hovering between life and death. The same is true for the commanders of an elite units of the IDF. They must be in a perpetual state of readiness. Even if he is with his wife giving birth, he must leave if suddenly called to save the Jews from their enemies. His wife, while giving birth, will pray for him to return safely and see their child, just as the entire nation would pray for the High Priest to succeed in his mission on Yom Kippur.

14. Ritual Purity

An impure person is not permitted to enter the Temple or even the Temple Mount before undergoing a purification process as detailed in the Torah. Why not? The reasons for the rules of purity and impurity are divine mysteries beyond our ken and we may never be able to understand fully. Nevertheless, a possible approach, begins with the idea that the Temple represented nothing less than life itself.

It seems purity is connected to life and impurity to death. The more developed the life form, the more severe the loss which comes with death, and thus the greater the accompanying impurity. Therefore, a human corpse is the greatest source of impurity, as humans are the most advanced life form. Lesser impurity can be contracted from animal carcasses or insects. Plants are a less developed life form, so there is no impurity if one comes into contact with a plant that has shriveled and died. However, if one uses plants to grow fruit and vegetables, or to make clothes or vessels, the level of impurity is raised to that below the impurity of dead animals. Another source of impurity is menstruation. It occurs when an egg, which had the potential to develop into a life, exits the woman's body (together with the blood and uterine lining which were prepared to support the pregnancy). This loss of potential life is why a menstruant is impure. An additional source of impurity is a seminal emission. When a man has a nocturnal emission, it is a waste of sperm, which had the potential to develop into a life. In all these examples, the loss of life or potential life is what creates impurity .

The purification process requires an impure person to submerge his or her entire body in a *mikveh*. Sometimes this process could be done the day after the person became impure, and other times it could be undergone only a week later. In a case of impurity caused by a human corpse, not only did the person need to wait a week before immersing, one also needed to be sprinkled on the third and seventh days with spring water containing the dissolved ashes of a red heifer. Unfortunately, today we do not have the conditions necessary to practice this ritual.

15. The Temple Mount

Due to the grace of God, after two thousand years of exile, we had the privilege of liberating the Temple Mount during the Six-Day War, on the 28th of Iyar, 5727 (June 7, 1967). Possessing the Temple Mount brings us one step closer to building the Third Temple. To avoid repeating the mistakes that led to the destruction of the first two Temples, we must focus on inculcating the values associated with the Temple (detailed above in sections 2-8). If we succeed, we will have the privilege of building the Third Temple, after which the Divine Presence will dwell in Israel and throughout the world.

In the meantime, the question arises as to whether or not

it is permissible to enter the Temple Mount. It is divided into two areas, the Camp of the Divine Presence and the Levite Camp. The first area is where the Temples and their court-yards were located. It is off limits to anyone impure due to a corpse. Nowadays, this includes almost everyone, because a corpse confers impurity not only upon those who touch it, but also upon anyone near it or under the same roof. And, as we mentioned above, there is no way to purify ourselves, as we lack the ashes of the red heifer.

Surrounding the first area is the Levite Camp. In this part of the Temple Mount, those who are impure due to death are permitted entry. However, those who are impure due to bodily secretions, whether semen or menstrual blood, may not enter unless they first immerse in a *mikveh*.

Many rabbis maintain that since it is biblically prohibited to enter certain areas and there is some disagreement as to the precise demarcations, no one should be allowed to ascend to the Temple Mount, in order to avoid possible transgression. Others maintain it is possible, and indeed a *mitzva* to deter-mine where entrance is permitted, and to take the necessary halakhic measures to allow it, i.e., to immerse. Thus, properly prepared, people should ascend to the Temple Mount to ex-press their connection to the most sacred place in the world for Jews, to reinforce Jewish sovereignty there, and to pray for the rebuilding of the Temple. I subscribe to the latter position.

16. Commemorating the Destruction

Our Sages ordained that we mourn the destruction of the Temple by fasting four times a year: the tenth of Tevet, the seventeenth of Tamuz, the ninth of Av, and the third of Tishrei (37:1-5 below). This is to ensure we do not forget to pray for the rebuilding of the Temple and the reestablishment of its values. Other laws commemorate the destruction as well. For example, anyone who builds a home is obligated to leave a small area (a cubit by a cubit, which is about 1½ square meters) facing the entranceway unpainted and unplastered; at the high point of every wedding, the couple break a glass (11:8 above); and those viewing the site of the destroyed Temple tear their shirts as a sign of mourning.

In the wake of the destruction and the exile, people needed to devote most of their energy to surviving, so Jewish life narrowed and many values were forgotten. Thus, the prayers for the rebuilding of the Temple are in fact prayers for the return of its entire set of associated values (sections 2-8 above). The road to rebuilding begins by deeply connecting with all these principles. By doing so, we will be blessed with the ingathering of the exiles, the rebuilding of the entire Land, and the rebuilding of the Temple, speedily and in our days.

17. When the Jews Walk in God's Ways

When the sacred values the Temple expresses serve as the basis for Jewish life in the Land, divine blessing will naturally flow to all Jews. Gradually, the nation will advance spiritually and reach indescribable heights. Jewish faith will wondrously link heaven and earth. The whole world will learn that life is filled with blessing when based on sacred ideals.

We will attempt to describe how this process can realistically occur when we let the Temple's values guide us. The Jewish people will recognize the value of the Torah, strengthening their faith and their desire to add blessing to the world. Understanding the significance and sanctity of the family, many more Jews will get married and enjoy a loving marriage, while raising many children in nurturing homes. Thanks to people's increased willingness to contribute to society through serving in the army and settling the Land, Israel's public security will improve. Appreciating the importance of study, many will devote more years to becoming experts in areas suitable to their skills, and the quality of their work will improve. Recognizing the importance of science, more Jews will study it intensely, and trailblazing scientists will emerge. Perceiving the value of hard work and its critical contribution to improving the world, employees will happily work conscientiously. Recognizing the merit of truth and integrity will lead to more honesty in business, which in turn will make it more worthwhile for people to open businesses and form partnerships, thus improving the economy.

Studying Torah daily, and additional study on Shabbat and holidays, will reinforce all these values, which in turn will lead to even greater growth and creativity. Not working on Shabbat and holidays, but rather taking part in festive communal prayer, and enjoying holiday meals together with family, will strengthen the values of faith and kindness. This in turn will encourage people to work hard to find ways and means to help the disabled and those suffering physically and psychologically. Consequently, all those unable to express their talents due to disabilities will be able to shine and make new and original contributions to society.

In other words, following the path of Torah and *mitzvot* will have amazing results. It will bring joy and blessing to families and inspire the educational system. It will add justice and kindness to society, meaning and values to the individual, innovation to science, prosperity to the arts, creativity and industriousness to agriculture and industry, energy to the economy, and honesty to business.

Even if Israel's gross domestic product increases only three percent more than other developed countries, and even if Israel's scientific advances benefiting humanity continue to be only three percent more than other first-world nations, and if demographic growth among religious Jewish Israelis remains stable, the results will be astounding within a few generations: tens of millions of Jews will live in Israel, and it will lead the world morally, technologically, and economically.

Jews of the diaspora will long to immigrate and join this successful venture. Descendants of Jews lost to us due to the terrible hardship of exile will explore their roots and return to their people and their Land. A powerful, populous nation will bring the messages of faith and justice to the world. We will pave the way for moral education and intellectual advancement for the good of humanity. We will innovate technologies that will improve both life expectancy and the quality of life. And we will have the privilege of seeing the realization of the prophetic vision: "In the days to come, the Mount of the Lord's house shall stand firm above the mountains and tower above the hills; and all the nations shall gaze on it with joy. And the many peoples shall go and say: 'Come, let us go up to the Mount of the Lord, to the house of the God of Jacob; that He may instruct us in His ways, and that we may walk in His paths.' For Torah shall come forth from Zion, the word of the Lord from Jerusalem" (Isaiah 2:2-3).

www.ingramcontent.com/pod-product-compliance
Lightning Source LLC
Chambersburg PA
CBHW061600120626
46550CB00004B/1557